Sport in the Global Society

Series Editors: J.A. Mangan and Boria Majumdar

# Playing on the Periphery

# Sport in the Global Society
Series Editors: J.A. Mangan and Boria Majumdar

The interest in sports studies around the world is growing and will continue to do so. This unique series combines aspects of the expanding study of *sport in the global society*, providing comprehensiveness and comparison under one editorial umbrella. It is particularly timely as studies in the multiple elements of sport proliferate in institutions of higher education.

Eric Hobsbawm once called sport one of the most significant practices of the late nineteenth century. Its significance was even more marked in the late twentieth century and will continue to grow in importance into the new millennium as the world develops into a 'global village' sharing the English language, technology and sport.

*Other Titles in the Series*

**Disreputable Pleasures**
Less Virtuous Victorians at Play
*Edited by Mike Huggins and J.A. Mangan*

**Italian Fascism and the Female Body**
Sport, Submissive Women and
Strong Mothers
*Gigliola Gori*

**Rugby's Great Split**
Class, Culture and the Origins of
Rugby League Football
*Tony Collins*

**Sport and Memory in North America**
*Edited by Stephen G. Wieting*

**Barbarians, Gentlemen and Players**
A Sociological Study of the Development
of Rugby Football (Second Edition)
*Eric Dunning and Kenneth Sheard*

**Australian Beach Cultures**
The History of Sun, Sand and Surf
*Douglas Booth*

**Lost Histories of Indian Cricket**
Battles Off the Pitch
*Boria Majumdar*

**The Cultural Bond**
Sport, Empire, Society
*Edited by J.A. Mangan*

**Sport in Australasian Society**
Past and Present
*Edited by J.A. Mangan and John Nauright*

**The Magic of Indian Cricket**
Cricket and Society in India
(Revised Edition)
*Mihir Bose*

**Leisure and Recreation in a Victorian Mining Community**
The Social Economy of Leisure in
North-East England, 1820–1914
*Alan Metcalfe*

**The Commercialisation of Sport**
*Edited by Trevor Slack*

# Playing on the Periphery

*Playing on the Periphery* is an innovative exploration along the edges of the modern sports experience. Using diverse and provocative case studies and covering a range of problems, it examines how the cultural content of sports that were once the epitome of Englishness – football, cricket and rugby – is reinterpreted by the distant cultures of a former Empire, and fragmented by the new media and economics of the modern world.

From a unique perspective and with a distinctive voice, Tara Brabazon considers sport's relationship with tourism, colonialism and popular culture. She shows how, through the media's filter – through photographs and film, stadia, shops and exhibition spaces – sport can acquire multiple and diverse meanings. Though it may appear peripheral, sport is a central force for memory, emotion and identity . . .

For all those interested in sport, media and popular culture, this is a stimulating new text.

**Dr Tara Brabazon** is Associate Professor in Cultural Studies at Murdoch University, Perth, Australia and Director of the Popular Culture Collective.

# Playing on the Periphery

## Sport, Identity and Memory

## Tara Brabazon

Routledge
Taylor & Francis Group

LONDON AND NEW YORK

First published 2006
by Routledge

Published 2017 by Routledge
2 Park Square, Milton Park, Abingdon, Oxon OX14 4RN
711 Third Avenue, New York, NY 10017, USA

*Routledge is an imprint of the Taylor & Francis Group,
an informa business*

Typeset in Goudy and Gill Sans by
Florence Production Ltd, Stoodleigh, Devon

*British Library Cataloguing in Publication Data*
A catalogue record for this book is available from the British Library

*Library of Congress Cataloging in Publication Data*
Brabazon, Tara.
  Playing on the periphery: sport, identity and memory/Tara Brabazon
      p. cm – (Sport in the global society)
  Includes bibliographical references and index
  1. Sports – Sociological aspects.    2. Mass media and sports.
  3. popular culture.    I. Title.    II. Series
  GV706.5.B72 2006
  306.4′83–dc22                                                    2005023718

ISBN13: 978–0–415–37561–0 (hbk)
ISBN13: 978–0–415–48492–3 (pbk)

# Contents

*List of figures*                                                    vii
*Acknowledgements*                                                   viii
*Series editors' foreword*                                            ix

Introduction: Back to the Boot Room                                    1

**PART I**
**Sport and tourism**

1   We're not really here: 'Homes of Football' and
    residents of memory                                                7

2   If Shearer plays for England, so can I: The National
    Football Museum and the popular cultural problem                  41

**PART II**
**Sport and history**

3   They think it's all over, but it isn't                            75

4   You've just been bounced at the WACA: Pitching
    a new cricketing culture                                         102

**PART III**
**Sport and memory**

5   Our Don and their Eddie                                          125

6   Bending memories through Beckham                                 154

7   On the Blacks' back                                        176

Conclusion: Leaving the Boot Room                          191

*Notes*                                                    196
*Select bibliography*                                      223
*Index*                                                    225

# Figures

1.1 'The Homes of Football', Ambleside 11
1.2 Green and Pleasant Landing 15
1.3 Ladies' Retiring Room 16
1.4 Neon Girls 20
1.5 Looking Up 21
1.6 The Kop 26
1.7 Goalkeeper's View of the Crowd 31
2.1 Red Café 52
2.2 Curving the static 53
2.3 Urbis from the street 55
2.4 The entry 62
2.5 Adding colour 63
2.6 Exhibition lighting 64
2.7 Exhibiting the floor 65
2.8 The first half 65
2.9 Hearing history 66
2.10 Sight and sound 67
2.11 History through touch 68
2.12 Tactile artefacts 68
2.13 Interaction 69
2.14 Extra time 70
3.1 The crossbar 78
3.2 Displaying 1966 84
3.3 The ball 85
4.1 WACA entry 103
4.2 Urban cricket 107
4.3 The WACA shop 119

All photographs by Tara Brabazon except 1.2, 1.3, 1.4, 1.5, 1.6, 1.7 (Stuart Clarke).

# Acknowledgements

Kicking a ball in a park, like writing a book, is often a solitary enterprise. Fortunately, many companions joined me on this journey through sport and space. I extend personal and professional thanks to Stuart Clarke from the 'Homes of Football'. He not only granted permission to use six of his remarkable photographs, but shared his time in an Ambleside interview. Similarly, I thank Kevin Moore from the National Football Museum and the International Football Institute for assistance with queries and confirmations.

Writing *about* the periphery *from* the periphery poses particular challenges. The diversity of source material deployed in these pages – analogue and digital, archived and ephemeral – was gathered through the support of numerous scholars. Particular thanks are extended to Dr Leanne McRae, Dr Dave Urry, Debbie Hindley, Carley Smith and all members of the Popular Culture Collective.

This book would not have been written without the inspiration and efforts of three remarkable people. My mother, Doris Brabazon, remains a life-long inspiration. Her commitment, belief and one-eyed devotion to West Perth Football Club and the West Coast Eagles showed me from an early age that women can love sport in a way unimagined by sneering men in suits. Kevin Brabazon, my father, shared his knowledge, time and passion for sport with his only daughter. One of my most evocative childhood memories is Kevin taking me – kitted out from head to toe in black and white – to see my team, Swan Districts, win the Western Australian Football League Premiership. He has nearly forgiven me, twenty years later, for West Perth being knocked out earlier in the competition. Without his varied interest in sport – encompassing all football codes, cricket, tennis and golf – this book would not have been written. It is appropriate that the research journey he started when I was a child is finished with his compilation of the index for this book.

The final thank you is to my husband, Professor Steve Redhead. Moving from North (of England) to West (Australia), he has been a true companion through the periphery. There is a light that never goes out.

# Series editors' foreword

*Playing on the Periphery* is an intriguing addition to the series *Sport in the Global Society*. It geographically complements Stephen G. Weiner's *Sport and Memory in North America*[1], also published in the series, but has its own analytical individuality and should be read for its ability to provoke reaction and stimulate response. It should be read, it is further suggested, in conjunction with the recently published *In Praise of Empires: Globalization and Order* by the distinguished international commentator, Deepak Lal[2]. All imperial coinage had two sides. With regard to imperialism itself, *Playing on the Periphery* presents one face; *In Praise of Empires* the other.

'Fond Memory brings the light/Of other days around me' wrote the balladeer Thomas Moore in his celebrated and sweetly sentimental, 'Oft in the Stilly Night'[3]. *Playing on the Periphery* takes a different view of memory. It views the past without sentimentality. The recommendation in the well-known Shakespearian couplet, 'Praising what is lost/Makes remembrance dear' is eschewed.

The reason is made emphatically clear. While, to an extent, through sport 'Stored memories provide a future for the past [and] Special moments common to friends, parents, siblings, lovers, whole towns and whole nations offer escape from anomie'[4], it remains true that these '. . . memories are mediated, in part, not so much through the culture of sport as the cultures of sport' and the '. . . global "collective memory" in sport remains stubbornly fractured and, on occasion, even confrontational. Memory transactions are far from being universal transactions. Sport still shapes "local" identities'[5]. Despite globalization sport remains culturally archipelagic.

At the same time, not too long ago, it was written,

> '. . . it is surely time to recognize the merging of memory, capitalism, consumerism and sport has produced its own "long cultural revolution" increasingly, inexorably and unrelentingly impacting on more and more millions as modern decades slip by. The human memory, stimulated in specific cultural circumstances feeds the appetite for sensations and much else. For this reason, capitalism through consumerism has been

able to utilize sport successfully in the pursuit of profit. "The vulgarity of the intruding masses" has been welcomed; the mass media spectacle has triumphed; moments made into memories are marvellously marketable.'[6]

*Playing on the Periphery* suggests that the modern media has been responsible, to an extent, for severing rather than sustaining memory, among other things, through its predilection for 'excess'. The media in an increasingly globalized world now considerably shapes projected images for our consumption. In this process, it has replaced a past emphasis on the boredom of 'fair play' with a present emphasis on the frisson of 'foul play' – on and off playing arenas. The motive is uncomplicated. To set an old industrial metaphor in a new industrial context, 'Where there's muck, there's brass'!

Finally, a bravura feature of *Playing on the Periphery* is the provocative use of generalization which jolts the reader continually into an interrogative frame of mind. This is an effective means of establishing a sharp mental dialogue with the author.

J.A. Mangan and Boria Majumdar
Series Editors
Sport in the Global Society

## Notes

1. Stephen Weiner (ed.), *Sport and Memory in North America* (London: Frank Cass, 2001).
2. Deepak Lal, *In Praise of Empires: Globalization and Order* (London: Palgrave Macmillan, 2004).
3. Thomas Moore, 'Oft in the Stilly Night' (first verse) quoted in *The Oxford Book of Quotations*, Revised Fourth Edition (Oxford: OUP, 1996), p.483.
4. See J.A. Mangan, Series Editor's Introduction in Weiner, *Sport and Memory in North America*, p.x.
5. Ibid., p.xi.
6. Ibid.

# Introduction
## Back to the Boot Room

Liverpool Football Club taught Manchester United how to be Manchester United. They, in turn, taught Chelsea how to be Chelsea. Through the 1960s, 1970s and 1980s, Liverpool transformed into an international footballing phenomenon. Without these preliminary experiments in global marketing, Manchester United would have had no template to follow. Obviously there are significant distinctions. The Theatre of Dreams has little of the Kop's aura. While United have had their share of effective and skilled managers, none – not even Ferguson – had the presence of Bill Shankly.[1] The footage of Shankly speaking to Liverpool's faithful captures the religious passion of a sermon on the mount. The ghost of Shankly – perhaps damagingly for the current club administration – still attends every game.

Many stories encircle his practices as manager. Some are enclosed in the famous Liverpool Boot Room. Seemingly a room to store the players' footwear, it was also the place where Shankly invited visiting managers for a whisky and chat after the game. In this cramped space he found out about player transfers, tactics and opponents' weaknesses. This book, *Playing on the periphery*, goes back to the boot room, to the sites of myth, memory and excess. It chooses as its subjects those sports, moments and stadia that are bigger than their time, casting a shadow over the citizens and histories that follow.

*Playing on the periphery* walks a distinct path in the burgeoning industry of sport history. It is drawn not only to peripheral sports, but also to sports on the periphery. It is not written by a white man from either Britain or the United States. This is a significant difference, as there is no authentic experience of the 'real' Premier League or NBA to be gleaned from these pages. I have not been ankle-deep in mud, scrambling in a scrum. I have not reverse-swung a ball at Lord's. Instead, each chapter focuses on the peripheries, edges and boundaries of sport. My eyes are drawn not to the trophies cabinet, but to the representations of success, loss, power and patronage. Distance from the United Kingdom and the United States offers odd opportunities. It is the media-tions of sport through film, television, popular music, museums, photographs and material culture that gain attention.

Sport is not an isolated social and political formation: it is part of popular culture. While popular culture is too often dismissed as trash, study reveals the relativity of aesthetic values, the implications of technological change, the political conflicts of daily life and the role of economics in the production of culture. Popular culture has a dynamic history, particularly since World War II. With the New Right winning the battle over national consciousness, sport is a crucial mechanism to strategically intervene in debates about difference, social justice and identity. This neo-conservative popular culture triggers more than popular nationalism, and has structurally intervened in public life. With an emphasis on consumerism and not citizenship, sport is used by politicians to salve unpopular policies[2] and is implicated in the domination of subjugated peoples. To reduce sport to 'mere' consumption or globalization is to dismiss the political negotiations that are possible through language, bodies and behaviour. The passion of sport and its sharp performance of difference is a reminder that the rules, codes and conventions of family life, interpersonal relationships and the workplace can be organized differently. Popular culture tenders a vision of how life could be. While the racism, sexism and homophobia of sport are excessive and harmful, they also hold a teaching function, delivering lessons in how and why symbols gain power and applicability through time.

While I am sketching these innovative future alliances, there are also unpopular glances back to the 'old medium' of photography, alongside the convergent potential of digitization. Sports media, encompassing – in a limited definition – journalism, blogs, advertising, film, television, popular music, websites, pop literature and photography, are the representational fodder of this book. These media and genres allow images, sounds and ideas to move through spaces bounded by political, economic or legal structures. Sports media play in, for and to the periphery.[3] This book, in working through diverse modes of representation, shows how all media – not just the visual – are integral to the study of how sport moves through space and time.

This book is not only 'about' sporting representations, but is drawn to the periphery, to those who play on the edge. Wayne Rooney frays the edges of heterosexual masculinity.[4] Brandi Chastain lifted her shirt, exposing the limits of feminine behaviour. Western Australian Cricket Association (WACA) bouncers are delivered at the brink of acceptable cricketing practice. Shankly's Boot Room, although in the north of England, has survived and thrived in popular memory beyond the narratives of a 'declining' port city. Peripherality – living on edges and boundaries – is increasingly fashionable and marketable. Such an interpretation attacks the notion that peripheral regions are characterized by low economic growth, a dependence on primary or manufacturing industries and a shrinking population caused through migration to core regions.[5] While some of the sports and locations in this book have these characteristics, it is important to affirm that peripherality can be attractive in popular culture as a marker of distinction and difference as well as representing social or economic barriers. Each chapter in this book captures a moment of media excess that spills beyond local parochialism, a current season or score. Football, cricket and rugby are of particular focus, but many sports dip in the well of memory to transcribe stories of class, race, nation and gender. Importantly, my work also continues the productive dialogues between sport and tourism, showing how these creative industries – when aligned – fuel the engine of the new economy.

Sports history and theory are publishing success stories. There are, however, two flaws in the field. First, there is a predominance of edited collections that prevent authors from developing more substantive arguments. Second, there are too many books that focus on a single sport, like football, cricket or rugby, without exploring their cross-code linkages.[6] I am interested in the passage of sports *away* from England, investigating why elite English sports – like rugby and cricket – became national sports in Aotearoa/New Zealand and Australia. There are also significant questions to ask about why 'working class' English sports – like football – have travelled less well to the Antipodes and the United States of America. This focus on New Zealand rugby, Australian cricket and English football summons interwoven colonial narratives and myths. In so many ways, the Antipodes are still at the end of the world. In a supposedly post-colonial environment, it is clear that – through sport – English truths punctuate the present, even at the outer reaches of the former Empire.

Sport is part of a new visual experience of living, but representations are in the eye of the beholder. Republican stalwart Newt Gingrich once stated that 'I raise my eyes and I see America.'[7] His experience is not shared by most. The act of looking is dynamic and intertextual, knitting the aural, visual, tactile, spatial and touristic. Sporting spectators see cultural differences which build into a lived matrix of place and identity. Therefore sport theorists, by focusing on the forms of representation, incite a meeting of epistemology and ontology, language and visual culture, history and cultural studies. The three parts of this book play between these categories. The first part – 'Sport and tourism' – investigates how understandings of space and difference operate within the footballing crowd. Working with Stuart Clarke's 'Homes of Football' project and the National Football Museum in Preston, UK, the problems of peripherality are revealed. The second part – 'Sport and history' – adds the variable of time to the mix. The relationship between sport and society, at its most general and precise, is probed. I investigate the painful stretch between two events of 1966: the English victory in the World Cup and the Aberfan disaster in Wales. Then, moving to the WACA in Perth, I show how the scars of colonialism graze the surface of one of the most volatile wickets in the world. The final part – 'Sport and memory' – continues the cricketing emphasis. Obviously, no understanding of world cricket is possible without attention to Don Bradman. The preponderance of biographies, news stories and documentaries warrant this attention. I match his career against a contemporary who could never match his fame. Eddie Gilbert, an indigenous cricketer who could have been one of the best fast bowlers of his generation, died alone in a mental institution, unable to speak. The parallel between the cacophony of words written about Bradman and the silences encircling Gilbert is a potent testament to the long-term consequences of colonization. This chapter is then followed by an analysis of the film *Bend it like Beckham*, placing attention on the Indian diaspora and British Asian communities. I also explore the rationale, success and decline of David Beckham's publicity machine and the reason for women's profile in US soccer. The book concludes with an analysis of the All Blacks, investigating the place of rugby within bicultural Aotearoa/New Zealand.

*Playing on the periphery* forges a path through the post-colonial sporting world, dancing through the rhythms that separate England and the Antipodes. My work stands against an easy globalization of sport and sporting media. By stressing the specific and the particular, the peaks and troughs of identity and community are discovered. Through popular culture and sporting memory, differences are made on the run.

# Part I

# Sport and tourism

Part

Sport and tourism

# Chapter 1

# We're not really here

## 'Homes of Football' and residents of memory

We are not
We're not really here
We are not
We're not really here
     Manchester City chant

The most interesting and disturbing of research cracks open the gaps, lights the shadows and hears the words left out of history. Put another way, revisionist scholars follow the lead of Manchester City fans, hearing those who are not really here. Football is the world game, but such a cliché undermines the local accents and inflections that build a community and forge (mis)communication. Sport as a creative industry is culturally pervasive, bleeding not only into popular culture and social allegiances, but into the realm of tourism, museums and shopping. While much discussion of sport and media-based globalization stresses the possibilities of convergent 'new media' such as interactive television and the Web, this chapter evokes a much smaller project: to investigate the 'old media' of football photographs. Instead of replaying the team shots of young men holding trophies aloft, we twist our focus from the players to their fans.

This chapter activates an interdisciplinary dialogue between sport, tourism and cultural studies. Both sport and tourism have suffered a lack of credibility within the academy. It is appropriate that these two 'trivial' discourses interact to create a new way of thinking about belonging, identity and community. To commence this study, the focus is an unusual one. 'Homes of Football' is a photographic project initiated by Stuart Clarke. For over a decade, he has captured the changing face of English football, directing his lens on both fans and pitches. His aim is to trap on photosensitive paper the small and the overlooked. He has followed a single goal: to chart the rise of shrines and seats following the Hillsborough tragedy of 1989. During the subsequent decade, the Victorian terraces have been replaced by all-seater stadia. Publishing books, Clarke has used his framing eye to freeze a view of football's fans beyond hooligans, scallies and scum airways.[1]

Sweeping from local games through to international matches, he offers a significant record of change.

> I have taken my artist's easel (in fact my camera) around and around the country. Recording in an entertaining way the welter of changes. I have also photographed the things that seemingly never change – the touchstones that give us a football vernacular. This might well be an international language and iconography, yet, if only by desire, I have chosen to focus on the streets and football clubs and football fans I feel I should know best, here in Britain.[2]

There is no singular or authentic identity as a fan of football. Instead, fans are formed from 'the emergence of industrialized, professionalized spectator sport'.[3] Not a 'real' or 'natural' record of fan behaviour, Stuart Clarke's photographs offer a marker of the changing commercialization of sport. His historical and archival role has been recognized by UK Prime Minister Tony Blair as producing 'outstanding photographs – this collection really is a gem'.[4] The issue remains: what has Clarke 'collected'? Such a question is answered when placing his photographs in the context of sport tourism, Hillsborough and the place of 'the crowd' in popular memory. He has captured a geography of consumerism, accidentally revealing how changes within football shadow the shifting allegiances of the working class.

## Sporting tourism

Tourism is the new final frontier for both cultural studies and sport studies. As a 'clean' industry of the post-Fordist state, tourism paves a journey into symbolic and metaphoric spaces, while trafficking in the iconography of the post-colonial. Moving beyond the pleasures and meanings of travel, the geographies of imagination spiral into view. To explore the visual experiences of living allows new questions to be asked of society, culture and identity. As Irit Rogoff asked,

> What are the visual codes by which some are allowed to look, others to hazard a peek, and still others are forbidden to look altogether? In what political discourses can we understand looking and returning the gaze as an act of political resistance?[5]

Images, and how we look at them, are not frozen in scholarly or disciplinary categories. Fine art discourses position photographs differently from photojournalism or multimedia presentations. Stuart Clarke's images jut into the realms of tourism and archival preservation. I asked him to explore the motivations for his photographic style.

**TB:   What have you been capturing? What have you been photographing here?**

SC:   I think I've captured several elements that add up to the final result, if you like. I've got a fascination with how the other half live, a fascination with British/English culture, the peculiarities of it, its humour and idiosyncrasies, and obviously a fascination with sport, in particular football, and travel too. So I suppose why I did it is that you put those four things together, I was an artist who used to draw, then took up photographs because it was easier and quicker and less messy than getting your canvas blown over in the high street. Photographs – why particularly football? Well, after this disaster known as Hillsborough, the Hillsborough disaster, the last of a series of disasters, everything was going to change in this country with regard to football and how it was structured. It was slightly in a pallor state, in that it was going downhill, but it was still much loved and it was a common language. People either like it or despise it, but mostly like it, but there was a conversation to be had.

I could photograph these other things until kingdom come, but you wouldn't really draw an audience, but here I'd have an audience but it would also test my art because it is something that everyone already knows what it's about. If people don't like what you're saying about their club, they'll tell you.

So I thought I'd have a social purpose, in showing the changing face of the game. I'd be the man on the spot. There was nothing stopping anyone else from doing it, but I just thought through my enthusiasm, artistry and knowledge of football that I perhaps have a peculiar angle on it.

I'd set myself ten years, and I've gone past that. This wasn't going to be a fly-by-night thing. I thought I'd put everything I had into it. And I thought that would be rewarded by shows and the trust of the football people who see people come and go all the time. Players come and go – bought and then sold the next minute. The photographs kind of outlived all that. They were far more about the permanence of belonging and supporting the cultural attachments in this country. We've lost a lot – most of the industries that we always think of as very English, like ship building and coal mining, those things were going. The only things that were left that were really important to people were football, shopping and occasionally going to church. You know people say football is a religion, and that becomes a bit of a cliché, but I certainly think that for many people it is a religion. I think if you said to most people, 'what do you believe in outside of your family?', perhaps they would say feeding myself, getting a drink, but my football team, and that is passed on from generation to generation. And that was the thread of Englishness or Britishness that I really wanted to pursue. (A) because it existed and was valuable and would get an audience, but (B) because it suited me too. It's something that I love, you know, and why not? If you find something that you really love then it is going to show by what you put into it. And underwriting all of this is that I thought I could make a living out of it. And here we are twelve years later and I've got this gallery. I'm not rich, but in many ways I'm rich. In my life, I've done something that lots of people would have liked to have done. I still haven't done everything I wanted to do. It keeps me hungry, trying to perfect it. I've got a lot more to do with it. If I had done something on any other subject, I probably wouldn't be able to make a living out of it and tour a show to seventy-seven exhibitions and art galleries, and still have four years of bookings and interest from abroad.

Not only has Clarke 'made a living' from his photographs, but he has also mounted a permanent exhibition in Ambleside, a major tourist destination in the Lake District in northern England. Most poignantly, he has been successful in creating a monument to what he evocatively termed 'the permanence of belonging'. His commitment means that commerce and culture, art and authority, memory and manipulation dance in front of his photographic lens. Images of this type are frequently claimed as art, requiring an aloof, aesthetic gaze. Such a judgement verifies the 'quality' of the prints. Stuart Clarke develops a limited quantity of ten 'original' images, being produced in various sizes. He also mass-produces postcards for sale in his Ambleside exhibition and for the National Football Museum in Preston.

There is a clear commercial component to Clarke's work, with the premises at 100 Lake Road in Ambleside functioning as museum, gallery and shop front. This location is also enhanced through a presence on the Web (www.homesoffootball.co.uk). An innovative, creative mix is formed, with the website being part commercial, part promotional and part fan

*Figure 1.1* 'The Homes of Football', Ambleside.

record. Beyond Ambleside and the Web, Clarke has also maintained professional and corporate connections, with official affiliations with the Football Association, the Football Foundation and the Professional Footballers' Association. The exhibition also tours, including a visit to Japan in the English summer of 2002 with the assistance of the British Council. In the path of the German World Cup, a show was held in Berlin in September 2005, with another to come in Munich in 2006 and a world tour starting from February 2007, including Cape Town, Rio, Calcutta and Beijing. Considering this international exposure, his images offer alternative visions of 'dangerous' English football fans, often banned from European competitions. He reveals a positive, quirky Englishness to counter the institutional racism that still persists, even in the Premier League. Clarke acknowledges a major audience for the 'Homes of Football' International Touring Exhibition:

> I certainly want to spread our wings as I think this unique British football perspective of 'Homes of Football' has appeal to . . . ex-pats.[6]

While such an audience may be significant if the 'Homes of Football' tours Aotearoa/New Zealand, Australia and Canada, a more immediate question is who currently visits his permanent Ambleside exhibition.

**TB:   Who do you think they [your visitors] are? Mainly English tourists, coming to the Lake District? Do you get the internationals?**

SC:   Well, actually, since the World Cup [in 2002] . . . so many Japanese people have popped their head in the door or come all the way in, and literally before the World Cup, not a single one. They'd walk straight past us because they didn't think that it was meant to be for them. Now that they've staged the World Cup, they understand it all. They understand that the English don't bite heads off and all that sort of stuff. They come in here to see if Mr Beckham is sitting down in a chair. And I honestly think that they expect him to be, or that he might be, or his cousin or something. There is a sort of childishness about a lot of the Japanese. I absolutely loved them.

In England, the biggest amount of support we get is from the North East, Sunderland, Newcastle and then Middlesbrough, probably in that order. Just ahead of the Lancashire trail of Blackburn, Bolton, Manchester, Liverpool, Everton, that is the Lancashire cluster. Then across to Yorkshire. We've got quite a few fans come from Barnsley, Huddersfield, Leeds. That's the biggest visitorship.

Then we've got people who support London clubs, coming up from London on team building, there's quite a few of those. Not that many from abroad, really. A few Australians, not many Americans at all. A few South Africans, New Zealanders. Not many Europeans, Portuguese, Italian, Spanish. Very few, actually, which is a slight surprise. Not many Irish. Quite a few Scottish, but less so in the last few months, with their teams doing so badly. I think they've just bid a hasty retreat.

**TB:   Hibs fans have to go somewhere . . .**

SC:   And then from the locality, Cumbrians, probably only about 3 per cent in the whole year. So I think some people come in and say, 'Do most of your visitors support Carlisle United?' And the answer is 'very few'.

Northern England has been an effective – if not economic – home of football. The global restructuring of manufacturing industries in the post-war period accentuated the rate and scope of economic decline in this region, intensifying the uneven effect of internationalized capital and labour. In the last 20 years, three cities in particular – Birmingham, Sheffield and Manchester – have stressed the cultural and creative industries in an attempt to jump-start economic rebirth. Birmingham moved from 'motor city' to the 'convention city'. Sheffield transformed from 'steel city' to 'sports city',[7] and Manchester from cottonopolis to museumchester. While the creative industries have initiated an impetus for growth, sport has remained a beacon of solidarity and commitment through troubled times.

Also, apart from Arsenal's and Chelsea's recent successes in the Premier League, the domination of Liverpool, Manchester United, Newcastle and Everton continues to represent a northern English sporting specificity. Regional disparities are revealed not only between developed and developing countries, but in the sporting geographies of northern and southern England. It is not strange that a 'home' of football is in Ambleside.

**TB:  As you know, I just arrived here [at 'Homes of Football' in Ambleside], and I'm left thinking is there any place further away from urbanized football? Who comes here, and why did you decide on Ambleside?**

SC:  There are so many football clubs in this country that [it's strange] to travel to a place like Japan where the game is so new they think, 'we'll have ten teams, one there, one there and one there'. This is part marketing and part whatever other reasons. But here you've got hundreds of clubs, many in the same city. It absolutely blows the minds of many visitors to this country. You know both Dundee and Dundee United are doing up their stadiums and buildings, and they're fifty yards apart. They're in the same street. And it defies logic, but that is part of the madness and beauty of English culture, which is very much 'whatever your neighbour does, we'll do better'. You can sort of look at them, but over the hedge. The guy down the road is fine, but you're a bit wary of the next-door neighbour. There's a slight freakishness about us all.

In siting it here, I did kind of think that it was neutral ground, football-wise. If I had it in Newcastle or Manchester, then the fans of those clubs wouldn't necessarily come. If it was in Manchester, then

Newcastle fans wouldn't want to come to Manchester to be told what their club looks like.

So I kind of thought, I live here in the Lake District, and I use this as my base for doing all these matches. Because when I come back I feel like I've still got some perspective in that as mad as I am on it, it won't totally overwhelm me. I think therefore we have a lot of tourists – we've had 80,000 visitors a year since we've opened, almost consistently. Yeah, it's crept up a touch in the last year because of foot-and-mouth [disease]. There is a bit of a tourist trail, football-wise it is sort of neutral territory, and it suited me very much to have it here.

I wanted to do something that was quality in a place that had breathing space and people would appreciate it. If I did it in Oxford Street in London, should I even be able to find the finances and things, it would be gagged by all these other signs. Here it sort of stands out. It glows like a ship berthed in the dock. People who don't know it is here sort of say, 'Wow. Why is this here?' There is a sense of 'I found it for myself', which I like, and is magical, which it is for people. People say you should go to that place in the Lake District, and they probably think that it is a corner shop, with a guy and a few pictures stacked up. And then they come and it is a lot bigger, which is a rather nice surprise for people. I do notice a few blokes, women occasionally too, say, 'Oh look, there happens to be a football gallery in the Lake District.' And they knew perfectly well that it was here. It was meant to be a get away from football weekend. And there they are, they can go walking, and enjoy all that getting away from it, and still have that thing dearest to them to have a look at.

Tourism has often been regarded as a clean, green industry, particularly in the Lake District. The image of such a destination is crucial to tourist marketing,[8] but 'Homes of Football' is able to cut through this reputation for nature, walking and fine dining to offer a footballing intervention. That is why Clarke's work is described as an exhibition or gallery, but rarely a museum. It is also a clear example of a post-tourism business: visitors no longer search for the authentic experience of a place, but the clichéd, the artificial and the voyeuristic. To find a football moment in a peaceful, serene district of tramping, elegant cuisine and gothic landscapes is odd, and tourism thrives on the distinctive and the quirky. He is also correct that the Lake District is a 'neutral' space that allows many allegiances to circulate beyond the boundaries of the terrace chant.

*Figure 1.2* Green and Pleasant Landing.

The image titled 'Green and Pleasant Landing' was taken of Ambleside United in 1997. Captured from the top of Loughrigg Fell, the subtle project of Clarke is embodied in a single image. The gothic scale of the Lake District is a backdrop and frame for a football game, dwarfed by the encircling panoramic landscape. The key realization offered through this photograph is that Clarke – through his books and websites[9] – creates a new cultural identity, the virtual sporting tourist. After the Hillsborough tragedy and the setting up of the Premier League, we are all tourists through the sporting past.

Tourism, even in the digital age, encourages particular ways of reading the world. Photographs are important transcribers of reality, appearing to provide miniaturized evidence of reality. Clarke's photographs maintain this documentary quality, simply 'presenting' the changes to football. While appearing real and truthful, all photographs hold an ideological function. The 'Ladies' Retiring Room' was taken in 1990. This photograph demonstrates Clarke's archival role. Taken at Gigg Lane, Bury's ground, the photograph captured the room where women were expected to remain while men watched the game. It was demolished in the remodelling of the premises. As football changed, Clarke catalogued these disappearances. In the selection of images, particular views of a past world are validated over others. 'Homes of Football' romanticizes the past, while tracking the changes to the game and its

*Figure 1.3* Ladies' Retiring Room.

spectators. Football, like all sports, is locked in a tense embrace: how we in the present excavate and understand that from the past.

Both tourism and sport inflect economic, social and cultural life. The local resonance is significant: do tourists visit the Lake District and 'stumble' across 'Homes of Football', or is the exhibition a primary reason for visiting Ambleside? The difficulty is that sports tourism is rarely tracked through a governmental policy, and is hard to monitor as a self-standing economic contributor, rather than 'value adding' to a visit.[10] As the tourist industry becomes more sophisticated and specialized,[11] it must market the distinctive and the new. For example, the first World Cup in the Asian and Pacific Region was held in 2002. The long-term cultural consequences of such a sporting shift are difficult to fathom. No longer can the game unproblematically represent only a European or South American face.

Stuart Clarke, in my interview with him, conveyed his experience as a sport tourist to Japan and how he carried English notions of 'the Orient' on his travels (see box overleaf). There is an implicit acceptance in his words that English modes of football remain central to global soccer. Japan and Korea become quirky, childlike and enthusiastic – a restatement

**TB:** You've talked about capturing Englishness and Britishness, but I believe you went to the World Cup [in 2002] in my part of the world. Do you think it was good for the game? What's your opinion on taking [the World Cup] to the Southern Hemisphere?

**SC:** I think before I went I just thought it would be a marketing exercise that I wouldn't like. No, I thought they had a real feel for the game. Emotionally they got very excited. They probably work very hard as a nation. Perhaps the English work quite hard, but it was a kind of release. They love the colour association with teams and all that sort of stuff. And they kind of had a great sense of humour, the Japanese. They probably noticed some of the absurdity of costumes and places, and things. So it wasn't that horribly packaged event. I didn't enjoy the American World Cup that much. More than a mile from the ground, you didn't even know it was on. It was a bit like, 'Come here for the World Cup.' And I was used to what happened in Italy which was, it just spread everywhere. It's got a life of its own and there are grannies in the street with flags just walking along at 9 o'clock at night for no apparent reason. It was just this great big happening. And to see it so perfectly controlled in America. And me trying to find out more about it on the TV. And I thought, this is the World Cup. This is something that I've thought is the biggest thing on the planet, and you are belittling it, as you are. So I didn't enjoy it in America at all.

But Japan was something else. And I didn't even get to Korea in the end. I decided to concentrate completely on Japan and create a portrait of the country receiving the World Cup. I've called it Sun Army, when the World Cup came to Japan. That's what I've been working on for the last few months. And Korea, where there was perhaps even more fervour, I didn't get there. I kind of cut it out, I thought as a culture, I'd get a bit confused. And also, I went to 17 out of 18 games so I did quite well. If I'd gone to any more, I think my eyes would have closed. So that's what we did.

of orientalist discourses. His 2005 book *England the Light* tracked how the team fared in Euro 2004 in Portugal. More significantly, the book conveys an intense pride in Englishness, glorying in the saturating red and white of the St George Cross.[12] For Clarke, England remains the Home of

Football: non-English fans are tourists to the game. Tourism, even to Japan, has not challenged English modes of sporting communication. Instead, the travelling has offered another venue where English sporting success can flourish. The level of exchange, dialogue, challenge and change in these authenticating notions and modes of sport and culture is questionable.

Through his English lens, Clarke grasps the colour and drama of the game, transforming the ordinary into the revelatory. His eye for the excessive and humorous provides the space to challenge the relationship between modern and postmodern, Fordist and post-Fordist, old and new, centre and periphery. In a post-Fordist environment, tourism is no longer a peripheral industry, but densely impacts on planning and government strategies for economic development. Consumption is prioritized over production, and new forms of credit permit consumer expenditure to rise. With all aspects of social life and identity commodified, 'consumers' rather than citizens rally against the mass production associated with Fordism. Peripheral regions such as Ambleside are able to capitalize on a desire by visitors to experience difference in the comfort of England. Most importantly, 'Homes of Football' is able to tether peripheral distinctiveness to nostalgia. As Bkingre and Sorensen have suggested,

> The idea of a loss of something valuable is maintained through tourism, because tourists search in other places for what they believe have disappeared at home, and when 'confirming' its existence elsewhere they are simultaneously 'confirming' the loss of it at home.[13]

'Homes of Football' is important because it verifies – through 'old media' – how diverse localisms and local experiences are gathered through photographs and assembled for the consumption of tourists. Stuart Clarke remembers football and fandom before Hillsborough, a lost 'world' that survives through his photographs.

## Keeping your eye on the ball

> Who are ya?
> Who are ya?
> Who are ya?
>     Football chant

To look at sporting photographs is to stretch time and to appropriate memories not directly experienced by the viewer. This semiotic commuting creates a database of choices about identity and social relationships. This is part of what Erik Cohen saw in experiential tourism:

The renewed quest for meaning, outside the confines of one's own society is commenced, in whatever embryonic, unarticulated form, by the search for 'experiences': the striving of people who have lost their own centre and are unable to lead an authentic life at home to recapture meaning by a vicarious, essentially aesthetic, experience of the authenticity of the life of others.[14]

In an era of the English Premier League and the Champions League, with globalized coverage and a loss of localized specificities, Stuart Clarke's photographs provide a brief insight into a moment of passion when a team scores a goal, or the dark corners of grounds lost through demolition, decay or 'renovation'. While many ways of seeing are summoned by Clarke's photographs, it is important to ponder how the virtual sporting tourist gaze grazes the surface of his images.

John Urry based his early and remarkable academic career on investigating how the tourist gaze 'is socially organized and systematized'.[15] Through photographs, the tourist gaze is framed, controlled and commodified. While men are assumed to be the obvious spectators to sporting photography, Barbara Creed has shown that 'the gaze of the female spectator (critic/filmmaker) is now more relaxed, confident and innovative'.[16] Phallocentrism, as a symbolic order, validates the phallus and those eroticisms which it appropriates. The insights of both feminism and men's studies have shown that plural masculinities are unsettling to this phallic order. In the realm of sport, and within Clarke's photographs in particular, men are featured in myriad guises, from the fool to the fan, and the true believer to the traitor. Through such images, sport becomes a way to summon nostalgic and ambivalent working class masculinity. Miriam Hansen has realized that

> [i]f a man is made to occupy the place of erotic object, how does this affect the organization of vision? If the desiring look is aligned with the position of a female viewer, does this open up a space for female subjectivity and, by the same token, an alternative conception of visual pleasure?[17]

The question is whether or not this role reversal allows women to appropriate the gaze, or actually confirms patriarchal modes of vision. Female spectatorship, particularly when cut through with class-based concerns, encourages awkward identifications. The Lady Chatterley gaze on working class men is undertheorized, with Lorraine Gamman suggesting that the female gaze move generally 'can literally throw itself within the frame and outside it to whoever is clever enough to catch it'.[18] With a male photographer primarily photographing men within the heteronormative discourse of sport, the resulting images can easily become excessive and camp. Little shutter space is left for excavating the limits and potentials of the feminine. Women's role in sport, particularly soccer, is tangential at best.

*Figure 1.4* Neon Girls.

The image of 'Neon Girls' at the Tranmere Rovers match in 1992 features two sisters serving at a burger stall. As fast food vendors, girlfriends, wives and mothers, the female body is removed from causing discomfort, conflict or contradiction in the realm of masculine competition. Clarke's work at its best captures the edges and shadows of sport. Women continually bleed into his photographic borders of sporting credibility.

There is a tension between how we see and what we are able to see. Photography is such a complex medium because it is a clearing house of the ideas and beliefs of photographers, the photographed and the interests of viewers. These readings are frequently contradictory, provoking either empirical or aesthetic interpretations. Greater awareness should be given to the role and function of surfaces and appearances. A photograph is able to slice a moment from time, and encourage excessive, hyperactive readings. John Berger has stated that 'photographs do not translate from appearances. They quote from them.'[19] Without this ability to quote and paraphrase, photography has no language of its own, but speaks through metaphor and performance. This discontinuity offers plurality and ambiguity in the sporting discourse, which relies on facts, statistics and certainties. While sports writing conveys an aura of knowledge and certainty, photographs simultaneously objectify and fragment the wor(l)d.

*Figure 1.5* Looking Up.

Photographs grant a magnitude and scale to the collective experiences of the working class, black and Asian communities and women in particular. An outstanding crowd shot, 'Looking Up', features Sunderland supporters in 1996 protecting their end and watching the goalmouth action. The photographer is not remotely relevant to this shot, but has provided an apparatus through which the viewer can gaze at an outpouring of collective fixation and commitment. While film rarely isolates and freezes a singular image, photography concentrates a view and a moment. By propelling photography beyond the aesthetic realm to show its historical and political function, it is a window – not a mirror – for society. It provides a view into micro-historical moments, disconnected from context, and available for political negotiation.

Football hangs on an ambivalent peg of Englishness. More than for other sports, there is a link between economic decline and footballing decline. The post-war period has witnessed the loss of both colonial power and foot-balling success for England at a global level. Former colonies have not competed against England in this game, as has occurred in cricket and rugby union. Football was never bedded into the sporting turf of Australia, Canada, New Zealand and the United States in the same way as cricket and rugby in the Antipodes. Sport is in the business of constructing competitive differences. Football – because little equipment and facilities are required – is cheap, providing a way for formerly suppressed or disempowered communities to summon a new representative matrix. Through cultural practices such as tourism, food[20] and sport, disempowered and formerly colonized citizens can be reconstituted and the symbolic order hybridized. Therefore, football has a dual function. It provides a competitive mechanism to judge England's place in the world. It also cuts up the terrain of England and Scotland, creating staunch regional and local belongings and rivalries.

Through the name of clubs and home stadia, local allegiances are maintained, creating an exotic past or a romantic landscape. Manchester United's 'Theatre of Dreams' is more than a ground in Old Trafford: it is a site of myth and excess. This iconic representation and cultural inscription mean that English football is often insular and self-absorbed. The Premier League and its global televisual rights reinforce the normalizing story that England is the home of football. Such an attitude is corrosive of innovation, and replays the colonial ideologies of home and abroad, citizens and foreigners. Stuart Clarke's 'Homes of Football' is a romantic presentation of sport and space. While he presents an incredible range of sporting stories throughout England and Scotland, there are not sufficiently plural cultural representations to grant the formerly colonized a role. The challenge for English popular culture generally, and sport in particular, is how to handle multiculturalism and post-colonialism within a new social and political order. In such an environment, there can never be an agreed version of a national past.

The changing relationship between people, place and power is tracked through popular culture. The Commonwealth was not a replacement for the Empire. Ironically – but perhaps not – the former Empire returned 'home' to play football. One-quarter of professional players in football leagues and the Premier League are black, most of African Caribbean origin, but less than 1 per cent of supporters of the top clubs are black.[21] Intriguingly, while the Sir Norman Chester Centre for Football Research assembled highly detailed information about the regions and earnings of fans and the gendered spread of the spectators, their race-based research was more intuitive. In 2002, they reported that 'we suspect that ethnic minority support is also growing, but only slowly and from a very low base'.[22] In a separate report to encourage 'The New Football Communities', they reported that there are only two ethnic minority employees in an administrative role within the 88 professional football clubs. Only one-third of clubs have written equal opportunities policies. Black players still face abuse by white spectators. Richie Moran remembered from his playing days that

> it always disturbed me when playing professionally that when I looked on the terraces and saw the features of middle-aged men contorted with hate racially abusing me, that self-same man was often standing

with his arm around his eight or nine-year-old son who was quite often calling me the same thing![23]

The face presented by English football is one of white power. Such an interpretation is confirmed in Stuart Clarke's photographs. While the greatest moment in English football is the World Cup victory in 1966, it is appropriate to remember the racial context in which this win was placed. Only two years after the victory, and spurred on by Enoch Powell's 'River of Blood' speech, the Commonwealth Immigration Act limited settlement to those who had 'patrial' ties with existing British residents. It was a way to restrict the immigrants from India, the then East and West Pakistan, and the West Indies. Stuart Clarke's images restate this black/white, player/spectator divide. His photographs overwhelmingly feature white men watching football. Whether in Liverpool or London, whiteness permeates his frame. Such a 'documentary' inflection restates football's whiteness at the level of officials, administration and management, but also fandom. Once more, the Empire performs for the colonizer's pleasure. As a memory prop, such photographs offer an idealized relationship between classes, genders, races and nations.

The low credibility granted to sports writing and journalism means that its social importance has been underestimated. James Walvin has suggested that 'football offers an outstanding example of the discrepancy between the historical role of a particular sport and its failure to find an adequate place in written history'.[24] Bodies like the Manchester Institute for Popular Culture and the publisher Frank Cass demonstrated a commitment to sport theory, particularly with a cultural studies inflection. Sports history has remained at a lower standard. Club histories and auto/biographies of celebrity/players offer little insight into either context or social change. At its best, football shadows the changes to urbanity, work and leisure. While the affiliation between public schools and rugby is clear, football provides powerful fodder for a discussion of working class history. The Cup Final of 1882, won by the Old Etonians, was a turning point where a southern gentlemen's team was challenged from the north by Blackburn Rovers. The success of football among northern and Midland working class men led to the professionalization of the sport. Crowds increased and the commercialization of football became possible. Yet few sources remain of how football changed the representation of white working class men. Photographs reveal how such power has been poached and renegotiated through sport. Particularly, crowd shots show the potential for collective action. Leisure spaces not only provide legitimated pleasure, but display how social control is imprinted on docile working class bodies. The spectacle of football provides not only a theatricality of display and performance, but multiple exchanges of looks, glances and gazes. Architecture – such as sporting stadia – helps to visualize power, providing a link between visuality and authority. Commentators, journalists, players and managers have a designated role and a legitimate function within the realm of football. The crowd rarely does. The next section of this chapter tumbles these debates about sports tourism, class, masculinity and photography into the greatest rupture that confronted the modern English game: Hillsborough.

## Crushed faces in a crowd

> Oh I am a Liverpudlian
> And I come from the Spion Kop.
> I love to sing, I love to shout,
> I get thrown out quite a lot.
>    The first Liverpool chant mentioning the Kop

A disaster, by definition, is an unexpected circumstance. Too often, the free-flowing emotions dissipate with the initial publicity, leaving little capacity to assess the long-term resonances of misfortune. When two fuel-laden airplanes crash into the twin towers, a tsunami engulfs Sri Lanka, or a coal slurry covers a school and houses in a Welsh village, national cultures warp. Through the medium of television, grief and confusion are conveyed to the viewing public. These short, sharp tragedies trigger pity and shock. The insight granted by single incidents rarely triggers long-term, dense reflection because few public discourses of death exist. The news media portray extraordinary deaths as self-standing 'acts of god' bubbling with the emotions of survivors.

The Hillsborough stadium was the setting for the death of 96 people who were crushed in the visitor's end of an FA Cup semi-final game between Nottingham Forest and Liverpool at Sheffield Wednesday's ground. Lord Justice Taylor, in his 71-page report on the disaster, made many recommendations. He crafted a well-researched document, based on 1.5 million words of testimony provided by 174 witnesses during 32 days of hearings. He cleared the blame from Liverpool's supporters and confirmed the errors of the police. This finding critiqued the press reports of the preceding weeks, which blamed 'hooligans' for causing the deaths of the crushed fans:

> Many fans who escaped onto the pitch alive were in a state of collapse or close to it. Most of those who retained their strength strove magnificently to assist the victims. They helped pull them clear; they helped with first aid; they helped carry the improvised stretchers.[25]

Lord Justice Taylor showed that the police had let too many fans without tickets into the small and barricaded space for Liverpool's visiting fans at the Leppings Lane End of Sheffield Wednesday's ground. Police then refused to open the gates at the front of the terrace when it was clear that fans were being crushed to death. This was the important determination in the report.

The reason why the police seemed to survive Hillsborough without severe reprimand is that Liverpool fans had some form. On 29 May 1985, a group of Merseyside away supporters attacked the followers of Juventus at Heysel Stadium in Brussels. Thirty-nine Italian fans died when a wall of the stadium collapsed. Fourteen Liverpool fans went to jail for their part in this tragedy. It was only on 5 April 2005 that the Kop and Liverpool Football Club addressed the consequences of their actions. When the Reds played Juventus in the first match between the teams since the tragedy, the Kop displayed a human mosaic which read 'amicizia', or friendship. Paul Kelso recognized the significance of this moment:

> Liverpool know more about tragedy than any football club. Their supporters have grieved for those lost at Hillsborough and campaigned tirelessly for those responsible to be brought to account. However, in contrast, their part in the carnage that occurred four years earlier had not been publicly and unconditionally acknowledged. Last night, collective amnesia pricked by the unavoidable reminder of a Champions League quarter-final, Anfield finally faced up to the most shameful night in the club's history.[26]

What is remarkable is that not only had it taken 20 years for this reconciliatory gesture to emerge, but it could not be avoided because of the fixture list. If Liverpool had not drawn Juventus, then the length of time before public condolence and guilt were expressed would have further lengthened. While most Juventus fans expressed gratitude for the gesture, there were others who, to cite Simon Barnes, 'were not . . . prepared to play the part that Liverpool – the club, the fans, the city – had prepared for them'.[27] While blame can be placed – firmly – on Liverpool fans, the events at Heysel were also caused by a complete lack of respect for the footballing crowd. A poor stadium, aggressive policing and poor planning all caused the death of 39 Juventus fans. Stuart Clarke's work is important because he actually photographs the cliché – giving the crowd a face and a context.

There is something about Liverpool's Kop – with the swaying and surging of the crowd – that encouraged intense community bonding alongside competitive hostility. The photograph of the Kop – taken by Stuart Clarke in 1992 – captures something of the scale, humour and collectivity of this footballing phenomenon. The security and safety concerns are obvious. When looking at the faces in the crowd, it is difficult to demonize fans as hooligans who 'caused' Hillsborough.

It is far easier to blame alcoholic hooligans than the police, poorly funded facilities or conservative and inappropriate laws. Margaret Thatcher's July 1985 legislation, Sporting Events (Control of Alcohol etc.) Act, was a mechanism to eradicate football hooliganism. This legislation made it illegal to drink, be drunk or possess alcohol on a coach or train heading

*Figure 1.6* The Kop.

to a football match. The Act was almost entirely directed at soccer, even though it mentioned sport more generally. Actually, the greatest quantity of drinking occurs at major darts tournaments rather than football. This Sporting Events legislation had a profound consequence, indirectly causing the Hillsborough disaster. Tony Collins and Wray Vamplew realized that

> [t]he draconian measures taken against alcohol had unforeseen detrimental effects on football. Sadly, it took the 1989 Hillsborough disaster to highlight that selling alcohol inside grounds could persuade spectators to come into grounds earlier, thus reducing congestion problems at turnstiles, and help improve the facilities available to football fans.[28]

Rather than drinking at the grounds, fans would drink alcohol – quickly – in a pub until just before kick-off, only to push into the ground at the last minute. Such legislative social controls over football are common. Through the nineteenth and twentieth centuries, as the working class became better paid, laws intervened in leisure time, restating a Protestant work ethic that rendered recreation sinful and wasteful.

Stuart Clarke framed Hillsborough as an origin for his photographic perspective.

**TB:    You mentioned already that the Hillsborough tragedy was a trigger. How so?**

SC:   I passed over that. It was a trigger in so much that the game was being slighted. Onlookers would say that football had it coming, the game was run down, they act like animals. Whatever sympathy you may have for the victims, there was criticism for the way that the game was being staged. And the danger then is just to rip up everything as it was and just try to put in a new system. Well, I thought some of that is going to happen, some of it would be welcomed, if I could sort of create something that was kind of soulful. But at the same time I then became a Football Trust photographer. In some ways I was holding onto some of the feeling, the nostalgia for the game and I was also running – and being paid by one of the football authorities – to put an end to it, with the seats and CCTV and things to make sure that the likes of Hillsborough never happened again. They thought that was great, because they said that we are not building seats for no one, you know, we want to see who the people are – we like our link with you. It is a very humanistic thing that you are doing. It works well for us. I sort of had my own artistic pursuit, and every other week, and even at the same time as I take my crowd shots, I would also take some of the facilities, like the seats, the building works. I've loved having that twin role. One foot in authority and one outside.

**TB:    And it is very hard to maintain. It is very hard to do with some sort of cred. What exactly is the relationship with the Football Trust? Is it a signed agreement? Is it a formal agreement?**

SC:   Yeah, it is, actually. At first it was very much, I showed a counterpart of yours – in social history at Leicester University, John Williams – some of my early work. And he said, 'Wow, this is great.' He goes, 'I get paid something by the Football Trust to do our work. I'm sure that you could probably too, because you're providing them with a lot of the stuff that they are probably going to need.' And so, after a year of working quite informally, after a year, we signed a retainer agreement.

**TB:    What year was that?**

SC:    Nineteen ninety-two. And I began all of this in 1989. So that's when I became their official photographer and I have remained with them for ten years.

We both had the same starting point in that the Football Trust were in situ well before the Hillsborough disaster, but suddenly real money was coming their way. Suddenly, they had a real kind of cause to turn the game around from becoming shoddy and dangerous. And I arrived at the same time if you like, trying to do something that tried to show that the game could ascend, but I wouldn't forget all the ticket sheds and all the crafted facilities of the Victorian era. They're going to be brushed away. I didn't want that to just disappear. I couldn't physically keep all these things; you know when they were about to break a shed down or something. I couldn't say, 'Oh, I'll take that home, you know.' You can't. I've kept a few things, turnstiles and things like that, but in the end I thought – it's my photos. That's the thing I'm best at. I can perhaps capture the beauty, the absurdity.

**TB:    And the complexity.**

SC:    Yeah, that's right – the social fabric that each picture tells a story to someone, if not the same story. Someone will look at the ladies' room photo at Bury and chuckle and say, 'yeah, that's funny', and they don't really know why. And then someone will explain to them actually, what it means is all the women are expected to huddle in there while the men were upstairs enjoying their football. And they'll say, 'That's shocking. That's not very nice.' And so you've got all these different readings about the same thing. I just try to capture all these things, and show the glory of the game presently. People often say to me, you know, 'Is it better or is it worse?' They just want to hear that it's gone downhill, it should never have modernized. Or – 'It's fantastic. I love all the gleaming seats and the safety.' And my response is I kind of like it all, really. And I like the past, I like the present, and I'm excited about the future.

As Clarke conveys in his testimony, in April 1989 one sentiment was agreed by those involved in football: the game had to change. Club costs were high through stadium upkeep and player payments. Little money was being spent on fan facilities, and attendance had been dropping at league matches for some time.

| Year | Attendance at league matches |
| --- | --- |
| 1948 | 41 million |
| 1967 | 30 million |
| 1985 | 16.5 million |

Source: Adapted from Robert Dwek, 'Superstadia throw lifeline to hard-pressed League clubs', *Marketing*, 24 May 1990, p. 2

An ideal solution to the financial concerns and dropping attendance levels was to multi-task the football facilities, to create a year-round leisure development plan, including conferences, museums and tourist attractions. The 'experience' and safety of football spectatorship also had to be improved. The swaying of the Kop and other terraces in grounds around England, Scotland and Wales had – post-Hillsborough – been determined unsafe. All-seater stadiums became the catch-cry, with profound consequences for the pricing structure of football attendance. It had always been cheaper to stand. As Doson and Goddard reported,

> Of the standing spectators who were in employment, 58 per cent were in manual occupations and 42 per cent were non-manual, while for seated spectators the proportions were reversed: 40 per cent manual and 60 per cent non-manual.[29]

This study, which involved surveying the spectators at Glasgow Rangers, showed that the social consequences of seater stadiums would lead to middle class, feminized, familial ideologies entering the game.

The 'architectural time-warp'[30] in which football clubs found themselves meant that stadia required a large financial injection to reduce the risk to their crowd. The demolition of Wembley in 2002, 13 years after Hillsborough, showed that incremental, rather than revolutionary, change was the preferred method for administrators. The Football Trust, which oversaw ground development, had only spent £264 million on stadium redevelopment up to 1993.[31] The rectangular grounds, an architectural style popularized by Archibald Leitch, remained the standard shape beyond the twentieth century. The rationale for the stability in stadia configuration, even after tragedy, has many origins. First, a lack of state funding meant that redevelopment remains slow. Second, planning constraints from local authorities had blocked change.[32] Finally – and understandably – fans have a strong emotional investment in their grounds. The best example of this connection with a stadium remains the Kop at Anfield. This space, and the community within it, is a living memorial to Lancashire men who died at the battle of Spion Kop during the Boer War.

It was obvious after Hillsborough that a huge investment was required in English sport – at all levels of competition. By the early 2000s, football grounds below the Premier League confronted far-reaching economic crises through the demise of ITV Digital. The loss of future income and a revenue stream from the media meant that a large number of players were released by clubs, squads were reduced and redevelopment schemes for grounds were further delayed. The Coca-Cola sponsorship of football was a method to stem the decline of the game. This commercial support was needed, as the economic consequences of these building programmes were profound. Leicester City, for example, built a new all-seater stadium at the very time that they were relegated from the Premier League in 2001/02, throwing the club into bankruptcy.[33] More than a decade after Hillsborough, smaller grounds still survive with their terraces, increasing the gulf between the Premier League and the rest. The uneven development is obvious, forgetting that the Taylor Report recommended that all football grounds should inevitably become all-seater stadia.

One of the overarching recommendations of the Taylor Report was that more money needed to be spent on spectators. One hundred million pounds of public money was allocated to improve the grounds. Instead of spreading this money among the 93 clubs, it was granted disproportionately to the (then) First Division clubs which, it was argued, attracted the large audiences. This process widened the gulf between the successful, well-financed, globally branded clubs, and the regional associations. As D. J. Taylor has stated, 'no one dares to offend the top half-dozen club on whom the game's prosperity depends'.[34] By 1996, professional football became a dynamic area of the UK's leisure industry.[35] Even with the continued decline of England's north-west economy, the rise in football prices post-Hillsborough had less impact on northern attendance than in the rest of the country.[36] Such was the profitability of sport that in 2005 there was an *Observer*-based call to reinvest the profit received by the government back into these industries.[37] A report commissioned by Sport England found that the UK government receives £5.517 billion in income from sport, but returns only £661 million

|  | Seated attendance | Standing attendance |
| --- | --- | --- |
| Manchester United | 68,217 | – |
| Boston United | 1,626 | 5,017 |

Source: Adapted from *Football Grounds: Aerofilms guide* (Shepperton: Ian Allan Publishing, 2002)

in grants from the exchequer and the National Lottery. In response to these figures, the former footballer for West Ham and England Sir Trevor Brooking stated that

> I would like to see a reasonable share of that £5bn being reinvested. It would cost about £2bn to bring the surfaces, changing rooms and drainage of all the 45,000 public football pitches in England up to scratch, yet at the moment only £45m a year is spent through the Football Foundation. At the current rate of investment, it will take more than my lifetime to get those facilities right.[38]

The consequences of annual funding allotments, rather than long-term investments and economic strategies, mean that building and improving facilities like stadia are beyond the planning of local clubs and organizations. Obviously this lack of strategic funding is ironic, considering that the Blair government used sport and its encircling industries to address 'social problems' such as obesity, social dislocation and violence.

The fear of the Kop and other terraces extends a long-term hysteria about the crowd. Throughout history, a crowd is viewed with either fear or political aspirations and opportunities. Both readings view the crowd from above. To reveal the faces in the crowd also renders history more representative –

*Figure 1.7* Goalkeeper's View of the Crowd.

summoning a history from below. Rather than criminalizing the crowd, Stuart Clarke has revealed its light, happiness, tension and personalities. The outstanding shot titled 'Goalkeeper's View of the Crowd' features the Manchester City fans at Blackburn Rovers in 2000, when they secured promotion to the Premier League. Through such photographs, 'hooligans' become citizens with lives, passion and joy, rather than a demonized other.

Through the development of the Premier League, working class fans were no longer the only target market. The changes to the working class through the 1990s meant that the relationship between consciousness, football and local allegiances loosened its grip. Not only was social mobility and dislocation possible in the new economy, but the determinants of class were also shifting. The Premier League was able to cream off middle class supporters, leaving little but nostalgia for collectivized working class football history. Vic Duke realized that

> [t]he advent of the Premier League in England, the impending Scottish 'Super League' and the increasing probability of a European League ... have led the elite British clubs to seek a new kind of football spectator. Executive boxes and expensive seating are cultivated at the expense of the traditional cheaper terrace supporter.[39]

Football's history has been based on the commitment, money and allegiance of generations of working class men to their team. After Hillsborough, this passion became dangerous and regulated spatially through seats, and visually through closed circuit television. There were so many journalistic, political and critical commentaries on the Hillsborough disaster: alternative interpretations were difficult to discern.[40] The money made from the new fans meant that older allegiances were not only nostalgic, but unpopular.

Photographs such as those by Clarke provide alternative readings of a crowd. While sporting fans may be demonized, supposedly trivial events such as a football match can become a transforming and defining moment in a nation's history. Clarke's photographs are able to travel the path away from the bloodstained fences of Hillsborough. He believed that Hillsborough is the point 'when it seemed the game itself nearly died'.[41] His work moves beyond the narratives of disorder, violence and hooliganism. Steve Redhead realized that

> [i]t would seem that the two most important foci for serious study of football culture in the 90s and beyond are not football hooliganism and macho posturing as such, but the conflicting figures of 'participation' and 'passivity'.[42]

It is here that cultural studies approaches can dislodge and disturb the easy labelling of spectators, audiences and the crowd as hooligans. Football fans are neither duped masses nor drunken disturbers of the peace. They are not docile bodies easily controlled by seats, drinking restrictions and mounted policemen. Stuart Clarke's photographs provide the evidence for Redhead's tracking of participation and passivity after a disaster. Before Bradford, Heysel and Hillsborough, the voices and interests of football supporters were rarely heard beyond the terrace chants.

The choice of a club to support is a statement about identity, particularly for working class men. Women are still institutionally excluded from football. Manchester United provide the best evidence for this claim. In 2005, they simply scrapped their women's side so that their Cliff training ground could become a Centre of Excellence for disabled coaching. The *Manchester Evening News* quoted an unnamed 'Old Trafford spokesman' to justify this decision:

> We have always made it clear the ladies' and girls' section was about community partnership and education rather than establishing a centre of excellence . . . But ultimately the hope is that the boys will progress to the first team . . . So naturally more resources are put into that area because it is our core business.[43]

With women's football located at the periphery of Manchester United's 'core' concerns, the decision to delete the team was justified by terms like excellence, resources and prioritizing 'the first team'. In such a narrative, women's football does not facilitate excellence, but creates community partnerships which can be destroyed when the 'core business' becomes threatened. United's decision was poorly timed, with the UEFA European Women's Championship being based in the north-west of England. Blackburn Rovers' Ewood Park, Blackpool's Bloomfield Road, Preston North End's Deepdale and Warrington's Halliwell Jones Stadium all featured games. Old Trafford was not listed as a venue for Euro 2005. Instead, the opening fixture was held at the City of Manchester Stadium, Manchester City's ground. In a continuance of the United and City rivalry, the Blues' Chief Executive, Alistair Mackintosh, expressed great support for women's football. He did not mention 'community partnerships', 'ladies' and 'girls'. Instead he stated that 'we are privileged to have the opportunity to showcase the best in women's football in the best stadium in the country'.[44] City 1 – United 0.

This division between Red and Blue Manchester has a wider context. While women's football was banned by the FA in 1921, with the decision only lifted in 1970, the ideological residue – through language and organizational support – remains.[45] For example, when Mark Bushell, of the National Football Museum, appealed to the public for objects relevant to women's football, the language and labels of identity were significant. He stated:

> It would be great to discover documentary evidence relating to the formation of women's teams after the ban was lifted. But kit, medals, diaries you name it, many mothers and grandmothers must have objects stored away that could help people understand the passion and intensity off [sic] the women's game today.[46]

Sportsmen are rarely referred to as fathers and grandfathers. To enclose women's sporting past into the maternal labels of mothers and grandmothers was inappropriate in 2005, and is not facilitating gendered equity in sport. The desire to promote women's football is extremely important to the future of the game. Relying on past languages to do so is unproductive.

This structural exclusion emerges not only at the level of players, but also among spectators. A survey of the FA Premier League reported that female season ticket holders were only 14 per cent of the total in 2001, up from 12 per cent in 1997.[47] In the same year, only 20 per cent of men attended football with their partners, far lower than for other codes of football, particularly Australian Rules.[48] Yet journalists wish to link a feminization of the game with the decline of the terraces. Crinnion reported in the *Guardian* during the 1998/99 season that 'More women will be sitting in the stands, watching the box, following the form than ever before. As a spectator sport football is being feminized.'[49] Obviously the loss of terraces has created the expectations that women (or ladies) prefer to sit at the football (with legs crossed?), rather than stand. Conservative notions of femininity and masculinity are being mobilized here. Stronger research would investigate how Association football offers information about place, family and masculinity, rather than (over)scrutinize the (few) women in the stands. Attention should be focused on how men's identity is shaped and coded through football. For example, the rivalry between Sheffield's Owls and Blades extends back to the mid-1960s. It involves the claiming of space and performing the changes and conflicts in working class identity that is too often reduced to the label of football hooliganism. Heterosexual masculinity is frequently excessive in its performances, particularly during an era of far-reaching social changes to working class communities. Football, as a stable basis of place and self when jobs and families are threatened, has in itself undergone a transformation post-Hillsborough. With it, the community symbolism has been either decentred or destroyed. Football is pivotal to the maintenance of identity, whether it be local, religious, gendered, classed or ethnically inflected.

Stadia are spaces of and for meaning. They provide a venue for thought and memory. As one of the very few sites that align the social and historical imagination, they are a frame for individual life stories and what Edward Soja described as 'spatial consciousness'.[50] While tourist spaces provide markers so that visitors can recognize 'home' even when they are away, sporting spaces provide a series of markers that are unrecognizable and foreign to outsiders. Chants, colours and languages mark those who belong. While sport is trivial, it has a powerful symbolic significance and consequence. For disempowered communities, sport is able to carry popular memory from week to week, and season to season. The shirts, scarves, songs and humour incubate a sense of place, even when terraces are lost, stadia are demolished and television coverage discards local sensitivities for globalizing coverage.

While 30 July 1966 is framed as the high point preceding the steady decline of English football, actually Hillsborough has enacted far greater social changes to the game. It was a confirmation of the unravelling of post-war consensus. The market became the mechanism for allocating resources, reducing the governmental role in controlling the levels of economic activity. Eric Hopkins recognized that

> [b]etween 1979 and 1990 the working-class electorate was subjected to a constant bombardment of right-wing propaganda in favour of individual enterprise, the supremacy of market forces, the need for cost effectiveness and the wickedness of the dependency culture.[51]

In the midst of this period, Hillsborough's dead seared the nation's television screens. The working class – it seemed – could not be trusted in leisure. The Premier League would offer safer, more middle class entertainment.

## Histories of the present

> We're on our way.
> We're on our way.
> How we got here
> We don't know.
> How we'll stay there
> We don't care.
> Manchester City chant, 1999

This chant exploded from a moment of ecstasy, when the victory-challenged Manchester City finally secured promotion from the First Division to the Premier League. Having moved between divisions six times in seven years, the City fans (rightly) tempered their enthusiasm with paranoia and depression. While Manchester United has become a brand, Manchester City is the best example of fans performing better and more consistently than their team.

Association football is an odd sport. From the beginning of its formal 'origin' in England in 1863, it was recognized that controlling the ball with the feet was extremely difficult and required special skills. It is far easier to move and manipulate a ball with the hands, as witnessed through rugby union, rugby league and Australian Rules football. With so few goals, the sensations of winning and losing are more ecstatic and tantalizing than in the other codes of football, which feature greater scoring opportunities. Not surprisingly, the popular memory of these stark successes and failures presents textured, tangy possibilities.

Sport encourages nostalgia. Torn between the white heat of the current results, injuries, suspensions, scandals and sponsorships and the warm glow of premierships and victories long ago, critical history is traded for pallid nostalgia. Clarke is aware his pictures have catalogued a lost past that is romanticized in the corporatized, all-seater, family entertainment football of the present:

> The pictures that I take are doubtless nostalgic and strive to show a warm affection for the purest form of the game, coupled with the people who made it happen. Such as my dad, who organized football at a basic and amateur level for half his life. But this good tradition, and sentimentality, is surely not enough when faced with bigger and better – THE PROFESSIONAL GAME. I share with you all this fascination with the professional game. How far can we go with it all? How big to build the stands? When should we move our club onto a greenfield site unencumbered by history? I wonder, like many, as to where it will all end?[52]

Sports history never ends, bubbling with back page headlines, player press conferences, corporate deals and player transfers. Clarke is conscious of his warmth for the past and its fans, but also aware of how this baggage can inhibit change. There is nostalgia for the regional past of football, before the corporatized, London-centric Premier League.

Photographs are a pivotal intervention between the banal and the extraordinary. Urry stated that 'our memories of places are largely structured through photographic images'.[53] Photographs – by cutting a moment from time – are able to prioritize particular venues, players, spectators and results over all others. They provide potent fodder for creating heritage, not critical history.

**TB:   What is the biggest – no, that's inaccurate – if I was to ask you what is the most significant change you've seen to the crowd since 1989?**

SC:   I think it is the seating thing. They've tried to, particularly the Manchester United fans, they're famous for standing up most of the time. You know, we're not changing; the seats won't get in our way. But what it's literally done is given you a space that you are meant to be in, in that ground. It's made it much easier for the clubs to control the crowd, and know how many people are there. And to make a bit more money, actually.

When I went to the football with my dad in the 1970s at Watford, you could swap ends at half time. You see, you were at one end and then when your team changed ends, off you go. That was part of the beauty of the old game if you like. But it was hard to police, you know. The two sets of fans could meet half way and decide that they weren't swapping. They'd have a chat on the way while swapping ends, and all that sort of stuff. So, it's a way of keeping people in their place. It forces perhaps some people to, but I am amazed how the common man has made the passage to the new style of game with all the prices and everything. Slightly more clinical surroundings and being on your best behaviour. I thought they'd be put off by that. But they've stayed on with a new lot of people too, the families feel happy to go along as well. That is why the attendances have been going up every year for the last eleven years. They probably won't quite reach 1948, which was the absolute mass with their cloth caps.

**TB:   You see those pictures.**

SC:   Yeah, that's one of my visual starting points is just seeing those old photos and thinking what a glorious game.

**TB:   There is an order to the crowd too. It's not out of control.**

SC:   Yeah, it's not out of control. I've talked to some of the old boys from that era and they'd say when someone was in trouble we'd pass them down. There was an order and respect. And in the 1970s and 1980s, it was like bulls tramping through a crowd if they wanted to. All that seemed to go out the window in many grounds. And disasters followed. It probably was not quite as nice as some of these people remembered.

Heritage sanitizes and sandpapers the weathered textured surfaces of the past. The desire to create a 'sympathetic remembering'[54] in sports history means that experiences are frequently encoded visually as images in the mind, such as the cloth-capped crowd in the 1940s. Photographs permit the presentation of a surface history that raises more questions than it answers. Robert Hewison has realized that

> [p]ostmodernism and the heritage industry are linked, in that they both conspire to create a shallow screen that intervenes between our present lives and our history. We have no understanding of history in depth, but instead are offered a contemporary creation, more costume drama and re-enactment than critical discourse.[55]

When we observe Stuart Clarke's photographs, the past becomes personalized and engorged, but also seductive. Clarke's great ability has been to freeze a collective moment or landscape and tether an emotion to it.

Local histories are frequently lost in the push for grand, nationalized stories.[56] The struggles of popular history in attempting to make the past accessible transform Stuart Clarke's photographs into a political act.

**TB:   What do you think you can capture in photographs that is not possible in other media, like the Internet, films and popular music?**

SC:   I love song, but I also used to love to paint and draw. So I often think, why photography? I quite often think I would have liked to have been a painter with an easel by the pitch and that would also cut me away from all the photographers who are there that have got a very different purpose. You know, they capture the moment, the players, the controversial moment and that. And they look at me – although a lot of them know me by now – but they look at me. I'm not a snob and they're certainly not snobbish, but we move in the same circle, but different circles. They can't really work out how I am using these old funny cameras, I don't seem to be rushing around quite madly in the same way as them with their laptops trying to send images down the line to their editors and they've got no excuses now because everything is digital. I dawdle around and take up these odd positions that they never want to go to. I go up – high up, in these slightly obscured positions, because I want fans in my way. But they want telescopic, clear and right behind the goal, while I'm working across the goal. You know, we kind of are using the same language, but we're kind of not. There is no one doing what I do regularly at the football grounds. It would be harder still for them now. Now it is very much closed doors. The marketing men have moved in, you know, let's try and make some money out of this. And definitely not let them wander around taking pictures. I'm a bit on a ticket of trust because of what I've done for years. I've got a bit of a privilege, which I've probably worked for and deserved.

Photography captures the moment in that defining way. It is also quite scurrilous, because you can give a moment great authority, just by the framing of something.

I can photograph the red wall at Barnsley and that becomes people's overriding memory or image of Barnsley. But they've had countless games, millions of people have walked through the ground over the years, but it is such a strong image. It is a bit like storytelling. You have to have an angle. But because it is a photograph, you do have a moment of truth, and a bit of authority about it.

Stuart Clarke's work is part of an increasing palette of sporting heritage, which creates a new alignment between past victories and present losses. What makes him a special photographer and significant in sports history is that he wants the fans 'in the way'. Those who follow him gain an enormous range of views and insight from these obstructions in his lens.[57]

Sport – like music – can rarely be written about with accuracy, let alone passion. Of all popular culture, it is not well supported by scholars or educational institutions. I am interested when sport commerce plaits with sports culture. Such a study requires the use of many disciplinary and intellectual frameworks – from tourism and museum studies to cultural and sports studies – requiring attention to photographs, television, the Internet, popular music, class and colonization. In taking seriously Stuart Clarke's 'Homes of Football', I have explored how footballing photographs tell alternative narratives about crowds, masculinity, leisure and social control. Stuart Clarke's photographs are outstanding because they move beyond sweetness and light, and hooligans and Hillsborough. He shows the fluidity of mind and eye required to understand contemporary sporting culture in its density and complexity. The passions of a crowd are so easily washed from history. Institutional memories drown out the joy, confusion, despair and loss of football fans. Stuart Clarke provides a tremulous echo.

Photographs generate a unique apparatus for interpreting the past, particularly the vanishing past. While Nick Hornby has offered a somewhat patchy 'voice' for the fan experience, Clarke's photographs have provided a face and body. He offers a reminder to all historians tethered to the written word that the material available to study the past is heterogeneous and rich.

**TB:   You've talked about the framing of a photograph in terms of a memory. How do you feel when these photographs are placed in art galleries or museums? What do you think that framing does to your work?**

SC:   Well, I put them up to create an image or idea. But people can walk through them in any way, and in any order. People will walk straight in and go to picture number twenty-six. It is no use trying to tell people what they should see first, or even think. And once again, I like that slight ambiguity. Some people might say – love the colour of the Barnsley red wall. Some people might see the broken glass on top of the wall. You know, maybe a bit of signage or graffiti which is a bit rude. But it springs a few little explosions.

Britain was the first industrialized nation. Now, instead of manufacturing cotton and steel, it is producing cultural tourism. Instead of winning the World Cup, it has lost the stadia that shook with past triumphs. The authentic experience of British sport is applauded only to be exploited. British sporting history transforms into a virtual theme park of triumphs, victories and successes. Stuart Clarke's photographs hint at alternative truths. Most significantly he maps emotion, linking subjectivity with community. Football teaches competition, respect and discipline. It also teaches hierarchy, power and violence. Spectators invest in the club, and the bond between fans and football is distinct from popular cultural relationships with other leisure industries. With the global brands of Manchester United, Liverpool, Arsenal and Chelsea taking out a patent over the planet, it is important to acknowledge that football clubs represent small and large places – towns as well as nations. Post-Hillsborough and the Taylor Report, stadia have become safe, sanitized and surveilled. Clubs have relocated and terraces are punctuated with seats. Long-derelict 'homes of football' once held residents who were riveted to the meanings in the sporting movement. The chanting echo is gone. The silent photographs remain.

# Chapter 2

# If Shearer plays for England, so can I

## The National Football Museum and the popular cultural problem

Football, like most popular culture, has a problem. Because it *is* life, and not only a *part* of life, it embeds itself into daily conversations, clothing choices, meals and metaphors. The chants become clichés and the colour of a kit transforms into a signifier of place and identity. Blue and Red Merseyside not only display support for Everton or Liverpool, but display indications of religion, family and perhaps class.[1] Our team provides information about 'us'. An Arsenal – Gunners – fan has different expectations and notions of success and failure than a supporter of Tranmere Rovers.

There is no barrier or separation between self and sport. Knowledge about results so tightly enmeshes into intricate family stories that there is no visible join. This tight weaving of players, managers, great wins and embarrassing losses into the fabric of identity poses a dilemma. When writing a history or creating public institutions like museums, an historian or curator is mobilizing not only aloof facts and cold objects, but also the throbbing life and joy of fans' lives. In most popular culture, fans know more than academics, journalists and museum curators. Sport is the intense confirmation of this principle.

The National Football Museum opened in Preston in 2001. It is a brilliant, evocative, interactive celebration of football. But it has confronted challenges. Eighty thousand visitors were expected in the first year: only forty thousand attended. While costing £15 million to build, it was left with little money to run on a daily basis. The current high-profile football stars with money and personal stature to contribute (and donate) have not visited the museum, yet every living member of the 1966 World Cup squad has acknowledged the institution's role and purpose. There is a significant point to be made here. Popular culture is of its present. It sucks (dry) the marrow of the contemporary, leaving the past redundant, banal or boring, like last season's trousers. While fans remember the Premierships, Championships, cups and medals, only a particular type of celebratory history is summoned, one which is directly relevant to present performances. A museum of popular culture, and particularly football, is tested by the fickle nature of the subject. When the present is all that matters and a glorious, nostalgic past is all that is required, a complicated problem emerges for a museum curator. This chapter excavates the problem of – and in – the popular, with particular attention to the sporting museum. The Preston National Football Museum is the case study into which the following analysis is poured, but the issues are similar for all information and knowledge 'experts' who dabble in the contradictions of the popular. The popular cultural past is owned by those who live it: it is not squeezed behind glass.

## Foucault's crypt

Museums were made for Foucault, and Foucault for museums.[2] Michel Foucault embodies all the contradictions of twentieth century intellectual life, and our bizarre fascination with obscure, difficult French thinkers. It seemed that during the 1980s a French accent and a black pullover were the foundations of academic fame. Add bizarre sexual practices and a fondness for Italian cigarettes and short, bitter coffees, and a legend is born. Foucault was an outstanding, innovative thinker, but he has come to represent, embody and theorize far more than he actually accomplished through his writings. It seems impossible to discuss sex, knowledge, prisons, madness, medicine, history or museums without tripping over footnotes to his greatness. The question is whether his work actually contributes (any longer) to a specific analysis of sport museums. The tragedy is that – behind the easy comments about power and resistance, dominance and subordination – museum studies is an outstanding, innovative and fascinating field. Significantly, Foucault is not always a handmaiden for their arguments.

The tight embrace between theory and practice, alongside a public fascination with heritage, has triggered an explosion of museums and a diversification of their activities. A new mapping of the field is taking place, instigating productive dialogues with cultural studies, tourist studies, design, the visual arts, public, community, social and oral history and popular memory. The museum is part of a unique vocabulary of designing knowledge. The construction of the Hellenistic Museum of Alexandria in 3BC provided a venue for scholarship, a site for scholars. Although this institution is long since destroyed, its memory was preserved through language: the Greek *mouseion* became, in Latin, museum.[3] The term returned through the 1793 French Revolutionary government, where it was used to describe the public collections of rare objects. Such a naming hailed the power of ancient Alexandria, while demonstrating a respect for the intellectual and a passionate reinscription of politics and citizenship. The Muséum d'Histoire Naturelle and the Louvre are the modern archetypes. While they function less as a collective of scholars, their aim is to collect objects.[4] From this origin, there was an attack on the powerful, with the private aristocratic objects being placed on public display. It was a revolutionary gesture. It held a pedagogic function, instructing 'the people' in the rules and possibilities of the French nation. The museum nationalized art, removing it from daily life. These origins punctuated the nineteenth century museum, particularly in shaping the bourgeois passion for collecting. The working class – supposedly – would be osmotically 'improved' through this contact with the spoils of the elite.

Museums are intellectually interesting because they are cramped presentations of pressure-cooked history, made by the winners and viewed by the losers. Didier Maleuvre realized that museums are '*essentially* historical'.[5] The role and place of popular culture, the working class, women, immigrant and indigenous communities are volatile interventions in this museum discourse.[6] Through these complex positionings of popular culture, sporting museums have garnered little critical attention. For example, Gaynor Kavanagh acknowledged that her collected essays revealed clear absences:

> Making histories of men, sports, buildings, gays and lesbians have not been dealt with, even though these are legitimate areas for modern history museum provision.[7]

Considering the sheer number and influence of sporting museums, from the Royal and Ancient Golf Club of St Andrews Sports Museum through to the Marylebone Cricket Club Museum and the Wimbledon Lawn Tennis Association, these facilities are an integral part of the venue. For the football clubs Manchester United and Arsenal, their museums are deliberately commercial ventures. To discuss the contemporary museum without a thought for sport is a problematic absence. Yet there are some analytical difficulties to address in museum studies before sport can flood the field.

The method and rationale of the collecting policies for popular culture are difficult to standardize. Through these challenges and decisions, museums are important thinking spaces for popular culture. As Moore has stated,

> Museums offer an environment to explore the meanings of popular culture in ways that academic texts cannot, primarily because the material culture can be directly experienced.[8]

Museums are an ideal space to collapse the gap between the academy and society. The popular cultural objects in a museum provide a way to transform public consciousness for shared objects into shared directives for change. The assumptions of daily life are interrupted by tactical pleasures and local resistances.[9]

The theoretical tangle emerges in debates between popular cultural studies and cultural populism. This debate is a negotiation of how popular culture should be researched, discussed and evaluated. Populism generally refers to an unstinting celebration of the popular as being intrinsically of value. This is a reverse snobbery that attacks high cultural criteria of quality. Simon

Frith and Jon Savage made the crucial realization about why popular culture
– beyond celebrations of populism – is important:

> The 'accessibility' of popular culture . . . describes not only the fact that
> 'everyone' can understand it, but that everyone can use it, has a chance
> to be heard, to develop their own language, however difficult or unpop-
> ular what they say may be.[10]

This is an important realization. The *use value* of popular culture is the key,
not the *qualitative value*. Populism – whether derived from the New Right
or disillusioned Marxists – infantilizes 'the people', 'the public' and 'the
audience'. The purpose of such an interpretation is to control the multiple
desires and opinions of fragmented and diverse social groups into a homogenized, controllable, representable 'nation'.

Museums are caught in a tight dialogue between knowledge and power.
Objects that have been worn, thrown and kicked are confined either behind
glass or within a building. Removed from a context, objects are granted new
interpretations that have little bearing on their original function, meaning
or volatility. Such a selection process is made more controversial because
of a dual difficulty: museums are becoming more reliant on large donors as
state subsidy declines, while at the same time curators wish to broaden the
collections to 'outreach' into the community. The notions of authority,
intention, interpretation and representation are not cleanly resolved in a
museum. Sir David Wilson, former Director of the British Museum, stated
that 'it is the objects which are important: they must speak for themselves'.[11]
But a soccer ball does not have a mouth. Formalist museums have been criti-
cized because when objects are allowed to 'speak', they voice the dominant
values of the powerful. In sport, such ventriloquism is difficult to sustain.

The diverse origins of the public museum – 'renaissance humanism,
enlightenment rationality and nineteenth century democracy'[12] – create odd
and conflictual directions and hopes. Museums were a product of modernity. Now in the much-marketed (post) postmodern age, the museum is
sandwiched between the local, national and global. Such a tight spatial and
ideological squeeze is triggering challenges. National institutions, such as
the football museum, are storing a society's treasures and signifying the
nation state. The complexity arrives when pondering how regional,
women's, minority and black histories are positioned. To build a museum
is to circulate society's rules in a controlled environment. Private memories are codified and commodified in public spaces. An even greater concern
is how intense local allegiances and differences are woven with the global
marketing of the Premier League.

Museums are unstable, managing ruptures of time which awkwardly cut
up the past and present. Such temporal jostling relies on a functional
ideology of progress to keep the volatile memories of visitors in check.

Whatever has happened in the past can be explained (away) by stressing the accomplishments of the present. Sporting museums order objects through the gauze of winners and losers, fair play and deception. Such a story can be sculpted because only objects that have survived through time can be shown. By displaying artefacts 'objectively', and shaping them through modes of categorization and classification, dissonant interpretations are repressed. In a time of ephemeral culture and the information age, museums represent a 'stuffy' permanence and stability.[13]

Through all these contradictions and paradoxes, it is obvious why Sharon Macdonald would remark that 'museums face an unremitting questioning about whom they are for and what their role should be'.[14] Museums display not only past objects but also past thoughts. The reason for the preservation of some items – without their context – is often inappropriate. By repeating the historical structures of human culture, the excesses of orientalist and colonial ideologies can be revealed.[15] Debates about museums are arguments about culture, and its production and conservation. They are also discussions about value.

To operate, museums require some sense of how words like 'the public', 'community' and 'consensus' function. Maleuvre showed how these words align to create a functional mission statement:

> Museums are institutions devoted to the protection, preservation, exhibition, and furtherance of what a community agrees to identify as works of artistic or historical value. In them, the artistic and the historical fuse into one seemingly immanent essence.[16]

In this fashion, 'official' and 'collective' notions of history conflate. It is no surprise that popular culture has infiltrated museums. Notions of cultural value have radically shifted in the last 50 years, and this movement has been tracked by both cultural and media studies. Museums, through their origins in revolutionary France, did not display popular culture, because it was marked as inferior and ephemeral. Instead, canonical notions of art and excellence were meant to inspire an aspirational working class. Simply because these museums were 'public', that did not mean that they were accessible. This confusion and ambivalence triggers an odd dance between 'the popular' and 'the national', and 'museums' and 'entertainment'. Once it is realized that *everything* has potential value, depending on the perspective of the viewer, the focus for a curator changes. The aim is to make a collection meaningful, and recognize that visitors can subvert intended meanings. Emerging from a desire for public involvement, popular culture is a site of negotiation.

The key couplet to be resolved in popular cultural museums is the relationship between experience and research. Is playing football and supporting a team all the expertise required to understand the game? The role of scholarship, reading and interpretation frequently seems foreign to the passionate intensity of scoring a goal or seeing a goalkeeper stretch for the impossible save. The bottling of this passion behind glass, with a neat card describing the contents of the panel, is not appropriate or satisfying. Yet individual memories of sporting moments can be wrong, and popular cultural museums must make compromises and revisions to personal stories that do not jolt or unravel popular memory too violently.[17]

The desire to democratize museums has existed for some time, but the theoretical underpinning and political direction of this goal are less well understood. While the popular cultural museum, based on sport, fashion or television, may attract a new audience, how will visitors benefit from the visit? It is timely to unravel the assumption that museums – intrinsically – are valuable. The best research into the role of popular culture in museums has been conducted by Kevin Moore.[18] He has recognized that 'popular culture, at least until recently, has tended to be relatively neglected, marginalized or conflated with leisure'.[19] Popular culture is more than triviality and light relief. It is the site where life's stories are told and negotiated. While curators think that they know what 'the people' want, Moore is far more reflexive about the identity of these 'people'. He also enfolds his passion for football, particularly Tranmere Rovers, into his scholarship. Through form as much as content, he shows that there is no clear line between theory and policy, scholarship and fandom. The distinction between high and popular culture has been perpetuated by many empowered disciplines and institutions and will take time to unravel. It is important to note, considering Moore's theoretical and political beliefs, that he became the curator of the National Football Museum in Preston in August 1997 and Co-Director of the International Football Institute at the University of Central Lancashire in October 2004.[20] He has aligned the public service imperatives of museums with the educational role he outlined in *Museums and popular culture*.

Leisure, recreation, tourism and education are the new big businesses. Most leisure practices exist at home: gardening, listening to music, reading and watching television. To deploy the term 'leisure' and not popular culture is to stress consumption, not creation. It is amazing how few records of past modes of working, playing and thinking have survived. Manufacturing – and the workers, equipment and materials that it produced – has been lost behind the shiny surfaces of new leisure complexes. Perhaps the most significant task of museum theorists is to monitor how the institutions represent the abstract, the staunch refusal, or that which did not happen. Museums require communication. Curators' tasks are made difficult because they must communicate not only with scholars, but also with many new audiences. Visual literacy is a required skill, extending into the capacity to form a relationship between objects and narrative.

Museums build a bridge between memory and history. Memories are organized around songs, photographs, furniture and buildings. For example, a story commences Gaynor Kavanagh's *Dream spaces*. She tells of a curator who found a box encasing a pair of shoes that were hardly worn. While he was able to date and catalogue the item, the question remains why they had not been used. Kavanagh continues the narrative:

> He looks up the name and address in the telephone directory and after a couple of calls finds the son of the shoes' former owner. He goes to see him and is told something about the man. He had been a bank clerk who had died in 1974 at the age of 79. He had bought the shoes so that he could take his wife dancing. He hated it, she loved it. She had died when he was in his early forties and he never wore them again.[21]

Objects – even ones as banal as shoes – tell stories. Within these tales are narratives of life, love, masculinity and femininity. Without the objects as a memory trigger, this story would have been lost. That is why popular memory is enmeshed in the work of museums. Museum time is not linear. It is not chaotic. It is circular, like a conversation, assembling linked ideas that mushroom into bigger narratives about the self and society. Material cultural objects – particularly those from popular culture – facilitate memory production and the building of identity.

## Footballing identity

All identities are relational and cannot be understood in terms of their intrinsic and essential qualities, but only in relation to other people and communities. In other words, 'Australia' has no self-standing meaning or content, but only gains significance when relationally judged against other nations like Aotearoa/New Zealand, Scotland, Singapore or Tonga. Therefore, terms like 'working class culture' or 'popular culture' are not intrinsically complete or meaningful, but placed in a dynamic and relational process. Sport has an organizing function in identity politics, configuring communities and enemies with great precision. It is also a site where rich community symbolism is not only created, but transmitted and reproduced. The tragedy is that – outside of 'soccer hooliganism' – most sociologists and cultural studies theorists completely ignore sport as a source and framework for understanding identity. As H.F. Moorhouse has recognized,

> Mainstream sociological analysis tends to ignore sport, including football. Where there is a lively subdiscipline, centering on football 'hooliganism', most social analysis does not bother with one of the great pastimes of the people, one which has divided and united groups in socially significant ways, and one which commands popular attention in ways that institutions which are regarded as more socially important (and are much more studied) do not.[22]

Football translates between tradition, modernity and postmodernity, while also summoning rituals of masculinity. Men and women possess different histories which occasionally align, but frequently rely on distinct representational rubrics. Women also have narratives and symbolisms for football, but these are too often ridiculed, decentred or ignored. While women are not playing in male leagues,[23] they occupy a series of important roles in administration, marketing, research, spectatorship and refereeing. Further, women's role as family members, facilitating the success of a masculine professional football, requires far greater attention.[24]

Football is unique. It is a team game without the pre-planned choreography of gridiron, or the batter/pitcher relationships of baseball. It requires a team-based interdependence which is probably only matched by Australian Rules or Gaelic football. National styles of Association football have also emerged. Comparing Brazilian, Italian and English modes of playing reveals distinct differences. Many of these distinctions speak to diverse class and race-based histories.[25] As Pierre Lanfranchi has suggested,

> In England football is the sport of the working class . . . For too long the 'continental' analyses of football have neglected a major difference they have with England: on the continent people do not play cricket. The polarities between town and country, amateurs and professionals, the Empire and the UK which these two sports bring out, have no equivalents on the continent.[26]

Football's English template is blocking interpretation of other modes and models. The implicit argument in the many chapters in *Playing on the periphery* is that English sport needs to be studied in a way that recognizes that other nations have distinct trajectories and histories. England is one of many 'homes' of football. While the Fédération Internationale de Football Association (FIFA) was founded by seven European footballing nations in 1904, by 1994 – the US World Cup – it had 179 member nations, and 44 affiliated non-members. We should stop theorizing football 'subcultures', but move to discussing footballing subjectivities.

A museum can reconcile these class and national challenges. Its symbolic spaces activate social and community dialogue. Popular cultural museums provide an opportunity to create belonging and allegiances for non-traditional audiences. While museums synthesize experience, barriers still block access and understanding. 'Those fans' need to be talked to, not talked over. Eilean Hooper-Greenhill reported that ethnic minority populations are highly under-represented in museum attendance.[27] Kevin Moore confirmed that 20 per cent of the UK population never visit a museum, 50 per cent visit at least one museum or gallery a year, and only 2 per cent visit eleven or more times.[28] Ironically, most of the objects on display in museums, although owned by the upper class, were made by the working class. Unfortunately, symbolic ownership is not so easily determined or granted, particularly in an era of heritage management.

## Heritage and haemorrhage

The past is fashionable because it is infinitely changeable. The plundering of earlier identities, events, fashions and styles stitches an awkward patch-work of images. The New Right, since the late 1970s, has fetishized a particular mode of history. Robert Hewison stated that 'we have no under-standing of history in depth, but instead are offered a contemporary creation, more costume drama and re-enactment than critical discourse'.[29] In actu-ality, critical or dissenting history is neither welcomed nor required by neo-liberalism or neo-conservatism. There has, however, been a willing and eager replacement.

In the last 20 years, heritage has become the word whose time has come. As a volatile thinking space, heritage raises questions of who owns and controls the present. It also leaves out the desperate and the dirty. Words like heritage, nostalgia and memory are silent detonators. Margaret Thatcher mobilized the word heritage to mould and shape a desirable history. Patrick Wright, from the standpoint of the mid-1980s, termed this a 'trafficking in history'.[30] The National Heritage Acts of 1980 and 1983 preserved a range of properties, and secured 'public access' for 'cultural consumption'. Thatcher attempted to revive the triumphs of World War II, extracting and discarding a critically interpretative history, restaging particular celebrated events, men and ideas. The grandeur of inheritance adds a scope and scale to a big past, rather than a little present. At a time when post-war consensus was being unsettled and principles of social justice undermined, public funding of museums started to decline while political celebrations of an exfoliated past increased.

Heritage is a readership strategy deployed by the powerful to restrict the meanings and interpretations of the powerless. Obviously history – not only heritage – is also an ideologically volatile construct. Both history and heritage are based on representations. Yet heritage summons a currency of exchange between producers and consumers, narrowing the potential for reinscription and disruption. For example, John Frow realized that

> [t]he heritage industry, which now includes monuments not only to ruling-class power but also to those idealized patterns of everyday life and work, has become an increasingly important piece of machinery for the construction of tradition.[31]

Postmodernism and the heritage industry are interwoven, creating a serene, opaque surface that prevents people from recognizing the debilitating and destructive determinants and conflicts in their lives. We need to be aware of the subtle shifts in meaning between the past, history and heritage. None of these words captures life as it actually was or is; they only facilitate the circulation of representations. When an object or part of material culture is 'retrieved' for presentation in a museum, an ideological decision has been made that tries to repress critical thinking and dissent that validated this selection. The problem is not a gap between representations, objects and real 'history'. There is no singular, real history to be (re)captured. Instead, there are multiple narratives, artefacts and ideas that formulate a web or matrix of history. Unfortunately, this plurality is difficult/impossible to represent in museum spaces. Nostalgia, or a desire for a simplified, pleasant past, soothes the trauma of this multiplicity. Susan Stewart has shown how nostalgia is a salve for the volatility of a critically edged history.

> The past has never existed except as narrative, and hence, always absent, that past continually threatens to reproduce itself as a felt lack. Hostile to history and its invisible origins, and yet longing for an impossibly pure context of lived experience at a place of origin, nostalgia wears a distinctly utopian face, a fact that turns toward a future-past, a past which has only ideological reality. This point of desire which the nostalgic seeks is in fact the absence that is the very generating mechanism of desire . . . nostalgia is the desire for desire.[32]

This desire for desire can make national identity insular, vulnerable and xenophobic. National museums can feed this tendency. Museums occupy a gatekeeping function in the nation state, protecting, nurturing and creating popular memories. Heritage is immersed in these debates because it operates at the level of the popular, through tourism, theme parks, memorials and museums. All these venues transform the past into a public, national celebration.

   This propensity – or economic necessity – to commodify a past is captured by the National Football Museum's initiative in 2002 to launch a Hall of Fame. Its task was 'to celebrate the greatest players and managers of all time in English football history'.[33] In the annual award ceremonies, 'the past' – a singular, celebratory national past – was celebrated. The inclusions in this celebration have corporate sponsorship. The companies that supported George Best's inclusion in the 2005 Hall of Fame received:

1   A once in a lifetime opportunity to meet George Best who will personally thank them for supporting his inclusion in the Hall of Fame. There will be an opportunity to have an informal meet and greet session with photographs and signatures . . .
2   A highly visible quality bronze plaque underneath the chosen Hall of Fame panel inscribed with e.g. 'George Best supported by (name or company name)'

3   Acknowledgement as a supporter of the Hall of Fame on the popular
    National Football Museum website . . .
4   Recognition in this year's Hall of Fame Programme . . .
5   Special opportunity to secure tickets in advance for this year's Hall of
    Fame Gala Awards Dinner . . .
6   You will also receive the plaque itself for you to keep as a wonderful
    reminder of supporting a legend.[34]

The use of 'legend' in the sporting discourse is not only tired and over-used,
but perhaps more accurate than the marketers intended. A sporting legend
is a dream, a myth summoned to simplify the stories of nations, events and
ideas. George Best was a fine footballer, but to include him in an English
Hall of Fame requires active forgetting of details such as the fact that he was
born in Northern Ireland, played for their national team and had a volatile
relationship with Manchester United. Yet for £3,500, a corporate donor gains
mixed-media advertising, and the 'feel good' recognition that 'The National
Football Museum is a CHARITY where all the monies raised go into the
conservation of objects and keeping the Museum FREE to enter for the public
to enjoy.'[35] The harsh reality of corporatization, that branding is required
to sustain a public good, is obviously another example of Naomi Klein's
evocative arguments in *No logo*, with the emphasis on consumerism, not citizenship.[36] Such sponsorship for George Best is even more ambivalently placed
when one recognizes that the research facility of the National Football
Museum is not open to academics or the public because of funding limitations.[37] That is, the largest and – arguably – most important football archive
in the world is unused because there is no funding to develop its facilities.
Celebratory heritage, with corporate sponsorship, is encouraged. Critical
history, facilitated by the use of the archive, is ironically closed for business.

Football heritage occupies an overt function in the branding of modern
culture, creating and sustaining an ideology of consumption, while obscuring
the unequal relations of capitalism. The conditions of consumption obscure
the conditions of industrialization. This masking of working lives and the
mode of production is made more serious considering that many players in
the Premier League are extremely well paid and being watched by and representing many working class communities. Brian Lomax affirmed that 'the
relationship between the football industry, football clubs and supporters is
complex'.[38] Fans are more than the customers of football or consumers of a
football museum. There is an intensity to the involvement, requiring loyalty,
time, effort and money. The bond between fans and football is distinct from
the relationship with other leisure industries. As a representational sport,
clubs name and claim towns and cities. Almost all the clubs in England are
named after a particular place.[39] This type of free advertising for a city or
town has been crucial for the creative industries of Manchester, triggered
through the fame of Manchester United. Fandom is now rarely restricted

*Figure 2.1* Red Café.

to a region. Television and the Internet widen out the catchment area so that a place and a team transform into a brand. The changes to football stadia since the Taylor Report also mean that they are now multi-purpose, multi-tasking facilities for leisure, shopping, tourism and sport. A visit to the Manchester United ground at Old Trafford confirms this diversity of role. Old Trafford is the home of a 'superstore' selling merchandise, a museum ticket and a guided tour. Dominated by red, it is an integrated experience of commerce, fandom and sport. The use of video and sound is matched by the 'conventional' display of photographs, kits and trophies. Even when static displays are put in place, excellent design strategies add interest and innovation.

The Manchester United Museum is outstanding. Whatever one's opinion of the team, the structure, media deployment and viewer involvement in these facilities are high. Just as the on-field play and management are professional, so is the museum. The use of old footage is excellent and is innovatively reconstructed for present purposes. It is obviously part of the marketing initiative of Manchester United Enterprises. It is a way to mark United as the multi-media team for the time. All other clubs become bit players and guest stars in United's history.

The United 'experience' demonstrates how good museum design and direction can contribute to sport tourism. Certainly it is nostalgic, encouraging sport heritage rather than history. It does demonstrate that museums are marketable and can be highly integrated into the sporting 'experience'.

*Figure 2.2* Curving the static.

There is a reason why English football is nostalgic: England and France dominated football for the first 70 years of its history. That level of influence does not currently exist. There is always a reason for looking back to the past. Popular memories hold a calming influence, a textual Prozac, to calm us as borders change, allegiances alter and our bodies age. Football is nostalgic, wistfully comparing the merits of different players from different periods: Pelé with Ronaldo, Best against Rooney. The irony is that this safe return to a time of success and simplicity is mediated through a highly advanced technological environment.

## Interacting with the dead

In 1994, Nick Hornby wrote of his concern and disrespect for sport museums:

> Football museums have a handicap that the British Museum or the Science Museum does not. An antique pot or painting is a direct and meaningful articulation of an ancient culture, and a working model of a steam engine is an adequate and instructive representation of the real thing. But football is necessarily about movement, athleticism, fleeting moments and huge crowds; a couple of old medals, a few international caps and a pile of old programmes – the staple of football collections – hardly capture the essence of the game.[40]

He could not have foreseen how remarkable the new museums were to become and how not only material culture would be deployed but also evocative footage, significant oral testimony,[41] tactile objects and viewer interactivity. Hornby romanticized the 'authentic' experience of football. Fans carry distinct desires and hopes to a match, and leave with different interpretations of the same scoreline. Also, most 'experiences' of football are already mediated through television and the Internet. Therefore, a museum – because of its open, interpretative framework and plurality of objects and ideas – can summon the complexity and diversity of football. For example, Nick Hornby has captured the passion of being an Arsenal fan. His ability to present 'the essence' of women's football, or even women's role in men's version of the game, has not been his strongest suit. Museums are able to capture this multimodal perspective.

The 'interactivity' bug has been immersed in technological change for the last 15 years. The Museum of the Moving Image (MOMI) in London, established by the British Film Institute,[42] was a pioneer, as was the Museum of Photography, Film and Television in Bradford. A judgement of dynamic or dull is not determined via a level of technological sophistication. Museums are multi-literate institutions, encouraging new ways of seeing, listening and touching. As Matthew Roth realized,

> Pandering to the alleged shallowness and short attention span of an audience accustomed to television and computer-based media neglects the opportunity to foster different ways of learning from looking at tangible objects, which have not lost their power even while other tools of communication have grown up around them.[43]

What Roth has not recognized is that the act of looking has changed. There is an historical gaze: in the nineteenth century, visitors looked at objects differently from today. Each medium encourages and develops new perspectives and literacies. The vivid visual experiences of a museum are now being matched by the use of other senses, particularly touch and sound. Touch is an underplayed sense in the museum discourse. Western thought is grounded in the visual.[44] The tactile has great potential as an educational tool and memory prompt.

The appropriate use of technology activates a delicate series of decisions for a museum. Technology must be carefully deployed, whether in education, the arts or museums. At times, unsuitable technology has actually fragmented the argument and agenda of the museum. A strong example of this concern is Urbis, the Museum of the City in Manchester. This museum explores people's experience of living in cities around the world. There are four floors of permanent, interactive exhibition. Unfortunately, the best feature of Urbis is the building. If a museum expunges all interest in artefacts (the content) and focuses purely on the 'wonder' of the form, then the result is invariably unsatisfying. For Urbis, there is no sense of direction or rationale. Museums are about ideas, not objects. Urbis does not have enough of either. The sound is clattering and obtrusive. The technology is self-standing: not an apparatus, but an endpoint. It is a rule to never start with the technology. Begin with the aim of the exercise, then choose the appropriate technology to realize that goal. There is too much 'gee whizz' at Urbis, and not a sufficiently reflexive interpretation.

Much nonsense and hyperbole surrounds the digital media, but when used well there can be a productive relationship between museums and new technologies. The buzzword that accompanied the 'digital revolution' is

*Figure 2.3* Urbis from the street.

interactivity. Museology theorists have researched interactivity throughout much of their intellectual history – how visitors 'explore' the collection – but have used different terminology. New media theorists must not impose terms and ideas on museum professionals that they have already been deploying in practice for many years. Innovative strategies are surfacing to investigate the relationship between the museum and media, museum and user.[45] Gay Hawkins and Julian Thomas have noted that 'the rise of the screen has had profound implications for the meanings and experience of museum space'.[46] Sporting museums require effective use of screens, not only for the presentation of archival footage, but to create an interactive inter-face for users to select options and navigational tools.

The digital media can be used for strategic educational purposes. Frequently, they are not deployed well, and are rarely considered in terms of a reflexive loop between teaching and learning. Activating such a process is difficult because empowered institutions are still dominated by print, while the most relevant mode of communication outside of formal education is visual.[47] Reconciling these communication systems in an era of convergence is pivotal, particularly in museums which require both signifying systems to work in tandem. Currently, 'new media' equates with excitement. This connection will – as with all past media 'revolutions' – pass. Gary Warner, who has been involved in the production of electronic media arts projects for over two decades, recognized that

> [t]here's been an arcane tendency to equate the experience of the museum with the experience of a shopping centre. That's a bloody awful comparison. Dangerous. The much more difficult path is to state that the museum is a place of cultural difference.[48]

Such a project is profoundly worthwhile and is theoretically possible. Visual – but also aural – media allow many meanings to emerge, particularly without the anchorage of a descriptive card which 'determines' meaning. These newer technologies can shift the centralized power of a museum, and its capacity to shrink a plurality of interpretations. By increasing the range and number of representational frameworks – from fashion to television to oral history and design – the potential for cultural diversity is realized.

Regimes of visuality are frequently regimes of power. When we cut up and fragment our view of authority, we unsettle familiar power structures. The movement from homogeneity and standardization to differentiation and fragmentation is facilitated through the passage from page to screen. Writing has always been visual, but convergent technologies tighten the link between written language and speech. To stress language alone is to neglect other modes of communication. Modes of seeing evolve historically. Visual literacy is an essential life skill, but changes like all other literacies. Sean Cubitt confirmed the remarkable social shifts triggered by video culture. He argued in *Timeshift* that there are profound social consequences shaped by this changing media:

> This book is about video in its relation to the building of a democratic media culture. Video, with its instant playback and its ability to record sound and image simultaneously, thrusts the instability of the present in your face and shouts in your ear: 'It doesn't have to be this way.'[49]

With videotape situated in a series of social relationships, visual literacy becomes ubiquitous and contestable. These struggles over meaning are intertwined with an increasing culture of surveillance. Put bluntly, we can choose from an ever-increasing range of pay television stations, but we will also be video-monitored as we go about our business at schools, workplaces and shopping centres. Similarly, while photographs objectify the world, there is a freshness and a shock of recognition that makes them disturbing. There is always a space between how a museum descriptor card identifies an object, image or footage and how it appears to a viewer without this information. While these written cues may frame an interpretation, viewer improvisation is common and should be encouraged. Photographs concentrate a view, but the free-flowing nature of film allows multiple interpretations to emerge from an event.

It is now possible to 'visit' a museum without leaving home, or at least a workstation. Dipping electronically into collections is not ideal, but is a metaphor for changing media literacies more generally. Nick Hornby's reading of a sport museum a decade ago is not only outdated, but redundant. To demonstrate how a football museum can function, these theories of museology, identity politics, heritage and interactivity are brought together in the final section of this chapter.

## Preston's nation

The National Football Museum at Preston is described as 'the spiritual home of the beautiful game' and 'completely devoted to football worship'.[50] It is highly appropriate that the museum is in Preston, as North End FC was the first winner of the world's oldest professional league in 1888/89. Although opened in 2001, it faced financial difficulties from the start. On the front page of the *Lancashire Evening Post* in October 2002, there was speculation that 'The National Football Museum at Preston's Deepdale today faced crisis amid speculation it could move to London.'[51] Poor attendance figures were seen to threaten the institution. Certainly there were problems during this period, including Railtrack strikes and the outbreak of foot-and-mouth disease. However, this poor attendance level was no surprise as the National Football Museum was the only national British museum out of 19 where an admission fee was charged. Kieran Howlett believed that attendance fees were the major problem blocking success: 'if entrance were free, thousands more people would visit the attraction, especially poor families who struggle to pay £6.65 for adults and £4.95 for children'.[52] In January 2003, with continued disappointing attendances, a decision was finally made to allow free admission for children from the local Preston area.[53] Howlett was proven correct: numbers increased. On March 2003, and facing remarkable local political pressure, the Blair Government finally granted the museum free entry for all, coming about through funding from both the Football Foundation and the North West Development Agency. In the first Easter bank holiday weekend with the new arrangements, nearly 4,000 people visited the museum.[54]

Further success followed this bumper Easter weekend. In the 2004/05 period, a target of 80,000 visitors was set by the Department for Culture, Media and Sport. The museum not only met this target, but attracted over 100,000 visitors to the exhibition.[55] The economic pressures felt by the Preston museum since its opening are not isolated. There is intense, centralized scrutiny of museums, with governments demanding accountability and efficiency. Corporate sponsorship is one way to alleviate the stress on these institutions, but too often this economic imperative has resulted in facilities being (re)located in London.

Beyond entrance fees, there is a more wide-ranging difficulty recognized by the museum's marketing manager. He stated that 'many people do resent the fact that the museum is in Preston and not London or the south of England'.[56] The acute concern that the museum may be lost from the region was expressed through myriad stories in the *Lancashire Evening Post*. On 17 December 2002, Kim Howells, the Minister for Tourism, stated that

> there is good historical reason to locate it at Preston at the home of one of the Football League's original member clubs. But we must recognize that location has played a part in the museum's financial difficulties.[57]

The Member for Preston, Mark Hendrick, believed that there was a concerted governmental desire to move the museum to London, to be encased in the refitted Wembley Stadium. While postmodern planning revitalizes the local, particular and peripheral, it seems much of the modern, centralizing imperative remains in contemporary football.

The tragedy of the museum's early financial failure is that it is highly successful by any other criterion. The display is carefully presented, well theorized and deploys a considered use of interactive technologies. It is the only national football museum in the world, and after seeing it football officials in Brazil, Germany and Norway are planning similar projects. Hunter Davis, the *New Statesman* correspondent, visited the museum and found it 'brilliant'. He also recognized the problems:

If it's so brilliant, as I maintain, and if football is so successful, rich and popular with millions, why have people not been queuing all the way along the M6? I wish I could answer that . . . Football-wise, as all football historians know, being in Preston is justified, but perhaps not otherwise. Who wants to go there? I've had specific reasons for four visits in 40-odd years, but I wouldn't have gone there otherwise.[58]

While the Ambleside location for 'Homes of Football', and its distance from urban football, has created a piquant surprise within the Lake District's tourist portfolio, the same strategy has not worked for the National Football Museum. Tourists, either from the United Kingdom or abroad, have not granted Preston a role in their visits. While the tourism industry is now highly sophisticated and specialized, the youth market is an important part of the sector. Researchers have shown that younger tourists are not interested in museums. Hunter Davis realized that:

Most football fans, especially new ones, are the same. It takes time for them to realize that there is a past. It's great that our National Football Museum exists but, like Martin Peters, it could well be ten years ahead of itself.[59]

With approximately 20 per cent of all international travellers identified as young people,[60] this is a sizeable slice of Preston's prospective visitors. If they are not showing historical interest in football, then that is a concern for the National Football Museum. However, the Manchester United Museum has many children visiting, and charges are made there. But Manchester is a different tourist destination to Preston. Publicity information for 'The Quays' at the Greater Manchester waterfront links Salford Quays, Trafford Wharf and Old Trafford as 'the ideal destination for culture, sport and shopping'.[61] The Lowry, the Imperial War Museum North and the Manchester United Museum and tour are linked to provide 'something to offer for everybody, whether you're a sports fan or a shopaholic, a culture vulture or a theatre buff'.[62] Through this strategy, sports tourism is granted a wider context and attractiveness.[63]

The distinction between tourism and non-tourism is not as clear as it once was.[64] It is rare for visitors to come to a city for a singular touristic purpose – such as visiting a football museum. Tourists are currently enacting multi-destinational trips, to increase the benefits of travel.[65] There is a desire to formulate a list of visits and itineraries, forming a coordinated approach to a region and a heterogeneity of travel experiences.[66] It is a way to rationalize the economic and time constraints: slotting as much into a trip as possible. Therefore, destination familiarity plays an important part.[67] If Preston is seen as presenting little of 'multidestination value' except the National Football Museum, then that will not be enough to encourage a trip. That is why

Stuart Clarke's 'Homes of Football' is successful: it slots into a Lake District visit. Preston is a fascinating place, in easy reach of Manchester, Liverpool and the Lake District. For an Australian writing these words, the short distances between cities would be an incredible boon to domestic tourism. However, distance is in the mind of the (English) beholder. Preston, it seems, does not have the multidestination appeal of London, or even Manchester.

The exhibition of football as a subject also poses specific problems. Because of the low fan participation from women,[68] 'family' tourism is more difficult to attract. The Sir Norman Chester Centre for Football Research reported that 'the proportion of adults attending with their partners or spouse has increased from 17% in 1997 to 20% in 2001'.[69] To expect women to make up 50 per cent of visitors, or encourage their partner to take them to Preston to see the National Football Museum, is stretching the reach of contemporary feminine interest. Similarly, the Centre reported that 'lower earners seem more strongly committed to their clubs than higher earners'.[70] Therefore, higher earners, who were less committed but were more able to afford the museum's entry fees and travel expenses to get there, would be more likely to visit the exhibition if it was 'easier' to access in London. The highly committed fans – earning less – were more circumscribed by the high admission fees when it opened. Preston's attendance suffered on gender and class-based grounds, increasing the 'issue' of the museum's distance from London. When the financial barrier was removed, some of these social obstructions to increasing the attendance were removed.

Cultural tourism, of which monuments and museums are a major part, is distinct from other modes of tourism. As 'serious leisure', it is far more reliant on the identity of the visitor. While beaches encourage a wide diversity of activities – sunbathing, playing cricket or football, picnics, swimming, walking or running – museum visitation rarely captures this range of interests. Sport, while part of cultural tourism, possesses its own specificities.[71] Because sports tourism is not often recognized, greater coordination is required at all levels of government.[72] It appears accidental or incidental, revealed through such 'enterprises' as the Barmy Army's tour of Australia for the Ashes test series or the planeloads of New Zealanders who fly to Australia, and Australians who fly to New Zealand, for the Bledisloe Cup. The British Tourist Authority and the English Tourism Council claimed that up to 20 per cent of tourist trips are related to sport, with up to 50 per cent of holidays containing some associated sporting participation.[73] There are myriad facets to consider: from active sports adventure tourism through to one-off sporting events. Sports tourism includes active sporting holidays, such as cycling, golf or fishing, but also more 'passive' viewing of games and events, and visiting sports museums. The question is, as Ritchie, Mosedale and King realized, 'Are sports tourists motivated by the events or match itself and leave the destination contributing little to the tourism industry?'[74] In other words, do visitors attend the museum or the game, and then depart, leaving little financially in the surrounding economy?[75] Such a question will continue to arise until definitive planning of sports tourism can be coordinated. The National Football Museum has an advantage as it is actually placed in a functioning football stadium. Such a strategy works for Manchester United, with their integrated superstore, ground and museum making a visit to Old Trafford more warranted.[76] There appear to be problems with Preston's transportation, image destination and subject matter that are restricting the attendance at and influence of a remarkable museum. Such a problem may be resolved when Preston North End is able to secure a place, and perhaps even more significantly a *secure* place, in the Premier League. The regular pattern of home and away matches, televised to a global audience, will increase the number of visitors in Preston to view a game and then see the museum. However, success and recovery cannot be assumed. The region is economically depressed, and finding money for regular Premier League game attendances has proved difficult for fans. Ken Worpole realized in the early 1990s that the British spending on leisure was increasing exponentially, but it was unevenly spread throughout the regions.[77] Such a tendency has only increased through the subsequent decade.

Football is central to English life, and is the national sport. Its status is similar to that of rugby in New Zealand and, debatably, cricket in Australia. Even through this popular cultural success, England holds an ambivalent position in global popular culture and sport. The resentment and anger about colonial excesses is part of the performative symbolism of football, cricket and rugby. In Wales, the sporting allegiance to rugby is a way to discredit Association football. Similarly in Eire, football is encircled by highly ambivalent politics of imperialism and revenge. Scottish football, even with movements for Celtic and Rangers to join the Premier League, established a completely separate competition from the English. National museums can create an insular, celebratory space of greatness that denies these conflicts.

Football is well suited to being represented in material culture. Fans objectify their allegiance through scarves, colours, kits, balls, programmes and endless match statistics. This enthusiasm and passion can be deployed in a museum experience. Consider the joyful obsession of Kevin Moore; besides being an outstanding museum theorist and curator, he is also a fan:

> At Tranmere Rovers in 1994 the pitch was sold off immediately after the last home game of the season. My partner and I queued with hundreds of other fans to buy a one foot square piece of turf each, which are now a carefully marked and tended part of the lawn in our garden. Each fan was given a 'certificate of authenticity' signed by the head groundsman. Two fans bought enough of the pitch to completely re-turf their gardens. Why? We now own a real, tangible part of Tranmere Rovers Football Club, we have bought in, we belong to the club, it belongs to us. If we ever moved house, we would dig it up and take it with us.[78]

This is commitment, and I am sure that the sport fans reading his words would act similarly if given the opportunity. There is an authenticating desire in sport, and it does have religious overtones. Ponder Moore again – this time moving allegiance from the Rovers to Pelé. He was part of a group assembling a 'People's Show' at Walsall Museum in 1990. It included a collection of shirts worn by players:

> As a member of the exhibition project team, I interviewed the collector in his home. He offered that I could put on a shirt worn by Pele, the Brazilian footballer generally regarded as the greatest of all time. I refused, because I felt I was 'not worthy' enough. I could only bring myself to touch it and be photographed with it. I ascertained that it had not been washed and therefore still contained Pele's sweat, which somehow seemed to be significant to me. This reaction may seem like madness to you, but I do not think it would be untypical of football fans. Would a Christian put on the Turin shroud?[79]

Again, this is an understandable reaction. What these stories are conveying, even for an 'expert' in museum studies, is that sport has a commitment and zeal. Recognizing such commitment, football can be an apparatus to welcome non-traditional visitors to the museum space.

Such an impetus and educative function are embedded in the structure of the Preston museum. Social and historical events are presented on the

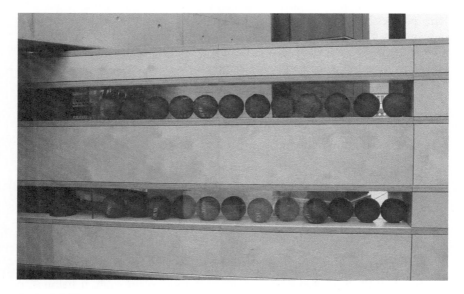

*Figure 2.4* The entry.

left of the visitor, with footballing history on the right. This soccer and society dialogue provides a useful contextual frame. To embody this relationship, the museum is structured in two halves. The first half is a presentation of football history. This interactive display is also the most elaborate presentation of football memorabilia in the world. The second half is an active, 'hands on' space for playing the game. Visitors can play table football, complete a Match of the Day commentary, conduct a virtual visit of every league ground in England, and see the history of Preston North End Football Club, in which the museum is situated.

Turning a style into an argument is the greatest challenge of popular cultural museums. The National Football Museum very carefully provides a

*Figure 2.5* Adding colour.

*Figure 2.6* Exhibition lighting.

context for objects. Museums have often been vaults, but the structure and architecture hold an important role in framing and representing the aims and goals of the institution. The use of stucco concrete and ball imagery adds difference and distinction to the museum's entrance. Importantly, colour and texture have added to the design innovation. Lighting is also an important feature. It signals many ideas in the exhibition – participation, a significant object, or change of era. Visitors stand on floor panels which then light up to provide information about the exhibition. Evocative iconography and a strong design sense combine to offer an innovative experience, one that I have not seen replicated in other museums. It has subtlety and simplicity.

The structure of the exhibition – in two halves and extra time (the museum shop) – means that the exhibition is not overly cluttered with too many small topics. Importantly, there is a distinct and overarching atmosphere to the museum. It is not a fluorescent-light-flickering experience. The floor covering is an exhibit of its own, marking out spaces and symbolism. It is a subtle, secluded, post-industrial presentation which creates remarkable opportunities for reflection, encouraging visitors' own memories of the exhibits. The darkness encourages nostalgia, as visitors pass down the corridor and into the past of football.

The use of sound is evocative and appropriate. Music from distinct eras fills the space. 'In the mood' swings with 'Rock around the clock'. These

*Figure 2.7* Exhibiting the floor.

*Figure 2.8* The first half.

soundtracks are not necessarily tethered to a single event or exhibit, but arch and float above the space and era. Further, booths are available in which to sit and hear oral history and testimony. The intimacy of the secluded cubicle is an innovative venue in which to hear the sounds of history. With the sensory overload of material culture in museums, it is both appropriate and innovative to provide visitors with a space and opportunity for reflection. The museum's realization is a clear one: oral history is not source material for popular culture, but part of popular culture.[80]

The exhibition space is cut up, individualizing and customizing the passage through the museum. There are many exhibits that involve the participant

*Figure 2.9* Hearing history.

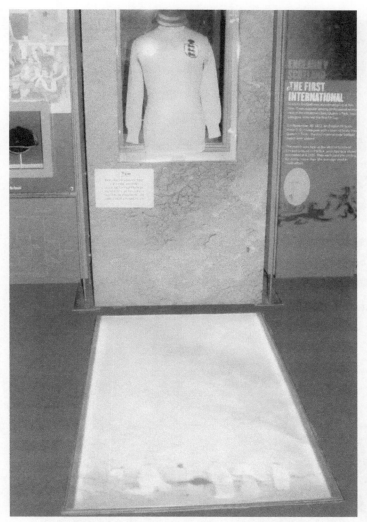

*Figure 2.10* Sight and sound.

standing on a square that lights up at their presence, to trigger oral information about the subject. In the exhibit shown above, the viewer is hearing
that this kit was worn in the first English international against Scotland.

The other great media innovation is the use of tactile objects in 'the
second half'. Visitors can touch footballs and shoes, giving a feeling for the
equipment and the sport. Visitors learn about the changes to football boots
and the other equipment. The ordinary is granted revelatory power.

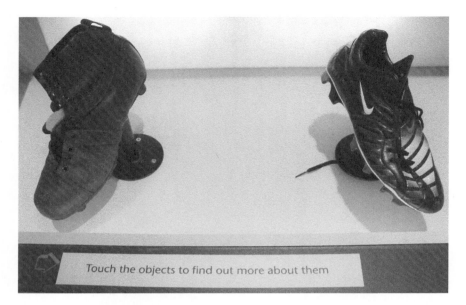

*Figure 2.11* History through touch.

*Figure 2.12* Tactile artefacts.

*Figure 2.13* Interaction.

The top floor of the exhibition features the interactive component. Visitors can record commentary, play board games and touch equipment. As can be seen by the photograph above, children in particular are able to utilize and develop motor coordination to formulate their own pathway through the information. The shop – extra time – which is placed at the end is part of the postmodern museum experience. A convergence between the museum's educational and commercial functions is witnessed. It can appear odd or inconvenient, but it is a way to reconcile the disparate roles of the institution. Museums were invented in a different time from ours. In our present, they are poorly funded and lack a strong public image. The media attention granted to the high-profile art museums in London, Paris or New York makes it difficult for other museums to attract coverage and criticism. Yet should they be funded: is there intrinsic value in a football museum? Ponder Kevin Moore's questions:

> Given the choice, would the public prefer that their taxes are spent on public museums or something else? What would attract those that currently do not visit or come to museums? If museums reflected popular culture more fully would this attract more visitors? Museums have generally acted on the assumption that there is no need to ask such fundamental questions, perhaps from a fear that it might be disturbing or even dangerous to do so.[81]

*Figure 2.14* Extra time.

Restricted public funding, and perpetual controversy about the location, meant that Preston's museum was built on these assumptions. Yet in a time of war, terrorism and large defence budgets, alongside the funding haemorrhage of education and health, perhaps museums have a more benevolent function than warships.

The benefits of museums can be justified in economic terms, for employment, tourists and day trippers. They can bring money into economically deprived areas. The problem is that the National Football Museum has yet to fulfil this great potential. Preston has been a marketing failure because the national 'patrons' of the arts – governments, corporations and foundations – have not found its product appealing. The functions of museums to collect, research, display and educate have been challenged by many social forces, including the proliferation of media technologies and formal education. While there are more museums now than ever before, they are being challenged by a creative industries policy matrix that deploys terms like cost recovery, performance indicators and financial mismanagement.

Universities and museums are facing similar issues. There have never been more universities and museums in society than there are currently. Both are threatened with notions of accessibility and a crisis of purpose. Both are punctuated with doubts about knowledge, about who owns the past, and how it should be represented. Similar solutions can be offered for both. A recognition that education and entertainment are not polar opposites, and that popular culture has an overt pedagogic (and democratic) function, provides a crucial starting point. Indeed, universities and museums can assist each other. In remarkable succinctness, Dipesh Chakrabarty realized that

> [m]useums, being public places where one does not usually require special qualifications to enter, have been more open to the pressure of mass democracies and have had to address more directly issues of experience.[82]

That is why museums face a crisis of purpose. From their modern origin in the crucible of the French Revolution in the late eighteenth century, museums have been based on the notion that an artefact is removed from its present ownership in private property, and removed from the context that originally gave it meaning. The problem is that football – and sport generally – is so heavily immersed in context, lived history and identity that visiting a museum to see objects distanced from daily life is perhaps too strange. The Preston National Football Museum is important. It is flaw-lessly constructed, innovative in method and considered in its selection of items. Such qualities are not sufficient in sport tourism. Like the singing in all-seater stadiums, it does not capture the volume, energy and discomfort of the past.

# Part II

# Sport and history

# Chapter 3

# They think it's all over, but it isn't

Paul Fussell, in his masterful study of Western Front memories from World War I, traced a path of stories, images, language and memory that survives in contemporary life. He showed how ink from the well of the trenches still writes our present histories:

> In this study of a small bit of that culture of the past, I have tried to present just a few such recognition scenes. My belief is that what we recognize in them is a part, and perhaps not the least compelling part, of our own buried lives.[1]

War is an event of trauma and rupture in normalcy that recuts the fabric of social structures. Other tumultuous events slice and shape identity as much as war. Such moments dislocate and contaminate those who experience them. Writing a history from discomfort and silence is difficult. Writing a history that justifies the emphasis of one moment over another is even more arduous.

This chapter enacts a historical conversation between two events in 1966. The aim is to show how two separate 'moments' from the year – the English World Cup victory and the Aberfan coal mining disaster – have left widely distinct markers on history and popular memory. The disjuncture between sections of this chapter is intentional, showing how temporally concurrent attitudes, ideologies and identities can exist in parallel, without troubling other events or interpretations. This historical dialogue confirms that 'facts' do not seamlessly fit together, even in retrospect. There is much academic talk about the relationship between sport and society, but we need to work much harder linking match statistics, names, dates, scores and venues with the dense contextual environment in which the game was played. The first part of this chapter establishes a critically interpretative sporting history, which distances itself from celebratory narratives of great players, managers and seasons. The research then splits into two trajectories: Aberfan and the World Cup. The aim is to show how these landmark yet diverse events linked by chronology write upon the present. Much intervention, interpretation and mediation is required to move from history to memory and memory to history. To stress sport in scholarship can – without care – undermine discussions of social inequality. The key is to forge the connection.

## Soccer in the shadows

It is a horrifying event: the soccer match played at Auschwitz between the SS and the SonderKommando, the special squad composed of Jewish prisoners who ran the crematorium. We are accustomed to sport capturing the pleasures, joys and passions of life. The playing of football in the courtyard before a crematorium is shocking in its starkness. In this context (as in others), it is difficult to disengage sport from society, and commitment from culpability. The struggle for historians, particularly those working with popular culture, is to assemble a method to evaluate the significance and value of source material without falling back on aesthetic judgements. An interest in history beyond the public sphere, moving into discussions of family, women, the workforce and leisure, changes our understanding of importance and relevance. Such a living history personalizes the past, immersing the self in the visual, aural and tactile. Playing football at the crematorium confirms the gritty complexity that meshes sport and politics.

Remembering requires consciousness. To write a history necessitates transforming the past into a discourse and constructing a relevance and importance in the present. Raphael Samuel stated that

> History, in the hands of the professional historian, is apt to present itself as an esoteric form of knowledge. It fetishizes archive-based research, as it has done ever since the Rankean revolution – or counter-revolution – in scholarship.[2]

Memory is more flexible than this configuration of history permits. It is like pre-fired clay, able to change its shape, texture and appearance at the will of the potter. Too many groups have been left out of too many histories. There is little allegiance or ownership of the historian's past. Yet public history has never been so popular. Sport biographies dominate the bestseller non-fiction lists. Popular memory moves between multiple contexts – existing in the grey zone of past and present – bobbing up in unpredictable and diffident places.

History, like all disciplines, is a framework for thought. There are always many possible histories circulating in 'the past'. Keith Jenkins made the pivotal intervention in historiographical debates, asserting that the question is no longer 'what is history?', but 'for whom is it written?'.[3] Events do not make history: they build into a narrative which justifies or explains an overarching argument. The vision of history, through photographs, film,

television and Internet-based media, adds new dimensions to our understanding of the past through a juxtaposition of sound, landscape and
dialogue. Such films as *Chariots of Fire* and *Sammy and Rosie Get Laid* tell
alternative tales of Thatcher's Britain. The ambivalent place of the working
class in both films reveals their unclear function in a crumbling industrial
environment. Geoff Eley described this as 'the pastness of working-class
culture and its seductive authenticities'.[4] As always, Eley summons a seductive turn of phrase. As we move through Aberfan and the 1966 World Cup
victory, we view antagonistic working class pasts fighting for relevance and
authenticity.

The 1960s and the 1980s were caricatures of each other: permissiveness
versus Victorian values. Alan Sked wrote that 'it was only in the 1960s that
people in Britain became aware of their "decline"'.[5] By the 1980s, the welfare
state and the principles of social justice established in the Beveridge Report
were shredded. Community goals and collective responsibilities devolved
into market imperatives and individual rights. Enterprise culture made
British industry vulnerable to the flows of information, capital and ideas.
Through the gauze of 1980s heritage management, only particular parts of
the 1960s survived through to the present. The glories of a World Cup
victory maintained an aura of greatness in English sport. The death and
destruction of homes, farms and children by industrial mismanagement in
Aberfan did not. Mining coal was no longer tenable: mining the past became
more politically beneficial. The miners' strike in 1984 dramatized the battle-
lines and exemplified the types of working class politics that would be
tolerated. Striking miners would be crushed: consumers and shareholders
would be encouraged. Authenticity – even working class authenticity –
existed only in a form that could be exploited.[6]

Any single year reveals a wash of possibilities. The events of 1966 were
more diverse than some. Walt Disney died. Indira Gandhi became Prime
Minister of India. Both these 'events' could convey stories of Americaniza-
tion or the passage from an Empire to a Commonwealth. Yet it was also
the year of a Labour election win, the release of the Beatles' *Revolver* album,
and the two 'moments' that are the focus for the remainder of this chapter:
Aberfan and a World Cup victory.

## Hat-tricks, crossbars and the crowd

It seems impossible now to grasp the whole event. England's victory in the
1966 World Cup can only be digested in images, such as an impossibly
young Bobby Moore holding up the Cup. In the Preston National Football
Museum, this image is enough to capture the 'spirit' of English football in
the 1960s. Bobby Moore was not only a fine defender whose accurate pass
enabled a goal to be scored in extra time, but also England's captain. Van
Deburg believed that

in any context, heroes come in many forms and serve various social and psychological functions. Scholars who have analyzed the heroic form tell us that the nature of a specific hero is directly related to the needs of an individual, group or political unit . . . heroes are mirrors of their time and place and serve as cultural barometers of societal hopes and fears.[7]

Blond, athletic, humble and a leader, he was also white, embodying the athleticism of a post-Imperial England. But Moore was not alone in his fame. There were other stars of the game. There was Hurst's hat-trick, with two goals scored in extra time.[8] The second goal was one of the most controversial of modern football. Hurst's ball hit the underside of the crossbar and bounced down 'somewhere' near the line. In a moment of high drama, the Swiss referee Gottfried Dienst had not seen the line clearly and relied on the Russian linesman Tofik Bakhraamov, who had seen the whole ball go over the line. Ironically, because of language difficulties, the two officials had to deploy sign language to confirm the decision.[9] The goal was awarded. The Preston museum preserved and presented the crossbar. To this day in Germany, the phrase 'Wembley tor', or Wembley goal, refers to something that is either illegitimate or unfairly awarded.

Besides the physicality of the ball, players and crossbar, there was also an extraordinary crowd at the final: 96,924 people crammed into Wembley

*Figure 3.1* The crossbar.

Stadium. The crowd was so excited that children ran on to the pitch before the final whistle, and before the final Hurst goal was scored. Finally, there is the mythic commentary – 'some people are on the pitch, they think it's all over – it is now' – that adds a soundtrack to the wash of images. It was a sea of red, only broken by the occasional blue and white of the Union Jack. It was an evocative television presentation for the time, beamed to more than 400 million people throughout the world. An international spectacle had revealed an English victory. Because of the hat-trick, the only hat-trick scored in a World Cup final, the disputed third English goal and the riveting commentary, a myth was born. At the time, BBC sport reported that 'It was a dizzy catharsis as everyone in the stadium realized that the World Cup and football had just come home to where it all began.'[10] England, the legendary origin of football, had followed through with a famous victory. The other great successes of modern football, the South American teams, were not in this picture of joy.[11] Yet these South American futures for football – like past disappointments – evaporated. The eighth World Cup brought football (home) to England where the game had been 'invented' 103 years earlier.

The World Cup is the epitome of football. Arguably, it is the one event – perhaps only second to the Olympics – that unifies (and divides) a sporting public. Martin Johnes isolated two dates in English history: 1066 and 1966. He stated that 'one event had a profound impact on the course of history in the British Isles while the other was just a football match. Yet soccer, like many sports, can be so much more than simply a game.'[12] The relationship between sport, nation and class is at its most intimate in such sporting moments. While the 1966 victory in the World Cup seems to preach exuberant national unity and success, there is an alternative historical thread fraying from this year.

## A study in grey and black

At 9.15 a.m. on Friday 21 October 1966, coal slurry rushed down a mountainside in Aberfan, swallowing a farm, 20 houses and a section of Pantglas junior school. Of the 144 who died under the tide of slag, 116 were children, most aged between 7 and 10. Half the pupils in the school and five teachers suffocated. Gaynor Minett, an 8-year-old in the school at the time, later wrote her recollections of the disaster in a school notebook.

> It was a tremendous rumbling sound and all the school went dead. You could hear a pin drop. Everyone just froze in their seats. I just managed to get up and I reached the end of my desk when the sound got louder and nearer, until I could see the black out of the window. I can't remember any more but I woke up to find that a horrible nightmare had just begun in front of my eyes.[13]

It took a full week for all the bodies to be recovered. The tales of horror were breathtaking. A pupil in the junior school remembers

> I was there for about an hour and a half until the fire brigade found me. I heard cries and screams, but I couldn't move. The desk was jammed into my stomach and my leg was under the radiator. The little girl next to me was dead and her head was on my shoulder.[14]

In the subsequent Governmental Tribunal of Inquiry chaired by Sir Herbert Davis, legal liability was cast entirely on the National Coal Board because of poor leadership, administrative incompetence and a failure to recognize earlier warnings. To come to these findings, the tribunal sat for 76 days, interviewing 136 witnesses and recording 2,500,000 words of testimony. Lord Robens, the chairman of the NCB, was cast as a villain early in the proceedings. He blamed an 'unmarked' natural spring below the tip, a spring that had been clearly shown for years on village maps. Witnesses demonstrated that there had been systematic concerns expressed about the tip's stability, which were ignored.[15] After the delivery of this report on 28 April 1967, no one was prosecuted, and Robens' resignation offer was rejected. He was seen by the government – a Wilson-led Labour Government – to be best able to manage the 'decline' of the coal industry while minimizing strike action, because he had support from the mining unions. Corporate manslaughter charges were not considered an option: accidents were accepted as part of the industry. The framing of disasters outside the lens of criminal negligence not only limited the legal rights of victims from Aberfan, but continued a trend witnessed through Hillsborough,[16] the *Marchioness* and the *Herald of Free Enterprise*. The NCB was able to escape culpability because of its power and influence. To denounce the obviously hazardous practice of tipping endangered the major employer of the region.

Unfortunately, this story only becomes more tragic after the light of publicity turned off Aberfan. Obviously much sympathy emerged towards victims. As McLean and Johnes noted, 'the loss of so many young lives, together with the underlying suspicion that this was the price of years of cheap coal, led to a widespread anxiety to do something to help'.[17] The disaster fund which was set up after the tragedy raised £1.75 million. Like the 9/11 money raised by the Red Cross, the passage of funds away from victims garnered controversy. In August 1969, the (Labour) Government made the Aberfan fund trustees pay £150,000 to remove the remaining National Coal Board tips above the village. In economic terms, the NCB nearly broke even: £160,000 paid in compensation to Aberfan's residents, but £150,000 returned through the removal of tips. A bereaved parent remembered this event 30 years after the disaster.

> They took money out of the disaster fund to pay for the removal of the tips, which was to me shocking. Absolutely unbelievable. And that's

always been in me. I think they [the NCB] owe us. They owe the people of Aberfan a debt. Call it a debt of conscience if you like. I don't think we should beg for this and we need the money. There is the Memorial Garden to be maintained. And the cemetery. For many, many years to come. Where is it going to come from in later years when we're gone?[18]

This tip removal was a completely inappropriate use of these funds, yet the Charity Commission did not intervene. The contemporary equivalent would be the 9/11 funds being diverted to pay for pilot security in United Airlines planes. The money diverted from the charity was only paid back to the fund in 1997, when a subsequent Labour Government was convinced of past errors.[19]

To make a ridiculous situation even more absurd, the Trustees of the fund had to determine if the parents were 'close' to their dead children, and therefore deserved money. Other injustices compounded this extraordinary treatment of the bereaved. The Bethania chapel was used as a temporary mortuary after the disaster and members could not return to it later to pray. A bereaved mother told of her experience identifying her daughter's body:

Until I went in [to Bethania chapel] I still had hope that they were just lost. When I went all the pews were covered with little blankets and under them lay the little children. They picked up the blankets and showed me every girl until I came [to her] and said she was mine. There wasn't a mark on her except a little scratch over her mouth, even her clothes were clean. What I missed most was the noise and fun around the house.[20]

Not surprisingly, the chapel's stakeholders asked that the building be demolished and rebuilt. The National Coal Board rejected this claim, and the structure was subsequently rebuilt by money from the disaster fund. Why the National Coal Board was not completely responsible for removing its own mess, and why the Government and Charity Commission protected their interests, would only be revealed much later.[21] Considering the ironies and tragedies of the Aberfan case, there was always going to be one more twist. Lord Robens continued his supportive relationship with the Government, being confirmed by Barbara Castle to chair a committee in 1969. The Robens Committee's task was to prepare for the Health and Safety at Work etc. Act of 1974. Pot-kettle-black.

Coal was king in Wales, and was interlaced with struggles for social justice. Public ownership and nationalization of coal in 1945 seemed the reward for years of worker hardship and exploitation. Yet nationalization was the framework through which to 'manage' pit closures, because British coal was 'uneconomic'. Such an assumption was proven false by the buy-out of Tower colliery by miners and supporters. It has continued to be a successful and profitable mine, raising questions about the economic rationale for all the other closures. Tower is now the only coal mine left in Wales.

What made Aberfan distinct was not economic success against the odds like Tower, but tragedy. The brutality of Aberfan demands an emotional reaction, and a vision to cope. In the stark iconography of September 11, there was an odd and inverted photocopy of Aberfan. The coal blackness was bleached paper grey. Aberfan is tethered to all subsequent tragedies because it was the first to be presented live on television. All the concerns and worries – about censorship, blame, compensation and retribution – were part of Aberfan, only to be repeated in Penlee, Hungerford, Lockerbie, Dunblane, Soham and the Twin Towers. There is something about the death and injury of the innocent, of children or adults in the prime of their lives, that triggers fixated interest, the giving of money and the laying of flowers. When disasters hit the television screen within minutes of occurring, a sharp public opinion is constructed. In understanding Aberfan, we comprehend not only the nature of personal and collective responsibility, but how the couplet of blame and retribution are negotiated through live television.

## What about the ball?

Of all sanctified objects at the alter of 1966, perhaps the ball is of the most value. After all, the Jules Rimet Trophy must be handed back.[22] Brazil won the World Cup in 1970 and were permitted to keep it, because it was their third victory. Unfortunately, it was stolen and melted down. Therefore, the ball is the only object, along with the kit (which was used for multiple internationals), that can signify the 1966 match. The ball itself was an unusual one. The majority of soccer balls are white, with the tan colour only being deployed in the days of snow-covered pitches before underground heating. This ball is red. For 1966, the ball was a specific intervention in the history of the World Cup. This special ball will always signify a particular victory, enhanced by the match being filmed in colour. The red kit of England, against the white of Germany, offered a evocative palette for footballing history.

Martin Johnes asserted that there is not a range of sources for sport history, particularly when compared with political or social history:

> Sports history does not benefit from the large range of sources available to political or more conventional social historians. This has meant it is, perhaps overly, reliant on newspaper evidence.[23]

Actually, sport has much in common with these other modes of history. Harold Wilson's prime ministership during this year is filtered through the

World Cup victory. Similarly, histories of class and masculinity are intertwined with football. Sports history is remarkable because of its diversity of
source material. There is a tactility to this subject area, and the media satu-
ration offers many different modes and sites of meaning. The World Wide
Web also allows diverse voices and views to be expressed about significant
sporting moments. If anything, there are more sporting sources – of a great
breadth and diversity – than are available in other historical sub-disciplines.
There are also important benefits from broadening out the database of texts
and evidence. As Kevin Moore realized,

> Material culture is in fact the most *democratic* form of evidence. Written
> sources are inevitably skewed to the higher social classes, and the more
> remote the historical period, the more evident this is. Material culture
> gives the only direct route into the lives of ordinary people in many
> cases; it is all that they have left behind. The problem is that curators
> often lack the skills to 'read' such material evidence.[24]

Curators are not alone in lacking a literacy of material culture. Great
meaning and history encircle the simplest of objects. The ball alone has a
story to tell. There is more to sport-based source material than media reports,
old footage and photographs. Moore goes so far as to believe that 'history
is in fact an inappropriate discipline in a museum'.[25] He asserts that the
training of undergraduates and postgraduates is dominated by documentary
sources, with oral history being an important intervention. A productive
interdisciplinary connection between cultural studies and history shows how
much meaning can be derived from supposedly banal textual objects.[26] The
stories and insights derived from a ball are both varied and diverse. The
one problem sport history does *not* have is a paucity of material and popular
culture. Instead, skills and literacies must be improved to utilize these texts
appropriately.

In the 1966 World Cup, a match ball was selected by the referee each
morning, with two reserve balls also allocated. Each was measured to ensure
correct size, a circumference between 27 and 28 inches. They were also
weighed, and had to be between 14 and 16 ounces. The ball chosen for
match days remains a unique signifier of the event. The ball is so relevant
because it is a record of the game played, the scratches, the bounce, the
colour, the seams and weather conditions. Moore has realized that

> [t]he ball symbolizes the game of football itself. At a deep level it links
> to the English self-perception as a 'nation of inventors', but nowadays
> we feel we fail to gain the fruits of such inventions, which are taken
> up by other nations. The ball, I would argue, has become a symbol for
> England's post-war decline; or rather, it is an object to stand against
> this.[27]

English myths encircle this particular 1966 football. Certainly there are many objects of material culture that capture moments of football: shirts, boots, programmes, match tickets, trophies, medals, photographs, oral interviews, scarves and banners. Like all sports, football is heavily objectified. When Liverpool's Kop raise their scarves to sing 'You'll never walk alone', there is a collision of affect, orality, tactility and memory.

For thirty years, the World Cup final ball was privately held, and only appeared on public display in 1996. The ball had been 'forgotten' until English football officials and the media decided to find it, as a way to celebrate the thirtieth anniversary of England's only World Cup win. The ball was in the cellar of Jürgen Haller,[28] son of Helmut, who played for West Germany in 1966. He justified the ownership of the ball via the German tradition of winners receiving the cup and the losers the ball. Further, the foot of Helmut Haller was the last to touch the ball when the match ended. In English competitions, the scorer of a hat-trick retains the ball, but Geoff Hurst did not make this claim at the time. Importantly, it had significance not only because of when it was used, but also because signatures were placed on it, including that of Pelé.[29] Unlike the trophy, the ball is a record of one game, win and loss.

Jürgen Haller had many media offers for the ball, and finally sold it to the *Daily Mirror* for an undisclosed figure. It was displayed at the Waterloo International Station, then passing to the Preston National Football

*Figure 3.2* Displaying 1966.

Museum. This is no surprise. Moore, in his *Museums and popular culture*, wrote about the ball in depth. When he became the curator, this was an object he wanted in the collection. Obviously 1966 is a feature year of the museum, and a diversity of objects is presented to 'commemorate' the game.

The surprise for me, as someone who had been researching the ball for some time, is that not enough attention or emphasis was given to this object. It is unique, and yet it is buried in a cabinet with more brightly coloured objects, and lost at the base of the presentation. The only signifier that 'this' ball is actually 'the' ball is the small information card at the base of its stand. Moore stated that 'few objects have such resonance in English post-war history; few are capable of still meaning so much with such little interpretation'.[30] This explains his decision in placing the object with little fanfare, but as a visitor who had seen the red ball in Preston brochures,[31] I did not know it would be 'the ball' until I saw it. I nearly missed it, having to be drawn to it by my companions on the visit. The excitement of seeing 'the real' is profound. Reconstruction simply cannot match the special relationship of material culture and visitor. Of all the objects in the museum, this is the one item that, as Moore realized, marks the moment of triumph in English football.

Soccer balls are remarkable objects. They are a significant surface for sponsorship. Like footwear and clothing, sporting equipment is an important surface for Nike and Adidas to claim visibility. In the 2002 World Cup,

*Figure 3.3* The ball.

Adidas bought rights over the ball, the Fevernova. It was the fastest and most accurate ball ever produced. It deployed a foam layering system that contained a tight matrix of gas-filled, individually closed balloons.[32] The aim of this system was to spread energy through the entire surface of the ball, making its flight accurate and predictable.[33] The Fevernova was the ninth consecutive World Cup ball produced by Adidas. Through these scientific and marketing innovations, the game of football is changing through increased opportunity for goal scoring. The World Cup has often been the moment of ball innovation. After the red ball of 1966, the Adidas Telstar was used in Mexico's tournament in 1970. Featuring 32 hand-stitched panels, it rendered redundant all other leather balls. The 1982 World Cup in Spain introduced the Tango España, with waterproof stitching. The water resistance was improved once more in 1990 with the Etrusco in Italy, which was a fully synthetic ball. Of all equipment, the soccer ball is a convergence of marketing, science and sport. But this explanation does not alone explain the significance in popular memory of the dusty red leather object kicked in the 1966 final.

Henry Wolf stated that 'with imagery there is a legacy'.[34] The image of objects is coded as a metaphor in memory. This ball therefore represents success, innovation, Englishness and the 1960s. By tracking the ball, we can observe the changing structures of representation. For Euro 1996, and after Switzerland drew with England 1–1 on 8 June, the psychic Uri Geller suggested that the English team members rub the 1966 ball for good luck. England then beat Scotland 2–0, to advance to the quarter-final. As a sanctified object, a national past embraces the ball, and extracts viable, pseudo-spiritual meanings.

Such sports heritage is more than a simple relationship between producers and consumers. Multiple meanings encircle these texts and sites, but to claim an object as national heritage is to restrict interpretations. Different representations exist of the ball, but by placing it in a museum diverse readings are quashed. By positioning it in a general display of the 1966 final victory, the remarkable passage of the ball after 1966 through Germany and Britain is not conveyed.

A soccer ball is a postcard and a souvenir of sport. It builds a bridge between origin and memory trace. It holds an authenticating function like few other objects. Authenticity builds a community experience. English football in particular has been able to capture and maintain interest. As Peter Young, who was a child in England before emigrating to Canada and the United States, stated, 'I love all football, but my favorite football is English football, not because it's the best – it isn't – but because it's the football I first knew.'[35] One of his primary memories of English football remains a mediated one, being the 1966 World Cup on delayed telecast with portions of the second half removed to slot extra time into American television schedules.

While memory is frequently idiosyncratic and individualized, myths grant individual memories a collective currency. The 1966 World Cup is such an event. It was evocative, passionate and potent. As attention to the ball demonstrates, an ordinary object became remarkable and worthy to be encased in a museum. Many traces of material culture derived from this sporting event have survived to be reminders of when England was on top of the footballing world. Only later would there be a critique of English power from across the Welsh border. Yet it would leave few traces, and nothing to celebrate.

## Tragedy on the television

The etymology of 'disaster' ties it to astrology and fate. As an 'act of God', too often free-flowing emotions of sympathy dissipate with the initial interest, without confronting the long-term consequences of misfortune. When coal slurry engulfed the school and houses in Aberfan, a small working class community gleaned attention from London-based media. The Prime Minister and the Royal Family all travelled to Aberfan. Johnes and McLean realized that it was the 'intensive media coverage, particularly television [that] ensured that the disaster was seen as a national one'.[36] Through the medium of television, grief and confusion were conveyed to a viewing public. For the first time, cameras presented live footage of the trauma as it overwhelmed the Taff Valley. The sludge was propelled from the valley and into the newspapers of the day. A rescue worker remembers, 'I was helping to dig the children out when I heard a photographer tell a kiddie to cry for her dear friends, so that he could get a good picture – that taught me silence.'[37] Similarly, a bereaved father remembers that

> during that period the only thing I didn't like was the press. If you told them something, when the paper came out your words were all the wrong way round.[38]

When analysed as a whole, the concerns of the journalists – about the display of intense emotion and (alternatively) the censorship of emotion – blocked a discussion of the cause of the tragedy. Debates about censorship and journalistic ethics prevented critical investigation of the disaster. The events in Aberfan were not created by a natural catastrophe or an unpredictable or blameless 'act of God'. Aberfan's disaster was preventable, but it became explainable within a coal industry village accustomed to unemployment and work-related 'accidents'.

There is something about the depth and freshness of this tragedy that is recognized in retrospect. D.J. Taylor, over 30 later, listed Aberfan as one of his three most evocative televisual experiences:

As a reliable conduit to the wider world, TV was responsible for some of the most vivid pre-teen experiences: the 1966 World Cup final, the Aberfan mining disaster, the 1969 moon landing – each was brought to me by the veneered rectangular box in the corner.[39]

It was an ironic choice of emphasis. A sporting success, a technological success and an industrial failure. Aberfan was not merely a disaster that cost life. It represented a twofold decline of Britain: industrially and socially. Coal built the industrial matrix of Britain. Perhaps this cost has created what Dean MacCannell described as 'the collective guilt of modernized people'.[40] Aberfan was distinct from the other great national tragedies in the manner the public perceived the events unfolding in the village. It was the disaster where cameras recorded the unerring screams of grief, the desperate search for a lost – presumed dead – child, and the building anger of a community suffering through a completely preventable 'accident'. The cameras intruded on grief and privacy. A bereaved father stated that 'I've got to say this again, if the papers and the press and the television were to leave us alone in the very beginning I think we could have settled down a lot quicker than what we did.'[41] He is probably correct. The poor handling of the crisis by the National Coal Board would not occur now. Whole sections in mass communication undergraduate degrees are based around the topics of crisis communication and risk management, creating a plan and strategy for media relations.[42]

This breach of grieving space, enhanced by poor media and communication strategies, also allowed those outside the community to share a memory, create a unifying historical bond, and raise some sympathy-triggered money. Whatever the response to the television images, newspapers and commentaries of the day were unified in a need to find meaning and reason in the loss of children. To view death and grief at Aberfan through the medium of television led to a reappraisal, however temporary, of the value and costs of industrialization. The long-term consequences of these revelations are more difficult to monitor. David Kinchin used the Aberfan tragedy as an early example of post-traumatic stress disorder. He stated that

> [t]his disaster is vividly recalled by many Britons because it was covered by television crews who arrived on the scene within hours. The full horror and traumatic consequences of the disaster were screened in millions of homes.[43]

A similar series of events also happened at Buffalo Creek, West Virginia on 26 February 1972. Once more, a slag dam was unleashed onto a community, resulting in 126 deaths. It was only after the return of Vietnam veterans that these symptoms started to be categorized and diagnosed. Then a retrospective diagnosis was possible for other conditions through the twentieth century, such as shell shock (1940), transient situation disturbance (1968) and Buffalo Creek Syndrome (1972). It was also viewed in the Lockerbie plane crash rescue workers. By this disaster on 21 December 1988, there was a greater capacity to grasp the symptoms and treat them more effectively.

Aberfan is a key moment in monitoring the long-term consequences of a tragic event, and provides a model for how *not* to handle a crisis in a small community. When Thomas Hamilton shot 16 children in Dunblane on 13 March 1996, a bond was created between the two communities in Wales and Scotland. Both suffered a similar trauma – the death of children. Such a resonance also emerged in Soham, when Holly Wells and Jessica Chapman disappeared. After 21 days of waiting for news, their bodies were found. In the immediate aftermath, social workers staffed an emergency line for Soham's children and families. Cliff Minett, remembering the days after the Aberfan disaster, stated that 'nobody came to my door to give me any professional help at all'.[44] It has been recorded by journalists and residents at the time that Aberfan children were restricted from playing outside, because it would cause despair for those families who lost their children. For many, though, Aberfan is the case study against which other tragedies are compared. After Soham in 2002, Phillip Hodson, from the British Association for Counselling and Psychotherapy, recorded that

> A community such as Aberfan will have benefited from being fixed and stable. In somewhere like Soham nowadays, people move in and out. There's much more fluidity. By the same token, there's much more publicity now too. The media plays an invidious role that both hurts and helps. The fact that there's no hiding place from information means that Soham knows that the rest of the world is sending them love and support.[45]

It appears some lessons have been learned, but at the cost of Aberfan's surviving residents. Hodson also underestimated the scale of Aberfan's 'publicity'. It is a question of scale and context. In 1966, a few television stations produced saturating coverage. Being the first news event of its type, it will be remembered – rightly or wrongly – more than subsequent tragedies.

Coal and coal mining are persistent images of industrialization. In Aberfan, the blackness of the slurry contrasted with the whiteness of the dead children. The event also fed into contemporary debates about the 'decline of Britain'. From the turn of the twentieth century, German industrial competition and naval building were a threat to British superiority. World War II only intensified the knowledge that Britain no longer ruled the world. After returning from the 'People's War', the soldiers discovered a nation of rationing, shortages and 'making do'. The cascading coal slag was falling on much more than a few houses and a school. It confirmed the lingering and destructive presence of nineteenth century industrialization in the present.

Greater controversy and impact surrounded the disaster in Aberfan than this (post)industrial explanation would justify. The television coverage was responsible for much of the resultant anger. A tragedy of this emotional intensity touched the lives of millions through quickly and badly edited visions of events. Alan Brien, in a *New Statesman* article responding to the events of October 1966, described the footage as 'pornography of violence'.[46] He, like many critics since that time, confronted the issue of ethics in broad-casting, questioning 'the treatment of reality, the genuine corpses and actual mourners, sandwiched between commercial and comedy half-hours'.[47] He correctly asked why television viewers were allowed into these people's lives at a time of crisis: intruding, probing and judging. Over the years, we have become news-literate about body counts, but in Aberfan this literacy was yet to develop. Can a community or nation personally untouched by tragic events experience grief? Sympathy and empathy emerge, as do voyeurism and curiosity. But when the bodies are simply unidentified corpses and a saddened community is indistinguishable from any other town, then viewers needs to ponder the rationale and depth of personal feelings. Through the window of television, onlookers become peeping Toms, perhaps dripping with sympathy and tears, but still peeping Toms. I am interested in the longer-term impact of these programmes. Too often we sap the feelings of disasters at a distance, and then withdraw when it is no longer fashionable, relevant or in the news. Aberfan's ghostly neighbours – the televisual audi-ence that 'witnessed' the events – did not view the calamity as a destructive force pulling apart a community, but as a 'television first' that captured extreme grief. Alan Brien asserted at the time that

> the overriding social task facing humanity today is to teach ourselves that strangers feel pain and pleasure, die and love, just as personally as we do.[48]

That such a statement was required after viewing the effects of death upon the town is a testament of what Engels described as 'so tender a conceal-ment of everything which might affront the eye and the nerves of the bourgeoisie'.[49] The growth of the southern English white collar work force through the 1950s and 1960s distanced these men and women from condi-tions beyond this region. This explanation may provide a context for the shock with which the footage from Aberfan was received.

Television allowed 'a collective witnessing'[50] of the disaster. Whether these televisual bystanders actually contributed anything to the healing of the tragedy, or forged an understanding of the brutal work involved in extracting coal, is less clear. There is not a natural, intrinsic sense of community created through television. Actually, it can establish boundaries of difference. Taylor affirmed that

> The point about TV is not that it is vulgar, or salacious, or exploitative, or a repository for every kind of human inadequacy ... It is fundamentally antidemocratic, just another of the many mechanisms at work in contemporary society whose effect is to separate one group of people from another.[51]

Television has provided a record of exploitation, dissent and struggle. Whether an event or programme is read as an expression of unequal power relations or justifiable treatment of the 'unworthy poor' is in the hands of the viewer. Class-based inequalities and consciousness are not blinked out with the operation of a remote control.

## The trivial and the serious

The World Cup spoke to the future through its stark televisuality, but also through its sporting commentary. Kenneth Wolstenholme's words were so famous because he was 'the BBC's commentator for England's finest hour – the World Cup final victory over West Germany at Wembley in 1966'.[52] Not only were his words significant, but the context could not have been more resonant. He maintained a long career in broadcasting, making way for David Coleman after the 1970 World Cup. Ironically, Wolstenholme only received £60 for this most famous of voiceovers. He was disillusioned with much football commentary after his tenure in the post, believing that it had become 'Americanized', with too much discussion.[53] Bobby Charlton realized, though, that Wolstenholme's few words became synonymous with the victory itself. He spoke at the time of Wolstenholme's death in Torquay at the age of 81:

> Sixty six is not just about the players, it's about Kenneth Wolstenholme as well. He always seemed to have been included whenever we got together, and I'm very sorry to hear that he's gone. But he's there forever, his words are there forever. He's down in history, and not every person can say that.[54]

His career was to be shaped by his words. The BBC even had Wolstenholme to introduce the video *Great Football Moments from the '50s and '60s*.[55] The question remains, though, how do such words survive through time, and what are their long-term consequences?

Football in Britain, as Pierre Lanfranchi has affirmed, was 'associated with a social class, i.e. the working class, the industrial revolution and the massive influx of unskilled workers into the new industrial centres'.[56] Classed identity was shifting radically in the 1960s through the development of new industries. Identities were being reconstituted, with new allegiances being formed with regions and the nation. John Sugden and Alan Tomlinson recognized the scale of this influence: 'sport . . . informs and refuels the popular memory of communities, and offers a source of collective identification and community expression for those who follow teams and individuals'.[57] The difficulty is that the zenith of English football was in the past. Even with the advent of the Premier League, English football is overshadowed by the Spanish and Italian competitions. The long-term consequence of 1966 is that it reinforces an isolationist framework, described by Chas Critcher as meaning that 'much of our thinking . . . is not what others do but what we used to do'.[58] The English mode of football is validated because of the World Cup success. Change and international improvements to the game are dismissed. A victory maintains the status quo. For this reason, 1966 has become 'the dead weight of history'.[59] All subsequent sides are compared to Moore's men.

Football is a significant national sport because it slots into many political agendas. In the United States, the desire to unify a nation composed of multiple immigrant populations requires a decentring of soccer, as it perpetuates more international allegiances. In Australia, soccer is a game of post-war migrants who continue links to England, Scotland, Ireland, Italy, Croatia, Greece or Serbia through the game. In England, football performs a role of 'origin' or 'home', a reminder of the glorious past of invention, innovation and (implicitly) colonization.[60] The deep structures of society are performed, circulated and reinforced through football. The history of post-war Britain is one of economic decline and a loss of international prestige. The community symbolism of lost greatness was only increased when Wembley Stadium closed. John Williams argued that 'the England national football team, especially, seems to symbolise key aspects of Englishness – and sometimes of hand-wringing national decline – much more than any of our other sports'.[61] The question is how sporting administrators and politicians manage the long-term decline of international footballing influence.

## Blame and retribution

An industrial revolution is not an event but a process. British industrialization is well theorized and discussed, commencing with Engels' interpretation of the social conditions in Manchester during the 1840s. Most of the subsequent historical debates locate the inequalities of modern capitalism. Britain industrialized first for a clear reason: the increased levels of demand could not be met by the social structures of the time. In other words, a desire for consumption was matched by a capacity to produce these desirable goods. Through the economic and societal transformation, economic growth rates were high, cheap goods were produced and there was a fundamental restructuring of the economy. Pivotally, the uneven developments of industrialization resulted in many time lags, which were both industry and region specific. British economic dominance peaked in the 1860s, when producing half of the world's iron and coal. Social conditions to generate this production were so poor that Engels thought that if a socialist revolution was to occur, it would be in England. The fire and passion of the Chartist movement in the 1840s seemed to verify his analysis. The reasons for a *lack* of revolution are controversial, but it is a maxim that working class social movements are invariably destroyed by conservative governments and the gradual improvement in social conditions through economic prosperity.

Industrial accidents change the perception of work and industry. They subvert simple statements about progress and improvement. Chernobyl and the Clapham Junction rail crash are clear examples. Frequently these disasters could be avoided if lessons were learned from previous industrial 'accidents'. When coal mining was threatened after 1945, and particularly through the Thatcherite period, safety concerns were decentred in a desire to fight to keep the industry viable. Only two major industries expanded during the 1980s: chemicals and electrical engineering.

The long-term, systematic nature of workplace deaths is difficult to monitor, but Ian Winstanley has compiled a list of all the mining disasters in Britain.[62] It is 28 pages long. It is horrifying to realize that every line on those pages, which features only a location and date, has a story and a tragedy behind it. For example, the Jarrow pit in Durham suffered three accidents in four years: January 1826, March 1828 and August 1830. The deaths arching back deep into the nineteenth century industrial revolution demonstrate how Lancashire and Glamorgan have particularly suffered. Aberfan is listed on the first page, as they are organized alphabetically. Yet Aberfan is more than a line in a list of mining disasters for two reasons. First, it was a mining disaster that did not involve miners. Second, full and brutal grief was captured on television without the controls or ethics currently taught in journalism schools. Ironically, Aberfan is the most recent mining disaster listed. The scale of closures meant that there were fewer mines in the post-war period to trigger tragedies. Currently, there is only one coal mine still operational in Wales.

Britain since 1966 has signalled a transformation in employment opportunities, with an absolute decline in the manufacturing workforce. Through industrialization, most of the population became reliant upon a male breadwinner. Yet in a post-Fordist environment, the service sector – with its feminine dominance – predominates.[63] Between 1911 and the 1970s, the number of collieries fell from 400 to 11. One thousand one hundred textile mills have closed since 1951. The 1984 miners' strike revealed the scale of this social, regional, economic and political rupture. Through the National Heritage Acts of 1980 and 1983, industrialization through museums and 'antique' machinery was only marketable and attractive in the past. The blackness of the past was scrubbed clean.

## Spectacle and counter-memory

Those who deny the link between sport and politics have their eyes closed and their ears blocked. Reviewing the press coverage of English football internationals against Germany and Argentina, it is not difficult to confirm this point. England has not won a major competition since 1966. As an *Economist* writer has realized, 'using football as a substitute for war has one significant drawback: English football teams have been pretty awful of late'.[64] Whatever the allegiance, from the conservative *Spectator*[65] to the leftist *New Statesman*,[66] football and politics are blended. Stephen Glover even tracked what he termed 'the footballisation of our culture'.[67] The potent realization is that this obsessive permeation of the sport has occurred at a time of little international success. While such footballing fixation makes sense in Brazil and Italy, it must lead to disappointment, vanquished hopes and an aware-ness of decline in English – indeed British – football. This lack of World Cup success since 1966 has fed the obsession for that next great victory which will prove that England is indeed all right. John Coghlan, in his wide-ranging investigation *Sport and British politics since 1960*, argued that 'probably the greatest single factor responsible for the development of a broader base to most sports across the spectrum of society is the desire for international sporting success'.[68] As the length between victories increases, the desire to win becomes more urgent. Sport assembles a social order, a template and map for living. It organizes a hierarchy of importance and influence. The nature of a game is that there are winners and losers, and failure can be due to a single point, or a fraction of a second. The hope that England can beat European teams, let alone those from South America, is a desire that power (at least in the realm of sport) has been maintained. The Blair Government policy document 'A sporting future for all' was an attempt to improve the sporting facilities for young participants in England, using lottery money to improve coaching and infrastructure. It is a Band Aid solution to soothe the 'something' that has gone wrong with English sport. Only in the 2000s did some international influence attempt to change British sport.[69]

The difficulty is that the 1966 victory created what Jason Cowley has described as 'a benchmark against which we will always be measured, and always found wanting'.[70] In the 1960s, England did seem the centre of the cultural world. Mary Quant, Carnaby Street, the Beatles, George Best and explosive consumerism made England fashionable and successful. New Labour under Blair was never able to remake little England, let alone Great Britain, into something new. London does not swing, and Liverpool does not dominate the musical beat. Winning the World Cup in 1966 was a success that the English football team may never again reach. Two players (Sir Geoff Hurst and Sir Bobby Charlton) were knighted, along with the manager, Sir Alf Ramsey. This prestige, victory, imagery and sound would be continually recycled. For the Italia '90 competition, the Manchester-based New Order released the 'soundtrack' for the English team. The song 'World in Motion' was a blistering, brilliant dance track, including a rap from the great winger John Barnes. The final quarter of the song is a chant that seemed derived from the terraces that, post-Hillsborough, were themselves a memory. Not surprisingly, Kenneth Wolstenholme's is the first voice heard on the track. His (misquoted) 'some of the crowd are on the pitch' is laid into the mix. Nothing more is required to establish the aura of 1966. That is the benchmark. Anything less than victory is a disappointment. Carrying around 40 years of disappointment is not only uncomfortable, but corrosive of innovation.

Such a problem could have confronted post-Bradman Australian cricket. While there would never be a better batsman, Australian success after 'the Don' started to focus on the team, moulded through the outstanding leadership of Richie Benaud in the 1960s.[71] The tight Australian sporting unit – through the eras of the Chappells, Border, Taylor, Waugh and Ponting – decentred the individual brilliance of Bradman and created a team-based mode of sporting success.[72] Bradman was and is respected, but his record is so extraordinary that a new way of thinking about Australian cricket had to emerge. The English myth of 1966 has created what Jason Cowley described as 'an entire culture of self-savouring romanticism'.[73] Looking back to the 1960s is dangerous, and must be collectively debilitating. The past is always satisfying – always superior – and therefore becomes a dysfunctional method for attaining present success. There is one major problem: the sporting context has changed. Ronaldo is not Pelé. Rooney is not Moore. The Brazilians have made that realization. The English have not. Each generation of English captains desires to raise the World Cup trophy. When Bobby Moore died in February 1993, thousands of scarves and flowers were laid outside the gates of Upton Park.[74] Punctuated by these tributes was the photograph of a young Moore, in red shirt, holding aloft the Jules Rimet trophy. He died at 51, stricken with cancer. The memory of his younger self outlived his body.

Sport is about change. Traditions morph on a yearly basis. The difficulty is that English sporting success is defined very narrowly. Shifts in the beautiful game have tarnished this easy nostalgia. Even Wembley became an all-seater stadium. The first match staged at Wembley after the terraces were removed was a friendly against Uruguay on 22 May 1990. Only 38,751 spectators were present. England lost at home (1–2), for the first time in six years. The fate of Wembley Stadium is a potent symbol of the administrative, governmental and fan dissonance of football. Wembley closed on 7 October 2000. By December 2000, the syndicate that was meant to create a new national stadium failed to gain bank finance. The plan was simply too large and unwieldy. The stakeholders in the project, the Football Association, Sport England and the Government, all backed away from responsibility. The FA, for example, saw their major role that of a governing body, not stadium developer. Yet it was the FA's influence that discredited the well-funded and developed plan for a national arena in Birmingham. They believed that 'premium seating' would be responsible for 70 per cent of the stadium income, and this 'will be significantly lower at Birmingham than Wembley'.[75] As is the case of Preston's football museum, there is a desire to locate 'national assets' in London. Also, there is a nostalgia associated with Wembley, a desire literally to revisit the site of past glories, that worked against Birmingham's strategy. Of the alternative Wembley schemes that were offered, the successful bid was 'a new simplified design at Wembley based on the design submitted by the Birmingham bid team'.[76] In other words, the plan assembled by the Birmingham consortium was so successful that it was actually used. The only element changed was the location. The stadium model headed south.

Sport is a spectacle; a way to manage bodies, public opinion and consumerism. It also maps our emotional lives, connecting subjectivities and personal impressions with wider expressions of community and belonging. It is ironic that in the decade after the World Cup victory, football was at its most violent. Jason Cowley termed this 'wounded nationalism'.[77] England did quite well in the Mexico World Cup in 1970, but failed to qualify in 1974 and 1978. It was an extraordinarily rapid decline. Part of the difficulty with English football is that the cult of 1966 has created an *expectation* of sporting success, not a desire or hope for good competition. This confidence has not been matched by performances. When watching a video titled the *Story of Football*, the English problem is revealed. It is as if no other nation has ever played football. England is the centre of the sporting world, when in truth it has not been successful in football, tennis or cricket for many years.[78] In this documentary, Gascoigne receives more attention than Pelé, and Michael Owen a greater emphasis than Diego Maradona. This is sporting chauvinism at its most dangerous. Gascoigne and Owen are fine players, but neither are in the league of Pelé or Maradona. What made the latter so superior was not only their skill and balance, but the capacity to use both feet with equal effectiveness and to finish a run with accuracy rather than disappointment. George Best is clearly of a different order but, like Maradona, was unable to stitch together private and public success. There needs to be a realization that the 'story of football' is not only – or even mainly – an English story. Only when such an acknowledgement is made can the present problems and strengths be corrected and deployed.

Bobby Moore is the symbol of this paradox. It is probably not possible to have a more successful career than that of Moore. He played more than one thousand games at a senior level. Upon his retirement from football, none of the expected successes in the media or business eventuated. Cowley showed how Moore's decline is a far wider and more significant symbol:

Bobby Moore was as much a victim as the rest of us of the myths of the summer of 1966: that thin-spun summer when class boundaries seemed to dissolve and the country floated on an invisible cloud of self-celebration. Nothing would be as good again, certainly not for Moore, nor for the rest of the players who have long since remained imprisoned by their achievement. Nor for the country, either, which, for all Blair's bluster about modernity and renewal, remains haunted by an inexplicable sense of loss; not present loss, but of something bound up with feelings that the best has gone – and it will never be so good again.[79]

The photograph of Bobby Moore is just that – a photograph. It is a disconnected moment, a ghost of a possible past that is reclaimed for whatever political narrative is summoned in the present. Photographs always soak in the interpretations required of them. Actually, photography is only a memory prompt. The question is how we place the faded image in theories of time.

All forms of communication embed watermarks of memory. These signals help readers find a context – their bearings – in a world created by a text, image, film or photograph. To be able to date an event allows us – as an audience – to be oriented in the world. When there are temporal gaps, such as between 1966 and the present, it becomes more difficult to establish bearings and orientation in the imaginative world of the text. The only way to explain the state of contemporary English sport is to provide an explanatory flashback to when 'everything' was all right, and the World Cup had come home. In such a narrative, there is no room for Aberfan. There is no room for the negative catalogue of events that follow it – the Commonwealth Immigration Act in 1968 and Enoch Powell's 'Rivers of Blood' speech, for example, – to scribble over the photograph of Bobby Moore.

This cracked cultural clock also has major consequences for the discipline of history. While heritage, museums and tourism are booming new creative industries, history has been in trouble for some time. In the early 2000s, English students were asked to list the ten most significant events of the twentieth century. Many of them included the English victory in the 1966 World Cup.[80] Such a ranking is not only worrying, but demonstrates that alternative visions of the past – of decline – were not relevant. Aberfan's disaster was not mentioned by the schoolchildren.

It is perhaps significant that sporting writers focusing on the euphoria of 1966 rarely scratch around to find the traces of decline within that same year. It is easy to align the greatness of English sporting success with cultural buoyancy. Only one writer in my research into both the World Cup and Aberfan actually linked them. Jason Cowley used the link as a final, punchy conclusion to his piece showing the destructive consequences of the 1966 victory. He stated that 'it is worth recalling, too, that 1966 may have been the high point of "Swinging London" but it was also the year of the Aberfan slagheap disaster'.[81] In connecting England and Wales, sport and politics, cultural resurgence and industrial decline, Aberfan displays a more accurate aura of the British future. While the Blairite rhetoric of 'new' Labour, the information economy, globalization and free trade may seem convincing phrases amid a neo-liberal agenda, the application of these ideas is more difficult to execute when nostalgia offers a cooling salve from the intense heat of the New Right's economic policies.

## Path of the slag

The coal slurry rolled onto the Welsh village 40 years ago. Aberfan represents more than a symbol of decline or burgeoning televisual literacy. It demonstrates how we accept mediated death. Very few British protested about the graphic displays of body bags and grieving relatives in the *Marchioness* tragedy: the interest, not anger, was focused on the death of 'beautiful people'. A 'disaster' exposes a moment of insight, a transitory glimpse into other people's lives. It composes a mobile, dynamic photograph: the viewer is aware that life had existed before the tragedy and will continue after it.

There is a popular memory of pit disasters in South Wales. Senghennydd and Gresford disasters both killed greater numbers, but Aberfan is remembered. Coal, the great symbol of Britain's past greatness, had destroyed children, the future. Martin Johnes and Iain McLean affirmed that

> Aberfan has become part of Wales's collective memory and was arguably a defining moment in the nation's history. Certain historical events assume such positions because of the signals they give out about our lives and place within society . . . The continuing social and economic problems of the South Wales valleys have ensured that the Aberfan disaster has remained part of the collective memory of the region and, indeed, of Wales. The tragedy does not belong to a poverty-stricken bygone age but a period of exploitation and deprivation that still exists for large numbers.[82]

The link between popular and collective memory is not as obvious as it appears. All memory is mediated. Collective memory appears more organic, connected with an authentic experience of events. Popular memory is not necessarily contextually grounded in social, historical or economic formations. It can occur in diverse times and spaces. Popular culture – whether music, film, television, food or clothing – carries ideas, visions and sounds like a vulture, only to land those texts within the experience of later listeners and viewers. This is a post-authentic memory that is not tethered to the intentions, ideologies or origins of the sender. To argue that all who have seen photographs or televisual footage of Aberfan 'share' a collective memory equivalent to those directly linked to the events via family or industry is not only naive but initiates a troubling humanism which suggests that we all 'share' a common bank of experience.[83]

Memory maps emotions. Collective memory affiliates feeling from an event with specific subjectivities. Popular memory is more fluid and hegemonic. Aberfan entered popular memory because it was a miners' tragedy that involved children. As the Pantglas school survivors grew up, they recognized the consequences of Aberfan – for the living. Ponder this testimony, and the process by which an individual experience is broadened to an authenticated collective memory.

> We were a generation that lost out. We lost out on our education and on our futures. I can't think of any of us who ever did really well and most of [us] just stayed and grew up in the village. We haven't gone far at all.
> We didn't go out to play for a long time because those who'd lost their own children couldn't bear to see us. We all knew what they were feeling and we felt guilty about being alive.[84]

Compare this testimony to a man remembering an earlier self, and his experience of Aberfan mediated through distance, time and television.

> One date stands out more than any other. It is the date when I realized that there is probably no god. In Christian terms it was 1966. I was twenty-four years old. At a place called Aberfan in Wales, a mountain of coal slag moved, became a landslide, and buried the local school. One hundred and sixteen children, some as young as seven, died.[85]

For this man's younger self, a belief system changed irrevocably. He used Aberfan to explain how and why he became an atheist. These types of memory – personal and popular – are distinct, and should not be conflated. Memory can be usefully sorted into categories or genres: personal, collective, institutional, social and popular. The experiences of others are not available to us. They are mediated, transmitted and translated, frequently through popular culture.

Aberfan's victims have been used and exploited by employers, the National Coal Board, Labour Governments and the print and televisual media. It was a rupture in ethics for journalists and for their audiences. The literacy of tragedy and its reportage was different after October 1966. When reading the historical material from the disaster, it appears that grieving parents were characterized as devastated puppets lashing out at their puppeteers. Their arguments and interpretation were shaped for other agendas. McLean and Johnes have expressed their scholarly interpretation at its most raw.

> The victims of Aberfan were ignored because they were working class
> ... they were ignored because the outside world failed to understand
> the depth of their trauma, and ... they were therefore dismissed as petty
> and quarrelsome ... Wales is a long way from Whitehall, and ... its
> neglect can be explained in terms of one or other of the models of
> centre–periphery politics.[86]

These men have argued throughout their research that Aberfan demonstrated the errors of corporatism. Big business, big government and big unions
colluded to displace the voices of working class citizens.[87] Certainly their
case is well made, rendered more serious and disturbing because a Labour
Government perpetrated these injustices. Importantly, they reclaimed
Aberfan as a periphery that mattered.

At the conclusion of the 1970s, Vernon Bogdanor and Robert Skidelsky
had already recognized the price of consensus in the political sphere:

> Consensus did ensure the emancipation of politics from the ghosts of
> the past; unfortunately it also imposed a moratorium on the raising
> of new and vital issues. For consensus also signified acceptance of tradi-
> tional assumptions concerning Britain's political and economic role in
> the world.[88]

Harold Wilson came to office in 1964 with the slogan '13 wasted years'. He
promised that – through economic growth – consensus could be established.
In such an environment, the Labour Party could then negotiate good conditions for the working class without struggling against the forces of capital.
Affluence through consumer goods was to signal the end of a polarization
between worker and management. These new world symbols, fed by skilled
scientific workers and a new 'technological revolution', were – like the industrial revolution – uneven in their application. The Aberfan disaster was
situated on the fault line of this transformation. Through the illusion of
consensus, economic decline was rupturing social structures. The disap-
pearance of the British Empire meant that the colonies could no longer feed
the need for world power status. The balance of payments crisis in 1964,
which led to the devaluation of the pound in 1967, alongside the debates
over entry into the Common Market, made a clear case for decline.

In reading the records of Aberfan written at the time and since, it is the
archetypal case not only of mismanagement – of the media, tribunal findings and charity money – but of misunderstanding. A Welsh working class
community seemed out of time and space in 1960s Britain. The scarved
women and stocky, strong men appeared to emerge from a different period
to the urbane and sophisticated worlds of John Lennon and George Best.
At the time, David Kerr, Labour MP for Wandsworth Central, stated that
'this tragedy has reminded people a long way from Wales that we are still

one nation'.[89] Actually, this television nation perhaps confirmed the opposite: the gulf between England and Wales, centre and periphery, middle and working class, white collar and black collar.

Politics saturates television so that it is no longer possible to see the join. Aberfan's television coverage was important because the mend was still visible. A literacy in televisual grief was being formed through the event. If Aberfan did change the 'national consciousness', then why did so few southern English citizens support the miners trying to keep open the Welsh pits? The relative lack of industries currently operating in this region outside of Cardiff currently means that the economic clock has stopped. The Beveridge Report in 1943 declared that the great achievement of World War II was the unity that would achieve victory. The People's War would create a People's Peace. Aberfan, mining closures and economic decline destroyed this New Jerusalem. The green and pleasant land was built on black coal. Aberfan is a historical translator between these images.

## A study in black and red

The iconography could not be more stark – the black wound of a coal slag and the red shirts of an English victory. That both emerged in the same year is not convenient to English football, or a theorization of the British economy. There is no unity to be recaptured from these fragments. The dialectics of a disaster rarely slot into a simple narrative of national sporting success. The gulf between Wembley Stadium and Aberfan cannot only be understood through a centre/periphery template. One represents a glorious past, and the other an underbelly of industrialization. In offering a critique of the authoritative narratives encircling 1966, Aberfan is a reminder – a frequently unwelcome one – that much of English economic and political success was built on colonization and exploitation. The blond, white-skinned Bobby Moore – holding the World Cup trophy – is an image that cuts away the black faces that built English power.

All images are an idealized representation of social relationships. Whenever exploring the composition of popular memory and history, we must ask who owns these images and their distribution. Every year enfolds contradictions, paradoxes and ambivalences. Every historian assembles an interpretation that suits current purposes. The tragedy will be when Aberfan fades from memory as one more mining disaster, while English fans continue to hope for another 1966, to confirm prestige, power and victory. It is difficult to live in the present, to confront inadequacies, disappointments, fears and confusions. While the red side of 1966 faces the sun of myth and nostalgia, the black face of coal and colonization is shadowed from view. The children have died in memory as well as being suffocated by the slag.

# Chapter 4

# You've just been bounced at the WACA

## Pitching a new cricketing culture

My memory is of a ball. The surface was scratched, shredded by bouncers and deliveries pinged into the slips. Sweat had worked the shine on one side to swing through the Fremantle Doctor. Now silent and stationary, this ball is encased in glass, untouchable and undeliverable. This tatty relic of cricketing culture is not like any other. It is polished by popular memories. It is not just a ball: it was once in the hands of Dennis Lillee. It was the last ball he bowled at the WACA, on his home pitch and in his home state.

Just as it is difficult to think of Sir Donald Bradman without Bowral, Giggs without Old Trafford or the All Blacks without the House of Pain, D.K. Lillee is *of* the WACA. It is a ground that forged clever spinners such as Bruce 'Roo' Yardley and some staunch opening batsmen, like Bruce Laird, Justin Langer and Graeme Wood. It is a pitch known for its bounce and speed.[1] A fast bowler's paradise, it was the home not only of Lillee, but of Graham McKenzie, Terry Alderman, Bob Massie, Bruce Reid and Jo Angel. It has been the happiest of hunting grounds for Jeff Thomson, Merv Hughes,[2] Brett Lee[3] and Glenn McGrath.[4] The wicket's pitch and bounce have – as a by-product of its reputation as a fast bowling nursery – created a dynasty of outstanding, aggressive and talented wicketkeeper-batsmen. Rodney Marsh,[5] Tim Zoehrer and Adam Gilchrist – or Marshie, Timmie and Gillie – were big hitters of over-pitched, under-pitched and loose deliveries. They have also shown a great talent to read a wicket, maintain concentration and understand the trajectory of the fast paced, short pitched bouncer. The WACA is one of the few – very few – pitches in the world known purely for its wicket. It has rarely disappointed its spectators. On 10 October 2003, Matthew Hayden made the highest score in Test history up to that time. His 380 runs, as part of a declared Australian innings of 735, added further gloss to the WACA's role in international cricketing history.[6] While Lord's is known for its slope, and subcontinental pitches take spin, there are very few wickets so associated with a style and mode of preparation and delivery. In the 1970s, enormous cracks emerged on the fourth days of WACA Test matches. From the 1990s, the new clay-bound pitch played much better, becoming so hard that it was almost shiny. What is frequently forgotten, though, is that this fame is incredibly recent: Test matches have only been played at the WACA since 1970. The reputation of the fastest, bounciest pitch in the world has been rapidly achieved.

This chapter bounces ideas off the WACA's hard surface, showing how history and geography rebound off the wicket. This sporting venue is a crucible, demonstrating that national cultures always conflict and agitate against local allegiances. Belonging and identity gain meaning in the liminal or in-between spaces. The multiple locations of a self – in a house, suburb, region, state, nation or trans-national spaces – activate social differences and diverse communities. The WACA is what Elspeth Probyn described as a 'zone . . . of specificity',[7] which allows a particular 'self' and belonging structure to be actualized, building a transitory – but powerful – community around a particular site. Through consumerism, identity is bought and sold. In our society of buying and selling, a stable identity hurts the market. We all must transform into desiring selves, requiring one more item from the global shopping mall to create a satiated self. This process of lack, loss and

*Figure 4.1* WACA entry.

desire never ceases. Transitory moments of insight and belonging are the only breaks in a wash of cultural, economic and political instabilities. Venues such as the WACA convey a shared narrative, story and history. Sport is one of the quickest ways to claim, speak and project an identity.

## Being Antipodean

The WACA encourages excessive journalistic rage, angst and intensity. In response to England's most inept batting performance of the entire 2002/03 Ashes series in Perth, Mike Coward stated that 'this England team is utterly beyond therapy'.[8] There was a justification for his disgust. The Test was over in three days. Brett Lee's hostile bowling resulted in three wickets for 78 runs at the end of the first innings. England was bowled out for 185. By the end of the first day, Australia was two wickets down for 126 runs – from only 23 overs. It was embarrassing. At the conclusion of this 2002/03 Ashes series, a joke circulated throughout Australia:

> What is the most useless thing in world sport?
> A ticket to the fifth day of an England Test.

It was that kind of summer for the English. This humiliation was made even worse by a football defeat of the national team by Australia's Socceroos. Association football, so long the third code behind rugby league and Australian Rules, finally received its just reward. If possible, beating the English at football was even better than winning the Ashes. It was unexpected, whereas there was a relentless predictability to the cricketing success. The *Sydney Morning Herald* even transformed it into humour. Their page one story featured the headline 'And it's a marvellous fighting comeback by the Poms – just kidding'.[9] There is a revenge narrative attached to these headlines. The colonial masters had been beaten, and the 'motherland' pummelled. To understand the enthusiasm of the crowd in the brilliant English Ashes victory of 2005, and the stunned pessimism of Australian supporters, requires a comprehension of how colonialism operates in and through sport. In formerly colonized nations, (re)discovering a centred, authentic identity is difficult. Amid the dense ironies of post-colonialism, it is no surprise that former sports of subjugation are renegotiated and claimed as activities of resistance and empowerment. Sport 'adds value' to the post-colonial national project. Suvendrini Perera has shown how cricket has been used for Sri Lankan nationalism, activating stories of displacement for the diasporic subject. She realized, being a Sri Lankan Australian, that cricket was part of her identity and was a potent site of difference between Sri Lankan and Australian allegiances. Importantly, she made the crucial realization – never quite grasped by the English authorities of the game – that 'cricket in the colonies, as in the colonizing country, has been a source not of unity and cohesion, but of division and antagonism'.[10] Her maxim is provocative and confirmed when focusing on the intense local allegiances within Western Australian cricket. 'National' teams must always negotiate through dense social divisions.

'Empire' holds an organizing function, tethering economic, political and cultural allegiances between territories with little in common except unequal power relations. Bats and balls were carried with bibles and rifles in the process of territorial acquisition. Cricket, more than rugby or football, is an English-speaking game.[11] Now that Great Britain has become little England, *Wisden Cricket Monthly* is once more filled with missionary zeal. Articles such as 'Spreading the gospel'[12] and 'It's time for cricket to go global'[13] make it clear that cricket's English elites have realized that while the sun did not set on the Empire, pink did not cover the entire map. The cultural (in)sensitivity to colonial differences survives in this cricketing publication, reminding readers that the 'MCC sent out its own missionary tours to foreign parts but matches were usually against local elites rather than Johnny Fuzzy-Wuzzy'.[14] With this attitude expressed in the 2000s, not the 1800s, cricket deserves to die on the vine. Thankfully, this insular, offensive and racist attitude has been critiqued in two ways. First, cricket has changed for ever because it has been claimed by the subcontinent and the Antipodes as an authenticating experience of nationalism. Second, English cricket is seriously and structurally in trouble. The county competition is failing, even after instigating two divisions in both the championships and one-day contests in 2000.[15] Twenty/twenty has been a more successful strategy to increase attendance. The problems, though, remain structural. Players are signed for 12-month contracts, and coaches are seasonally employed.[16] This means that a continuity of line-up and strategy is difficult to accomplish, and player loyalty hard to justify and maintain. Compared to the fitness, skill and intent of Sri Lanka, Pakistan, India, Australia and New Zealand, the (formerly) colonized have entirely invaded the pitch. For India and Pakistan, cricket enters popular culture and performs conflict, change and difference.[17] Importantly, too, Wales has maintained teams and an infrastructure. Like rugby, Welsh cricket is a working class sport, not an elite contest. As Mike Fatkin, the Chief Executive of Glamorgan Cricket Club, stated, 'we're desperate to beat England at anything'.[18] The reason for this desperation is obvious. Colonization required a dual process: civilizing and subjugating. Through sport, England revealed its differences from the peoples it invaded and colonized. This 'boundary dispute'[19] triggers a range of representations, of strength and weakness, civility and 'fuzzy-wuzzyness', resilience and compliance. There is a sad realization made by Bee Wilson that 'the archetypal England team would travel the world without ever tasting it'.[20] Mike Gatting was known to pack Branston pickle wherever he played. It is no surprise that even the great historian Eric Hobsbawm likened the decline of British power to Britons' failure in team sports.[21]

The troubles of English cricket gained public recognition during Mark Taylor's tour of 1997. The English bowlers were termed 'blunt as infants' scissors in the penetration department'.[22] Lord's became the 'symbol of all that is good – and embarrassing – about English cricket'.[23] Nostalgia for English pastoral outfields and polite applause did not create Australian superiority in world cricket. It was a commitment to professionalism, coaching and training,[24] and a reclaiming of particular Australian symbols in cricketing history, such as the baggy green cap. Tony Greig also linked the success of the team with media broadcasting:

> The way Adam Gilchrist plays doesn't just happen . . . it's because as a little boy he'd been listening to guys like us, saying you've got to play horizontal-bat shots, you've got to pull and cut, you've got to take the initiative. Without being too big-headed about it, I think what we've done with television has been fantastic for Australian cricket.[25]

I am the same age as Adam Gilchrist, and I can confirm Greig's testimony. To understand the passionate enthusiasm for cricket in Australia, readers must share a televisual summer. It dominates radio, television, newspapers and conversation. The legendary commentators – Richie Benaud being the Obi-Wan Kenobi of the team – taught a generation of Australians about cricket. We learned about leg spin, line and length, hooks and pulls, slip fielding and catching in the outfield. The game was and is mediated, but is also owned. Probably Simon Caterson expressed this contradiction best: 'cricket enabled Australia to assert its independence on its own soil, even as it confirmed its sense of British-ness and still does'.[26] The one-day game – the Australian contribution to the sport – made cricket exciting again. While the rest of the world embraced the Kerry Packer revolution – the night games and the coloured clothing – England lost its role as a global cricketing innovator, reclaiming some of the initiative through 20/20. The class bias of the sport, its inflection as a game of the leisured classes, is not replicated in Sri Lanka, Pakistan and India. There is an honesty in these crowds, an affirmation that professional sport is actually in the business of entertainment.

The greatest difficulty in creating a post-colonial environment is to rein-habit and reclaim the land. Cricket has (re)invented Australia for England. Stereotypical representations of loud-mouthed, arrogant Australians are now matched in English consciousness with the (post) Waugh aura of professionalism, competitiveness and ruthless brilliance. It is no surprise that the WACA displays the excesses and contradictions of Australian identity. On match days, it is filled with abusive chants and offensive banners. It is a brash, bouncy, populist stadium – bustling in the city centre. The enormous lights can be seen tens of kilometres from the ground. The WACA is part of the geography of Perth and captures much of the pride, parochialism and aggression of this state with a capital city on the coast and a parched landscape stretching into the desert. Western Australia is isolated from the rest of the continent. Its industries are different, as are the climate and terrain. Paranoia also frequently surfaces, particularly around sport. The collision of east and west – whatever the game – results in a brutal affair. It was even hypothesized that the recent refit of the ground was caused by eastern states' hostility to the WACA:

> Whether it was well-founded speculation or just smart politicking on the east coast, there has been periodic talk of Perth losing its Test match. Even more unsettling for the WA Cricket Association was the scrutiny of its Test match attendances by Australian Cricket Board executives and auditors. Clearly, word filtered across the Nullarbor that there was a need for change and the ground is now more intimate and appealing and certain to host Test matches for many years. Certainly, the calls for Melbourne and Sydney to get an extra Test match will be less strident.[27]

The Nullabor is a long stretch of desert road that connects (or separates) the two halves of the continent. The WACA remains a space of pride, difference and exuberance for Western Australians, probably because the ground and its Tests had to be won after years of struggle.[28] They remain

*Figure 4.2* Urban cricket.

under threat, with Darwin and Hobart now bidding for regular Test hosting rights at the expense of Perth. The point is that cricket continues these struggles over space and meaning. These fights in Australian cricket makes one point clear. Lord's is not 'the home of cricket'.[29] The game has many homes, histories and spaces. English writers and spectators always view cricket differently. Only when playing and watching the game on the periphery can we recognize social, sporting and political changes.

## Warriors from the West

Australian marketing executives have two great talents: producing advertisements that sell beer and sport. For the 2002/03 and 2004/05 seasons, the campaign supporting the Western Warriors, the Western Australian state cricketing team based at the WACA, was provocative. Based around lilting but energetic Irish folk instruments, it is a call to war. The players smear war paint on their faces and follow Adam Gilchrist into an open field. He then throws a bat high and long into the air. It lands – having been transformed into a sword – in the WACA ground, surrounded by lights. The slogan 'Catch the spirit' connects sport and war, folk and urbanity, aggression and Western Australianness, into a tight and effective bundle.

Most cricketing books do not catch this spirit. It is remarkable that such an exciting game produces such dire prose. There is a need to break the dominance of Wisden and autobiographies. The season reviews are the worst: page after page of scores, caught and bowled lists and parched commentary. Jonathan Rice's *One hundred Lord's Tests* completed the usual test-by-test review, with bland, narrative accompaniment. Outstanding pictures were included in the book, none of which were discussed. He even stated that 'I have tried to keep personal observations out of the text'.[30] Obviously such objectivity is not possible. There is a confidence in writing about Lord's that fosters many assumptions, including the idea that English truths are 'naturally' relevant to international supporters.

Cricket is where we find it. There is a need to do something different with the literal and metaphoric wicket. The best writers capture the sweat, heat and agitation that peppers even the mildest of cricketing contests. For example, Andrew Hignell's outstanding book *Rain stops play*[31] creates an innovative linking of cricket and weather. Not a season review, the book explores the stories of such events as the fifth Ashes Test at The Oval in 1968. In the era before covered wickets, the crowd and the officials swept gallons of water off the playing area, even wringing sponges, so that Derek Underwood could bowl out the Australians. This victory ensured that they shared the series. Cricket writers rarely think about such topics. They are drawn to narrative history, or more precisely chronology. Time becomes more relevant than space. If writers placed attention on the spaces of sporting competition, then they would be able to understand social meanings with much greater effectiveness. Colonization has always been about spaces: discoveries, invasions, ownership and dispossession. But it is also about representation, and the flight of the imaginary. The Australian continent was a mystery for the European imagination. The isolation of the western half only increased this aura.

Because of this isolation, Western Australia has done it tough throughout its sporting history. It was kept out of the National Soccer League until 1997, while multiple teams from Sydney were admitted into the competition. Before the league nationalized into the Australian Football League (AFL) in 1987, the best Western Australian players were poached to compete in Victoria. In cricket, this isolation is even more profound. The WACA was only included on a provisional and half-time basis in the national Sheffield Shield competition in 1947. This state of affairs was then replaced by a decade of enforced WACA subsidy of visiting state teams: in other words, paying opposition players for the inconvenience of coming to Western Australia. The consequence of this treatment was that it fired up the hostility of the team, administrators and spectators and intensified the training. Considering this recent inclusion in the national competition – or even not considering it – their success has been remarkable. In the first year that Western Australia was admitted to the Sheffield Shield competition on a restricted basis in 1947, the team won. They would then win again in 1968, 1972, 1973, 1975, 1977, 1978, 1981, 1984, 1987, 1988, 1989, 1992, 1998 and 1999. In the 30 year history alone, 1967–97, the WACA had won 12 shields, twice the number of New South Wales, who had been in the competition twice as long. There has also been great success in the one-day competition, with Western Australia claiming this trophy three times more often than Queensland, the nearest rival. This is a remarkable sporting success story, with all the usual parts of the narrative: underdog makes good and victory overcoming hostility. Such sporting narratives offer insight into Western Australian history more generally.

Western Australia was only 'settled' by colonizers in 1829, but was an unstable community throughout the 1830s. The colonists tried to establish a little England, planting European crops and gardens. It did not work too well. Not surprisingly, cricket was played. The Western colonies confronted difficulties. The small population and the isolation from the major centres in the East hampered the development of particular sports. Still, the WACA as an association was established on 25 November 1885, and the ground opened in 1893. The first match was played on turf wickets in February 1894. Still Western Australia was lagging behind, because the Eastern colonies could represent themselves as 'Australia' and then play Test matches against England. Before the WACA received its first Test match against England in 1970, the great players such as Bradman rarely appeared in the West. Between 1956 and 1960, the WACA paid a total of £10,104 in subsidy to eastern states teams. Up until the 1970s, the WA state team played its four Sheffield Shield games in other mainland capitals on a single 'tour' each season. Bob Simpson, the one-time national player and coach, held a 'lurking feeling that Western Australians were sometimes more fervent about playing for the state than for Australia'.[32] There is a justification for his concern. The great partnerships of the national team – Lillee and Marsh, Laird and Wood, Martin and Gilchrist – were Western Australian alliances. It is no surprise that Bob Massie's remarkable Test, where he took eight wickets in each inning was assisted by Rodney Marsh's keeping. He had kept to Massey's bowling since grade cricket. He knew precisely how the bowler could swing and seam the ball. As with Yorkshire and Lancashire, the isolation from the population-dense areas of the country has granted Western Australian players a marked difference and distinction through distance. There are seven men who have played more than 100 Sheffield Shield/Pura Cup matches for Western Australia: Tom Moody, Mike Veletta, Graeme Wood, John Inverarity, Tim Zoehrer, Geoff Marsh and Jo Angel. When Angel reached this milestone, his captain captured the Western/Australian relationship:

> Not only has he been a quality cricketer for his state, but he has been a quality person. He is a most reliable teammate and friend to everybody. The character and courage of Jo Angel epitomizes all the good things about Western Australian and for that matter, Australian cricket.[33]

The parochialism is obvious, but so are the ideologies and characteristics invested in the team.[34]

Enfolding these ideologies, the isolation and success against the odds is the WACA ground. The legendary Dennis Lillee received the remarkable figures of 8 for 29 against a Rest of the World team in 1971. Lillee – literally – beat the world. Perhaps the most famous one-day game played is the Gillette Cup 'miracle match' of 1976. Western Australia made only 77 runs, but then went on to dismiss Queensland for 62. Dennis Lillee bowled Viv Richards, a visiting 'international', for a duck with his fifth ball of an over, following on from four bouncers. There are other stories, of Geoff Marsh who scored 355 not out against South Australia. Terry Alderman gained 14 wickets against New South Wales in a Shield game, eclipsed by Ian Brayshaw's 10 for 44 in a single innings against Victoria. Peripheral sporting spaces are built on such stories. Most of the tales within the WACA are of remarkable bowling against the odds.

The WACA has had far greater autonomy and success than most local, regional or state-based cricket organizations. It has two great factors in its favour. First, the WACA has had freehold ownership of the ground. Originally holding 29 acres,[35] part of this lot was sold to the Trotting Association in the early 1920s. Many sports have been played at the ground, including rugby league, baseball, Association football and Australian Rules. Currently, though, only cricketers use the field. Because the land is held freehold – and media rights are so lucrative – there was no extreme necessity to hire the ground out regularly.

The WACA's history is particularly stark when comparing the case of the Lancashire County Cricket Club. The LCCC has established an entire facilities arm, including a conference and banqueting centre. The Old Trafford Lodge has 68 bedrooms and is frequently utilized by Manchester United fans on match days. The LCCC has held concerts at the ground, starting with Simply Red in 1992 through to Robbie Williams in 2001 and the Move concerts in 2002. The Chief Executive explained the rationale for multi-tasking the facility:

> It is now beginning to dawn on most clubs that cricket cannot survive on cricket alone and those that try are heading down a long dark tunnel. Here at Old Trafford just to run cricket alone . . . costs in excess of £2 million. That's before we take into account the huge annual maintenance costs for the upkeep of an international ground – well in excess of another £1 million! . . . We are fortunate to have a football club like Manchester United close at hand. Their match days help us to fill our car parks and restaurants throughout the winter months and they too are part of the financial jigsaw.[36]

Importantly, Manchester United do not mention the other Old Trafford in any of their publications. They do not need to. The LCCC is desperately trying to broaden out its business interest. It is the only international ground in England with planning permission to build floodlights, but they have not yet been built. Yet this potential means that the ground may never suffer the disrepair of Headingley, the home of Yorkshire cricket.[37]

Most cricket grounds have problems because they are unused up to 300 days a year, but this 'space' provides potential for multiple income streams. This question of unfulfilled potential is raised at the WACA: 'It's a state landmark that stands dormant for much of the year, but is the WACA Ground an expensive white elephant or untouchable turf?'[38] The facility remains relatively debt-free, because the Association is a one-sixth shareholder in Australian cricket. The revenue raising of the Australian Cricket Board ensures that the WACA receives a one-sixth share of television rights, even when the Australian team plays overseas and media rights are sold. Therefore, it is difficult to demand changes from a sporting association with an adequate income stream. Unfortunately, the Labor Sports Minister during the refit of the WACA, Alan Carpenter, tried to persuade the Association to shift to Subiaco Oval – the home of Australian Rules football – to play tests and one-day matches. He stressed the quality of 'drop-in' pitches.

> If they want to stay at the WACA that's their business. They own the ground. They have significant revenues from the ACB TV rights and

don't have financial difficulties. But they would have created a problem for themselves by continuing to develop a coliseum-style stadium which isn't warranted for cricket in WA.[39]

Subiaco Oval is confronting financial challenges. It is not surprising that a state government would like a regular tenant at that venue, particularly one with the income stream of the Australian Cricket Board. However, Carpenter has not realized the scale and importance of the WACA. He has also underestimated the second great advantage that the Association possesses. The WACA encases one of the most famous pitches in the world. Asking the WACA to use drop-in pitches is like suggesting to Mohammad Ali that he should have taken up kick boxing. He might have beaten his opponents, but that is not the point.

## Pitch of life

For the 2002/03 Ashes tour, the WACA pitch was at its fastest for 20 years. The famous bouncy wicket was also plumb, thereby ensuring even bounce. In such an environment, there is a rawness to the confrontation between batsman and bowler on this wicket. Bowlers are frightening, charging in with the Fremantle Doctor at their backs, also carrying the speed history of Lillee and Thomson with them. The aggressive fast bowler always has a home at the WACA. For batsmen, the ground offers great value for shots, particularly when playing straight. What has made the WACA famous is not its facilities, members' enclosures or scoreboard. It is the pitch that gleans notoriety, and it is worth attention. In a *Cricket World* rating, of the top 20 bowling performances in test cricket, two were at the WACA, and three were at Lord's. Considering the few Tests hosted in Perth, when compared to over one hundred at Lord's, it is a remarkable record.[40] With sport tourism a burgeoning and developing area, the global branding of the wicket in Western Australia has enormous potential. It is important to note that a Bangalore-based organization, SportzVillage, has created a niche market for sports-related tour itineraries for schoolchildren aged from 9 to 15 years. Such an initiative has a wider context in India, with an estimated 100,000 Indians travelling internationally to watch sport-related events.[41] The primary sports of focus are football, golf, Formula One and cricket. Obviously the WACA, with strategic partnerships, must tap into this burgeoning industry and audience.

The WACA remains marketable in sports tourism for the pitch. The WACA wickets run true north–south and are maintained by the seven-member Turf Department. Their responsibilities include preparing the main arena, practice and training facilities and the WACA gardens. The wicket block is 30 metres wide and 30 metres in length, incorporating ten pitches. The soil comes from Waroona and is specially chosen for its 85 per cent clay content. Special grasses are utilized on the wicket block, creating a hybrid Windsor Green and Winter Green with some native varieties. Similarly, the outfield was planted with Winter Green couch during the 1985 makeover,[42] and now also contains some native varieties as well.[43]

This curatorial care betrays an ill-kept history. When the ground was first granted to the WACA by Governor Broome in 1889, it was a swamp. Even when the terrain was raised by half a metre, the rise and fall of the Swan River caused the pitch to hold moisture. This problem, when combined with the poor clay, meant that the first wickets at the WACA were a spinner's paradise. The pitches were then replaced with wicket soil from Merri Creek in Victoria and Bulli in New South Wales in 1908. Only in 1920 was local soil located from the area of the Harvey River. At this point, Nick Bell acknowledged that 'there was a noticeable improvement in the wicket and the fast, true, and even-paced bouncy "WACA WICKET" legend was born'.[44] The soil is actually what has caused this cricketing environment. The influential curator of the WACA from 1998 to 2005,[45] Richard Winter, explained how these wicket conditions are formulated:

> The WACA pitch is renowned for its exceptional pace and bounce. This is due mainly to the physical and chemical characteristics of the soil used. The clay content of the soil is up around 80% and it is a montmorilinite clay, renowned for its ability to drain when saturated and to set very hard when prepared as a cricket wicket. These characteristics, along with Perth's hot, dry climate and grass type allows the pitch to bake hard, which promotes bounce and produces an excellent shine, which creates pace. The downside of this is that under extremely hot conditions, cracking can become quite prominent, resulting in uneven and erratic bounce that can be quite dangerous. The key ingredient to controlling this risk is to maintain a vigorous turf root system and to monitor soil moisture very closely.[46]

Establishing an even bounce is important, not only for international games, but to ensure that the Western Warriors have strong performances in the state and one-day competitions. Much of the financial stability of the WACA organization is carried by the Warrior performances. They require a consistency of wicket and outfield.

The WACA has witnessed many changes. It was expanded and rebuilt as it became a Sheffield Shield cricket ground in 1947, and again as it became a venue for Test matches. In the mid-1980s, the turf was completely removed and replaced by a perched-water system, instigating good drainage. Lights were added in 1986. Through the refurbishment, the members' enclosure was moved from the northern to the southern side of the ground encompassing the refitted Lillee Marsh stand and its surroundings. In 2002, the WACA instigated the largest refurbishment of the ground. It was successful: the first Test match after the refit saw a record crowd of 22,523 on the first day, 29 November 2002, and the atmosphere improved enormously. The capacity of the ground was slightly reduced and the grassed embankment increased. It was an ironic inversion of the all-seater stadia now dominating English football. The concrete and plastic were reduced, the 'stands' became grassed and tree-speckled spaces which triggered far more pleasant viewing. The refurbishment also changed the shape of the oval, reducing its size. Originally 185 by 140 metres – which allowed for football – it is now a fat rectangle 150 by 140 metres. Removing 15 metres from the western and eastern ends of the ground ensured that spectators are closer to the play. In this refit, 5,000 square metres of new turfed areas were laid. A new players' pavilion was also established, along with a Lord's-style balcony so that players can sit in the view of fans. Food facilities were also improved, including both food halls and cappuccino bars. This is a remarkable, hybrid cricketing innovation. A 'village green' effect has been established, arching back to a pastoral myth of cricket, while improving the spectator comforts through seating and hospitality suites.

These facilities have been matched with coaching improvements. In 2002, Dennis Lillee was asked to head the Fast Bowling Academy, funded through a joint partnership between the Department of Sport and Recreation and the Western Australia Cricket Association.[47] It is a talent identification programme to ensure that the young fast bowlers for which the WACA is known are able to have specialist coaching, without succumbing to back injuries in particular. The WACA justified this initiative by stating that 'the idea is to harness and develop their talents to a level that will continue the tradition of WA producing quality fast bowlers who can make the most of the WACA's bouncy pitch and make life uncomfortable for opposition teams'.[48] Dennis Lillee's stature in world cricket is unsurpassed in terms of quick bowling, enhanced by his reputation as a defier of authority. His era, the 1970s, was a remarkable time in Australian cricket. Lillee and Marsh's leering moustaches enhanced the popular iconography of the game. This period saw cigarette sponsorships and mythic drinking regimes of players. When World Series Cricket was launched in the 1978/79 season, the 'C'mon Aussie C'mon C'mon' song became a number one single. The lyrics named both Lillee and Marsh. The son of a Perth truck driver, Lillee made the WACA conditions famous. However, he is also known for other mythic incidents, including the Javed Miandad kicking controversy in 1981/82 at the WACA.[49] Others have produced remarkable spells at the WACA – including Glenn McGrath's 300th wicket at the ground, which was part of a hat-trick – but few can match Lillee's affiliation with the pitch.

It is no surprise that when the financial future of the WACA started to become more tenuous through 2004, Dennis Lillee again bowled to the rescue. He was named President of the WACA by the end of that year. Beverly Ligman reported that 'Lillee was the undisputed heart of Australia's attack for more than a decade – now it seems he will play a major role in the re-invention of the WACA for a new generation'.[50] His radical desire to open the WACA for public open space during winter and sell the land surrounding the ground for development is one way to stabilize the financial future of the Association. His goal is 'to ensure that the WACA regains its standing as a leader in cricket on and off the field'.[51] Lillee is mobilizing his reputation and the passionate histories of the WACA pitch to refocus the financial future of the ground. The strategies he has instigated bear many similarities with those of Lancashire County Cricket Club, focusing on membership drives, corporate sponsorship and event management.[52] Yet once more, the potential of sports tourism is underplayed.

Throughout cricket, it is the ball that does the talking for bowlers and batsmen, but the wicket allows the dialogue to commence. The cricket ball is a potent missile, 156 grams propelled at a batsman at speeds beyond 150 kilometres an hour. For a dry continent, Australia features a remarkable diversity of wickets. Different conditions, such as the high humidity in Brisbane or the dry heat in Adelaide and Perth, create distinct atmospheres. Pakistani wickets are known to be flat and dead, encouraging the remarkable talent of Pakistan's bowlers to move and swing an old ball, utilizing an irregular bounce. The bouncing WACA wicket nurtures fast bowling, big hitting, good slip fielders and confident keepers.

Considering this global reputation, it is odd that the WACA has not been stressed as a tourist destination. The Association is starting to develop a series of initiatives, including regular tours of the ground, a new visibility for the museum and, by 2003, a superb website. While a functional site existed before this time, the current 'virtual WACA' is well structured and developed.[53] All parts of the site are well linked through hypertext, and there are great opportunities for expansion.[54] Fixtures, news, a sporting calendar, sponsorship and information about Cricket WA are all included in the package. This site will become even more important in the future. Communication and information systems are necessary for sporting tourism and creating 'virtual visibility' before a visit to Perth.[55] While the WACA is an assumed part of the Western Australian landscape, for sporting tourists it is a primary destination in the state. Unfortunately, the state's tourist department has not recognized this role in a similar fashion to the city of Melbourne. In the 1980s, a decision was made to turn the capital of Victoria into an 'events' capital. Sport is the primary focus of their campaigns. It is currently a A$1 billion a year industry, and cities such as Manchester are looking to Melbourne's strategy as a guide.[56] Unfortunately, Perth is yet to follow this lead. The branding and visibility of the WACA could not be bought and – in future years – should be recognized as a resource to be mobilized.

Tourists seek novelty, and sport is often the basis for change, excitement and innovation. The key is to align sport and tourist organizations, creating a shared agenda.[57] The consequences of globalization are that local specificities – or sites of interest – become even more important.[58] Through the rich representational fabric of sport, the WACA is able to activate nostalgia and cultural tourism. All tourism is saturated with representations. Postcards, souvenirs, T-shirts and caps are part of the authentification process. As the WACA website increases in its commercial role, it may provide the trigger for a considered strategy to deploy the visibility for tourism. While the WACA is part of cricketing folklore, its museum is a neglected part of the Association's initiatives. If tourism is seen to be a part of the WACA's future growth, then the objects and ideas encased behind the glass may be released to convey far more wide-ranging economic initiatives.[59]

## A living museum

Sport is a culture of the present which fetishizes the now and creates shallow links with a hyper-relevant past. 'Tradition' is only important when either challenged or confirmed by current events. It is never possible to capture a singular past with objectivity and clarity. University historians tend to hold authority in what happened in the past, gaining credibility over popular memory or 'common sense'. Such authoritative silences crush the chattering collectivity of the past. The strength of a museum is that it opens the past out to multiple readings. Power and patronage disengage experiences of sport, transforming the memory of a great catch, innings or wicket into a commodified event within leisure, recreational or educational businesses.

The key is to fathom why the WACA museum currently has a low profile, and ponder some proactive strategies to address this problem. One reason is leadership. Kevin Moore's expertise and importance in the National Football Museum in Preston is without question. With such a model as a guide, the WACA Museum is a site of potential, not of actuality. It is run mainly by volunteers. For much of 2003, the museum ran curatorless after the resignation of Tracy Maitland. However, because of the quality of its material exhibits, there is a far greater visitorship at the WACA than at the Lancashire County Cricket Club Museum, which only opens on match days during the season. Also, Australian cricket at all levels of competition is far healthier than the county cricket scene.

Most companies would dream of holding a global brand like the WACA. There is a sense that the WACA is aware of this power, but hesitant to exploit it. This phenomenon is most clearly revealed in the WACA museum. Established in 1979 after restoration and refurbishment of photographs and memorabilia, the first official museum display was only established in the Prindiville Stand in 1985. It was moved to a larger venue in the Farley Stand during 1988. It has maintained very conservative curatorial strategies. Simple relationships between objects and narrative are formulated, which are inappropriate when handling popular culture such as sport.

The WACA museum has eight separate display areas, emphasizing cricket, but with mention of the other sports that have been housed in the arena, including tennis, football, hockey and athletics. There are rooms dedicated to international cricket, Sir Donald Bradman, local history, the Centenary of Federation and a Sheffield Shield display. Patrons have assisted the museum, with the International Room completed with the assistance of the Office of Citizenship and Multicultural Interests. Dennis Lillee has been a long-term supporter of the collection, and his influence and commitment can be seen in the objects and photographs displayed. The tours, which run three days a week, permit the visitor to walk on the turf of the WACA. Clearly, the structures are in place for a successful tourist venture to be actualized. The 'problem' is the museum's building and the mechanism through which items are displayed.

The current museum is situated in the house where the ground's curator used to live. The resultant exhibition is a cluttered presentation of outstanding and fascinating objects, which simply require expertise in display, to order and grant meaning to the balls, bats and photographs. The WACA holds a rich depository of objects. A greater array of ideas is required to grant the materials context and meaning. Museum architecture is important, providing a frame for ideas and objects. The old house has provided neither the room nor spatial unity to allow the collection to develop. Few sporting museums have such potential as the WACA, but at the moment it is a vault, rather than a venue. The relationship between objects and ideas requires careful rethinking. The current desire to present the artefacts of material culture as self-standing and self-evident is not in keeping with the capacity of the WACA name and reputation to move beyond the conventional and conservative audience for cricket. The key problem for museums, and particularly institutions wishing to activate sport tourism, is to ponder how to open the collection to disenfranchised groups.

Cricket is such a fascinating case study of social diversity in Australia because it allows a discussion of values, or who is being represented and believed. All nations are based on unspoken assumptions, and these values are not innocent, transparent or unproblematic. It is significant that the WACA is located in central Perth. It is not a rural, pastoral or idyllic setting. It gives the ground a tougher, grittier context, rather than the gentle crack of willow hitting leather. Australia is a highly suburbanized nation,[60] resulting in words like 'community' being emptied of meaning and capturing little explanatory force beyond consumerism. There is an ambivalent and confusing relationship between city and country in museum culture. While the bulk of Australians live in cities, the rural environment has played a major role in the construction of a national identity.

Museums freeze moments in time, and attempt to create a narrative around them. The problem with many sport museums is that there is a static and conservative display of materials and collections. Visual culture offers such potential, but the WACA Museum – like many cricketing institutions – over-utilizes photographs. As historical documents, visual culture is better used as part of a mixed media presentation. As Rajchman has argued, 'it is a matter not simply of what a building shows "symbolically" or "semiotically", but also of what it makes visible about us and within us'.[61] While spatialization is one technique to exercise power, it can also be a way to build identity and allegiance.

Museums hold an educational function, working in the space between knowledge and entertainment. The WACA Museum is increasingly marketing itself towards school groups. Such an imperative rewrites the earlier histories of museums, which were based on collectors, founders or funders. Educational strategies require distinct initiatives, goals and media to be deployed that are different from a 'general public' audience. Museums – particularly sporting museums – must focus on the issue of the audience. The WACA website states that 'school students will learn a lot about sport and history when visiting the WACA Museum'.[62] The materials distributed to these groups require attention. No detailed pedagogic frameworks, curriculum or course materials have been developed. Old models of passive learning and absorbing information have been assumed. To take education seriously, the form and content of a museum must change, altering the direction of exhibition development, community outreach, volunteer management, fundraising and teacher training. Knowledge does not emerge osmotically from museum objects, but is produced and negotiated. Cricket in Australia is enmeshed in popular culture, particularly television and the Internet. To present objects behind glass cases and in a static display demonstrates little understanding of the changing sporting audiences. The adaptations of the museum environment must create spaces for visitor interpretation of facts. Cricket museums around the world are probably the most conservative of all sports in their presentation, particularly when compared to Association football. However, the WACA Museum has the potential not only to be an 'accidental' site to visit on match days, but also to be enhanced through the refit of the stadium. The benefit of being in the centre of Perth, for example, is an advantage not shared by Manchester United's ground in Old Trafford, which requires a Metro ride from the city.

To improve the WACA Museum, new premises are required. Obviously, after the multi-million dollar refit, such improvements may be of only minor concern. But if the WACA is to focus on cricket alone, with football going to other ovals, then the uniqueness of this function must be stressed. The way to 'occupy' a stadium that is not filled for much of the year is to take sports tourism seriously, opening the establishment out to the expansion of leisure opportunities. Diversification is pivotal not only to survival but also to expansion. Interestingly, when the former curator Tracy Maitland took on the management of the WACA Museum, she approached UWA's marketing lecturer, Jill Sweeney, to organize a marketing plan. Dr Sweeney gave this project to her marketing class. The students made their suggestions:

> diversifying what is on offer at the museum, to include a variety of sports and possibly become the WACA Sports Museum of Australia; tactics to encourage visitors to browse longer and spend more time in the recently developed shop; promotion through web-based directories and community and education-based media.[63]

The last two tactics are the most viable, and have actually been commenced. The refitted website has created a series of hypertext links to the virtual museum off the home page. The casual virtual visitor gains awareness of the museum's presence at the ground. Also, the shop has been expanded.

Ironically, this commercial venture may provide the greatest lift to the museum. Just as Manchester United fans visit the superstore at Old Trafford and then discover the museum, a similar tactic could work for the WACA. The first stage must be not only web-based promotion of the shop, but the ability to buy merchandise from the e-WACA.[64] The problem with the marketing students' ideas was that including a variety of sports serves to dilute the specificity of the WACA brand. It is a site of cricket. There are other venues for football and soccer throughout the state and the world. The specificity of location and destination is an advantage that would be

*Figure 4.3* **The WACA shop.**

blunted by generically widening its interests to all sports. The international experience with football demonstrates that spectators to games are a primary base for the museum's visitors. An innovative focus for the future could be a development of an educational suite for schools, similar to the phenomenal package distributed to teachers and students for the Twickenham Rugby Museum.

Museums provide a venue for entertainment and empowerment. The WACA is part of the history of Western Australia, and offers an incisive intervention in discussions about identity. While visitors' experiences may be unpredictable, the museum could offer a way not only to restore the history to cricket, but also to activate an avenue for social interaction, reminiscence and personal involvement. The WACA Museum almost has too many objects of significance. All the attention has been placed on the 'content' of material culture, and little attention has been placed on the 'form', the methods mobilized to create meaning. To establish the best model of presentation for objects requires an answer to Sharon Macdonald's provocative question: 'whom they are for and what their role should be'.[65] A rationale must be established for displaying particular objects. An audience of schoolchildren has different needs to the general tourist, or those on a package tour for the Ashes Tests. Further, methods must be established to explore the silences, gaps and omissions in museum history.

Dipping electronically into collections is possible through the Web. Through this medium, the museum is a site for a global and local dialogue. Photographs and video can be mediated through the Internet, enlarging exhibition formats and design possibilities. New media agitate the relationship between museum and media, museum and user. The commercial imperative of the WACA website should increase the exposure and potential for the museum. The key problem for the organization is to find a way to capitalize on its global branding not only for economic, but also for educational, benefit. The shop at the end or start of the museum is actually integrated in the experience of the visit.

Clearly, the role of the curator has changed, and markedly. The contradictory desires – to welcome community 'stakeholders' to the museum while also activating a strong curatorial voice – is difficult to resolve. The WACA Museum is sandwiched between old and new traditions of cricket and, through neglect, has been unable to move to new premises or creative innovative strategies to exploit a remarkable collection. With careful curatorial oversight, popular cultural strategies can be used to render Western Australian cricket both accessible and entertaining. The museum or the WACA generally has not capitalized on this initiative. The tourism authorities in the state have not recognized or realized the potential of sport in bringing visitors to Western Australia, or 'value-adding' to their stay.

## Wickets of memory

At the end of a one-day series, a final was held between England and Australia at the Sydney Cricket Ground, 23 January 2003. England made a score of 118, all out. Gilchrist and Hayden reached this score without losing a wicket. Gilchrist scored twenty runs from one over, the fifth. The miracle worker had an amazing game even by his standards. Five catches, one stumping and 69 not out. It was one of his most dazzling, definitive innings. A banner in the crowd – an Australian one-day cricket tradition – confirmed the impression of all watching his wizardry: 'Gilchrist is the messiah'. Indeed, he is the cleanest hitter of the ball for his generation. As his career has progressed, he has come to represent the best of Australian cricket (and the nation) as 'the family man'.[66] Yet he is more than this. By the end of the Australian domestic season in 2005, his Test average of 52.67 ranked him fifth in Australia's all time greatest list. What makes that average extraordinary is that he attained it while batting at number seven. The speed at which he has scored grants him a stature beyond what his final career average will convey. Concurrently, his wicketkeeping is often underestimated. He is currently fourth in the world for total dismissals. Before the end of his career, he will overtake Mark Boucher, but Rod Marsh and Ian Healy's record may be more daunting.[67]

Australia is fortunately placed in global cricket: each of the six states features great pitches. Such a mesh of localisms forms a tight dialogue between sport and the nation. Any mapping of sport in Australia requires a considered discussion of how a regional identity is formed. The nationalizing of the Australia Rugby League and Australian Rules football was an example of economic rationalism, but regional rivalry has remained. Perhaps it is through cricket more than the football codes that the distinctive isolationism in Western Australian identity is best displayed. The WACA's pitch has consistent pace and bounce and is – arguably – the fastest wicket in the world. Brett Lee – probably the quickest bowler of his generation – delivered the fastest ball ever recorded by Channel 9's media facilities on 22 December 2002 in front of a sell-out WACA crowd. The sheer speed of the ball attracted both awe and applause. The myth continues. That pitch has life.

# Part III

# Sport and memory

# Chapter 5

# Our Don and their Eddie

It was probably the most remarkable over in cricket, but for all the wrong reasons. Don Bradman, the cricketer who became more than a man, faced Eddie Gilbert, a missionary Aboriginal who had not been granted the rights through citizenship to be a man. They played out a script that only Australian cricket could write. On 6 November 1931, New South Wales played Queensland at the Gabba. Gilbert, carrying the curiosity of the white spectators and the hope of fellow 'inmates' at the Barambah mission, summoned his speed, dexterity and fitness for one remarkable over. The first ball removed the New South Wales opener Oscar Wendell Bill, caught for a duck. Bradman then took strike. The second ball, he blocked. With the third, Bradman fell to the ground trying to avoid the Gilbert missile. There is a surviving photograph of the legendary batsman crumpled on the wicket. The fourth ball whizzed over Bradman's head. Ball five was described by Bradman as the fastest he ever faced. The bat was knocked out of his hands. On the final ball of the over, Bradman was caught by Waterman, bowled Gilbert, for a duck. Gilbert completed the over with the figures of two wickets for none. Bradman strolled back to the pavilion.[1] Bradman went on to walk into national iconography, often described – particularly by politicians – as the greatest Australian who ever lived. His accomplishments are remembered, lauded and discussed. Bradman folklore is a secular religion. Gilbert died poor, alone, anonymous and in a mental hospital.

This division between 'our Don' and 'their Eddie' is a stark presentation of the race problems that have cut up and scarred Australian history. It is completely appropriate that such an event should emerge through cricket, the great colonial game. This chapter forges a dialogue between Bradman's and Gilbert's lives, intervening in the narrative of nation, race and memory. I want to apply an idea explored by Toby Miller that 'when Australia became modern, it ceased to be interesting'.[2] He suggested that Aboriginal Australia provided Europe with a photographic negative of itself. Through the early British 'discovery' and settlement of the continent, 'Australian' – as a description – signified Aboriginality and blackness. He argues that the reason racism in Australia has been so ruthless, corrosive and destructive is because the meaning of the word 'Australian' had to be twisted and transformed from signifying blackness to whiteness. The singularly brutal racism against Aboriginal people by white colonizers was a mechanism to affirm and confirm the difference and hierarchy separating white Australians and British settlers throughout the Empire. White Australian racism – amid colonialism – was a way to perform difference from Britain. The consequences of this racial history are remarkable. Miller realized that

> once Australia was a sovereign state, and able to deny Aboriginal people citizenship, it was merely one more place filled with whitefellas. 'Australians' were transformed in northern hemisphere theory from dashing blacks living out of time into dull Anglo-Celts living out of place.[3]

With institutional racism established through removal from traditional lands, the formulation of missions, the restriction of languages, movement, religion, education and occupations, the specificities of indigenous Australians were crushed but, thankfully in a post-colonial environment, not lost. White Australians are only significant and different in the history of British colonialism because the racism was of such a scale that it continues to pervade the present life expectancy, educational level, maternal mortality rates and incarceration of indigenous citizens. To test Miller's thesis, this chapter weaves two cricket stories to explore why Donald Bradman has been claimed as a national icon, and to establish his role in the iconography of the colonial project in Australia.

Researching Don Bradman has an addictive quality. Most of the cricketing world has an opinion on his greatness, and invariably shares it in prose. There are reasons for his influence, and they survive to this day. There is no other sport where the gap between the best player and the next best player is as vast. Phil Mollon believes that 'he was like Tiger Woods, Babe Ruth, Muhammad Ali, and Pele all rolled into one'.[4] The famous 99.94 batting average is nearly double that of the next best player. While individual scorers in specific seasons may reveal a strong average, over time his batting stands alone.

Sport is not only about results, averages, winners and losers. The context in which he played granted him a cultural leadership that none, excepting perhaps Gary Sobers, could match. He played, scored and flourished through the Depression when few succeeded. He returned to playing cricket after the People's War, when Britain had won the war but lost the peace, suffering from rationing, rebuilding and despair. Finally, during a time when Australia was desperately trying to establish a separation from 'the motherland', he not only beat the English at their own game, but maintained his accent while doing so. Culturally, this was significant. He was a public figure during an era when Australian actors, news readers and politicians adopted a clipped, mock Home Counties accent. To deny the oz-tray-lee-un elongated vowels and cut-bread-sharp consonants is to reject the landscape, history and troubled immigration patterns that shaped the accent. Bradman – while speaking at Lord's or to the King – spoke the King's English with an Australian inflection. He owned Australian differences while playing an English game. There are still surprises when reading the historical documents discussed throughout this chapter beyond the hagiography and extraordinary statistics. This is odd, considering the scale of the Bradman 'industry'. His stance on race is especially remarkable, particularly for his context. By piecing together oral histories, letters and websites, a different picture of the man can be created, beyond the truth or falseness of his Freemasonry-inspired disdain for Irish Catholic cricketers. With so many conflictual renderings of the O'Reilly saga, there appears little left to write or reveal.

In any book exploring sporting movements and moments on the periphery, Don Bradman must be mentioned. So many people have made so much currency – monetary and social – out of a five-minute conversation with the man that the minutiae of innings, deliveries and dismissals creates grinding research. But odd 'slips' and 'asides' still peep through other writers' agendas. A different Bradman can emerge. It is his perspective on race that interests me, particularly when spliced against his contemporary, Eddie Gilbert. There is little material on Gilbert's life outside of the bowling crease or Bradman's race-based 'politics'. These stories are on the periphery of both these great men's myths. They deserve centred attention.

## One Nation?

Australian cricket – for all the broadening of televisual audiences into the working class, women and migrant populations – has not altered its squad in keeping with the ethnic diversity of the nation. While the team carries the symbolism and hope of Australia, it is revealing to ponder the moments of shame for the team. The betting scandals from Mark Waugh and Shane Warne, the drug scandal where Warne (again) supposedly popped a diuretic given to him by his mother, and Darren Lehmann's racist outburst during a match against a visiting Sri Lankan team do not display the 'best' of the nation. There are many excuses why 'good blokes' would behave in this way, and justifications, brief punishments and public apologies always seem to smooth the troubled sporting waters.[5] Malcolm Knox, a former cricket journalist for the *Sydney Morning Herald*, explained in an English paper why he had suffered enough of these excuses:

> We're not yet at a stage of cultural maturity where we even know what racism is. Our prime minister John Howard is supposedly a decent man who hates the racist epithet. Yet each year he sanctifies the white man's military tragedy (Gallipoli) while denying or excusing the black man's

military tragedy (the colonization massacres). Racism in Australia is insidious, unadmitted . . . Lest this be taken as paranoia, one need only look at the make-up of Australian cricket teams at senior levels. The most common name in the Sydney phone book is Lee – and they're not relatives of Brett – yet all our teams can boast is the occasional Kasprowicz or Di Venuto. If you want a cultural snapshot of Australia in the 1950s, look no further than cricket.[6]

It is therefore no surprise that the cricket team can so easily slot into national iconography. It represents an earlier, simpler Australia before mass immigration and the instigation of multicultural policies. As a form of sporting assimilation, cricket has no peer. The continual cultural ruptures from the safe 1950s to the troubled 2000s create representational confusion in cricket. The current team's success means that whatever is required to ensure that victory, and whatever happened in the past, can be explained or reduced in its significance by stressing the accomplishments in the present. The baggy green caps encase histories of colonial struggle and resistance, alongside fair play and sportsmanship. Ponder Justin Langer's allegiance to the cap's history:

Sitting in the visitor's dressing room at Lord's in 1997, an interesting situation presented itself. Ever since I was a young boy, I have had a burning ambition to walk through the infamous Lord's Long Room wearing a baggy green cap. As I sat waiting for my turn to bat during the one day international, I looked down at my Australian helmet and batting gloves lying together at the foot of my chair. In an instant, it struck me that here was an opportunity to realize a childhood dream. Without thinking too much about the consequences of batting without my helmet, I walked over to my kitbag and replaced the modern protector with my cherished baggy green cap . . . To most observers my action may seem very insignificant, but in reality it goes deep to the core of the way Australian cricket has such a rich history of achievement.[7]

For the first match of the new millennium, Steve Waugh organized that his team would wear replica 1900 baggy green caps. Symbolic ruptures cut through this traditionalism. Bradman and bodyline are pleated with Shane Warne and text messaging. These 'tarnishes' can be washed away because all these 'larrikin flaws' have delivered the game into present victories. Certainly there is little 'intent' or 'malice' that structurally excludes diverse groups from the cricket pitch. But a glance at Australian Rules football, rugby league or soccer teams shows a greater diversity of players than has ever been seen on a cricket field. While Bradman is clearly the greatest player of cricket, it is also obvious that only particular players from specific social groups are even identified as potential cricketers. There may have been outstanding cricketers who were women, indigenous or from migrant communities who never had an opportunity to hold a bat or bowl to a wicket. To mention cricket is to signify fair play, decency and self-discipline. A world of values is summoned. It is clear that cricket also reveals a racial history, which obsessively categorizes, ranks and judges. The cricketing statistics block a clear headed evaluation of how race, ethnic, religious and gender-based prejudices have punctuated the game. Peter Kell was correct in his analysis, but the consequences of his words are frighteningly far-reaching:

> Australians have a powerful belief that sport is one of the few social institutions where everyone still gets 'a fair go' . . . Far from being a source of unity . . . sport in Australia has always been a source of divi-siveness and a site of exclusion. Sport has reinforced anxieties and fears about outsiders . . . heightened irrational fears about Australia's Asian neighbours, China in particular. Some sports have been utilized as a tool of established elites, with imperial and anglocentric linkages.[8]

Such an interpretation brutally shifts a simple celebration of the Australian cricket team, the doggedness of Steve Waugh,[9] the precision of Glenn McGrath, the flair of Adam Gilchrist and the blind speed of Brett Lee. Looking at the post-war teams, it is obvious that they have been invested with the ideologies of an old Australia, signified so clearly by the 'tradition' of the baggy green caps.

The audience for cricket has certainly changed and many spectators possess lived memories of migration, loss, dislocation and diasporic identities. This type of experience is difficult to see in cricket because the game has been invested with the performance of a single grand narrative: coloniza-tion. It embodies – better than any other sport – the tether of English colonizer and Imperial colonized.[10] Anglo-Celtic-derived Australians are in an important position in this equation. As discussed in the WACA chapter, Anglo-Australians are both colonizers and colonized, dominating and dis-possessing the indigenous population, but remaining colonized by the English. The lack of public support for becoming a republic, with a British Queen or King of the day remaining as the Australian head of state, merely confirms this perpetual inequality. Such a position grants Anglo-Australians a dual cultural literacy of colonization, occupying the role of translator in world sport.

Sport is necessary to establish the hierarchies of race, gender, nation and sexuality. A ranking is created with precision, through competition and scoring. Arjun Appadurai realized that 'nowhere are the complexities of this [colonial] dialogue more evident than in the vicissitudes of cricket'.[11] Not only is there a reaffirmation of English power as the 'inventors' of the game, but a field of play where the colonized can rank and judge themselves. In other words, the hierarchy of power has been so internalized and normalized in social structures that the colonial masters no longer have to organize the competition. The colonized continue their own disempowerment by ranking and judging themselves through colonial criteria. It is therefore appropriate that the Australians are the bouncers for international cricket, just as the New Zealanders are the bouncers for international rugby union. These colonial games have become the national sports.

While English cricket is attempting to be more racially diverse in the selection of teams, best signified by Nasser Hussain's captaincy, it is clear that Australian selection patterns have not followed this lead. Also, English cricket has had the benefit of outstanding critics such as Mike Marqusee, who have been prepared to track and attack the racism in the game.[12] The Australian team's success spanning from Mark Taylor's captaincy[13] has blocked a considered and critical reassessment of why cricket means so much at this point of national history. Race and nation, as social variables, are locked in a seductive dance. Immigration and indigenous policies that restrict entry, impose language restrictions or prevent movement are all methods to create a myth of homogeneity, and a 'clean fit' between race and nation, whiteness and Australia. Peter Mewett posed a fascinating distinction that separates Australian identity from other nationalisms:

> History is replete with examples of how sporting events and the successes of athletes have been used to bolster national esteem. In the case of Australia, I suggest that sport plays a somewhat different part, because it comprises, through a notion of the Australian as a physically excellent person, an aspect of this nation's identity . . . Australian sport, or, more accurately, athleticism, is intrinsic to national identity, whereas elsewhere sport is often a vehicle used to parade other symbols of nationhood.[14]

To construct Australian distinctiveness, indigenous citizens are denied a voice, land and language. Some iconography and instrumentation are appropriated, such as 'dot painting' techniques and the didgeridoo, but they are cut away from context and social function. Cricket remains important, because it is an advertising campaign for the Australian nation, selling 'Australianness' to England and the (formerly) colonized others.

Importantly, Packer's innovations in the 1970s brought the working class to the sport. Through this change, a particular type of masculinity was promoted. Nikki Wedgwood attended a New Year's Day match when Pakistan played Australia. She discovered that 'in the Doug Walters' Stand, anyone who was not actively doing hegemonic masculinity was considered "fair game" by those who were'.[15] While such suffocating structures are perpetuated, it is remarkable how often England's 'others' revolutionized the game. For example, women played a cricketing World Cup before the men. The first tournament was held in England during

1973, two years before the men's competition. Yet innovation is not the key to unlocking the ideology of the game. Cricket, more than any other sport, is obsessed with its past and tradition. The desire for social cohesion has meant that in Australia, the national sporting imaginings are deeply bound with normalized and unstated systems of racial exclusion. The extraordinary attention to the Invincibles' tour of England is granted more importance than the struggles facing indigenous peoples to claim citizenship rights at the time, or the battles faced by migrant groups struggling with Australia's assimilation policies in the 1940s and 1950s. In the first Bradman/Gilbert intervention of the chapter, the focus is not only on Bradman's achievements, but on the success of early indigenous cricketers in the game.

## That's not cricket

It is difficult to know how to interpret Birley's 'social history'. While the book's cover refers to its 'wit' and 'humour', I must have missed it.

> Australia was foremost of the cricketing colonies, and it had its cultural strongholds, such as St Peter's College, Adelaide, which was deliberately modelled on Rugby School. Cricket was also administered to Aboriginals, as part of 'the civilizing process', by missionary schools. Unfortunately, by the same token, it became an important route to social improvement for the less privileged, and at its higher levels seemed to have fallen into the hands of mercenary-minded types with no breeding.[16]

The desire to lock Australian cricket into an elitist English history is inappropriate. Sport is used by colonizers to impose practices, truths and ideals on the colonized. Arbitrary rules become the basis of the social system. When they are followed, the ruling position of the colonizer is validated. The first indigenous person who was recorded playing cricket in Australia was 'Shiney', in Hobart in the 1830s. Upon his death, his skull was sent to a museum in Ireland, only to be returned for burial in 1992.

Too often there is a reverence for batting in cricket, focusing on the aesthetics of footwork and willow. Australia, though, has a fine tradition of bowlers. The art and artistry of fast bowling are frequently downplayed, particularly when compared with leg spin. Not only is a level of fitness not necessary for spinners, but an intense concentration is required for the quicks. An attempted yorker can easily become a full toss and dispatched, at speed, to the boundary. Too often, it is the great batsmen who embody the best of the game in each of its eras. Trumper, Bradman, Richards and Steve Waugh verify this point. Even Gary Sobers, Imran Khan and Richard Hadlee were all-rounders. The quick bowler seems destined to be 'the brawn' to the batter's brain. Australia's tradition of fast bowlers is another way in which the practices of the team have been demeaned within a colonial relationship.

The first cricket tour of England was undertaken by indigenous players from a not-yet-nationalized Australia in 1868. Forty-seven matches were played: 19 games were drawn and the visitors both won and lost 14 matches respectively. The indigenous team was captained by Charles Laurence, a Surrey cricketer who had stayed in Australia after English players toured in 1861/62. While Laurence took 7 wickets for 91 runs in a match against Surrey Club at The Oval, Johnny Mullagh scored 73 runs. He finished the tour with 1,698 runs and 257 wickets. There was tragedy amid the success. One of his teammates, King Cole, died on the tour. Jim Crow and Sundown were sent home ill. For those who remained, their treatment by English spectators, to our eyes, was inhuman but captures the racial hierarchy of the time. For example, at their match at York, they were not invited into the luncheon tent. At Lord's, the situation became even more destructive:

> People flocked to see the team, but the greatest attraction was the Aborigines' athleticism and their apparent desire to display their skills with spear and shield. The 'action' began after stumps were drawn, but sometimes, as happened at Lords in June 1868, there was a bizarre turn of events. MCC members gleefully discarded their to hats and tails and gladly paid a bob to get the chance to 'stone' an Aboriginal cricketer. Side-show alley had come to Lords . . . Dick-a-Dick used a shield to fend off and deflect the cricket balls tossed at his upper body and head . . . The members lined up in turn: each man threw full-force from about ten paces.[17]

Even through this disempowerment and tragedy, it is important to remember that the first 'Australian' cricket team was this indigenous touring party. What is remarkable is that the 'antics' of indigenous cricketers with a spear and shield were not seen as a threat, whereas the Maori haka has always been more ambivalently viewed. It is a war dance, and it is not only ritualistic or performative. It introduces and frames the battle on the pitch. It is not a side show. Therefore, a distinctive interpretation of Maori and indigenous Australians has been perpetuated through sport.

In remembering this first team, Geoff Clark, the former Head of the Australian and Torres Strait Islander Commission (ATSIC), remarked on

> how difficult were the circumstances they faced – in all aspects of life, not just cricket. White laws stripped them of virtually any control over their own lives. Endemic racism blocked or destroyed their careers. Disease, poverty, dispossession and crime decimated their numbers. For the 1868 team there were no ticker tape parades or lucrative contracts. They returned to obscurity and early deaths.[18]

One year after the team's return, the Victorian Aboriginal Protection Act forced most of them onto reserves and into obscurity. Johnny Mullagh was the exception. He escaped the reservations and played cricket for 25 years. He was not only the top scorer and wicket taker of the 1868 tour, but he took five wickets in an innings 21 times. Despite this success, he was only granted one chance to play for Victoria, against England. He top-scored with 36 runs. Dying in 1881, he was acknowledged with a memorial which overlooks the Glenelg River.[19]

Jack Marsh's cricketing career was a distinct case from Mullagh's, but betrays many confluences with Gilbert's. Both had great expertise with a boomerang, sharpening their reflexes and wrist dexterity. Marsh was 'discovered' entertaining tourists with his boomerang and started to play cricket. Playing in New South Wales from the end of the nineteenth century until 1905, he led the national bowling averages for his first season. Like Gilbert with Bradman, Marsh bowled Victor Trumper, the best batsman of his time. But at the very point where he was about to be selected at state or even national level, he was no-balled by two umpires for chucking. This damaged his career, and he only appeared for NSW on six occasions. He had one more moment of fame. In a 1903/04 game against the English touring side, and playing for a Bathurst XI, he finished with 5 wickets for 55 runs.

As Mike Colman and Ken Edwards discovered, 'the English men . . . declared him not only a fair bowler, but the best they had faced on tour'.[20] Marsh became an alcoholic and was bashed to death in an Orange hotel in 1916. He was 42 years old. The two men charged with his manslaughter walked free of the court without conviction. Marsh is buried at an unmarked grave in Orange Cemetery.

Even less is known about Albert Henry. He opened the bowling for Queensland in 1902 as the first Aboriginal to represent the state in cricket. Born in 1880, he died of tuberculosis in 1909. Remarkably – and there is a pattern forming here – he was accused of chucking when playing for South Brisbane. A trajectory was being established for Gilbert through these early, tragic pioneers in indigenous sport.

The blueprint to these stories, which is continued by Eddie Gilbert, is caused through institutional racism where calls of chucking meant that umpires could destroy a bowler's career. This charge can be made if he 'appears' to be throwing. It is ironic that this claim has been made about indigenous bowlers in Australia, the Sri Lankan off spinner Muttiah Muralitharan and Shoaib Akhtar. It was never made against any of the bodyline bowlers. Instead, their actions were referred to as 'unsportsmanlike'.[21] Mallett, the former Test spinner and coach of the 2001 indigenous team, tracked this pattern from Marsh to Gilbert:

> Marsh was acknowledged as the best bowler in the world at the time and he was no-balled out of the game . . . I suspect it was [racism]. He was only no-balled to keep him out of the Test side. An umpire can no-ball someone for throwing even if he doesn't throw.[22]

'The system' could not handle these young indigenous men. Because they were bowlers rather than batsmen, it was easier to mark the differences in identity by also seeing differences in action and removing them from the game. The story could not be more starkly placed in relief than through the batsman supported by 'the system' throughout his career.

Donald Bradman, at his most basic, was a right-handed middle order batsman. Born in Cootamundra, New South Wales, and dying on 25 February 2001 in Adelaide, South Australia, he played 52 Tests, 19 in England. Famously, he accrued 6,996 runs, at an average of 99.94, knocking 29 hundreds and 13 fifties.[23] Bradman's first tour of England was in 1930, beginning with a score of 236 against Worcestershire, the highest debut first-class innings by an Australian batsman in England. He scored Australia's first Test century of the tour at Nottingham, then made 254 runs in the Lord's Test, and following with 334 in the third Test at Leeds. The final Test at The Oval saw him score 232. Not surprisingly, Australia won the Ashes. Donald Bradman was 21 years old. He finished the series with an average of 139.14 runs, a world record for any series. Three years before this tour, Lord Desborough, former Conservative Member of Parliament and former President of the Marylebone Cricket Club, stated overtly his – and England's – position in the world:

> As long as the English race, and those in charge of it, did play the game and as long as those underneath assisted, no doubt that in cricket as in other things, England would maintain the position she has secured in the world.[24]

It is difficult to ascertain the role of 'those underneath', but Bradman must have come as a shock to this English ideology. It is no surprise that a tactic was developed to counter this scoring. It was termed by the Australian press as 'bodyline' and it became the word by which the 1932/33 tour would be remembered. Jardine was the wrong captain to be sent on an Ashes tour. As Richard Wilkinson related, he 'personified British upper-class arrogance. He referred to Australians as "the working-class who got away" and to Bradman as "the little bastard"'.[25] Bradman, who left school at 14 to work in a real estate agent's office, was matched against Jardine, an Oxford-educated lawyer. He intended to intimidate the Australians and undermine Bradman. He did neither, but is probably responsible for transforming the Ashes series into one of the most significant in sport.

To this day, it appears that many English players, while appreciating Bradman's skills, believed that the Australian myth was overplayed. Eric Bedser, an English bowler, stated that 'you know with all due respect to the Australians, in London Don Bradman would be one of many so-called celebrities. You've got the top of the acting profession and the top of the law and everything else'.[26] Donald Bradman had an international career that spanned Depression and war. In 1930, he scored a world record 452 not out at the Sydney Cricket Ground in a first-class innings. The scale of his dominance in the sport in

Australia is perhaps only matched by the status of Gary Sobers in the West Indies, who emerged at the time of independence.[27] Bradman's career also had controversy. He was a Freemason,[28] and conflicted badly with Bill O'Reilly, a former teammate, who believed that Bradman undermined the Catholic members of the Australian cricket team.[29] Racial differences were not possible because no indigenous players were included in the squad to provoke this prejudice. Religious differences became the fount of trouble.

Understanding the nature of Aboriginal sport is the singular most controversial and difficult topic in Australia's cricketing history. Because individual indigenous men and women have been successful in different regions and times, a network of support, resistance and community could not be formed. Whether investigating the cases of John Twopenny and Bullocky from the first tour of England, through to Jack Marsh, Albert Henry or Eddie Gilbert, each created a new start, never leading to a systematic movement of indigenous men into cricket. Each new player confronted the same old prejudice. Rugby league was different. There was money to be made from the sport and there was a critical mass of players.

There is an intense need in racist societies to reduce the identity of non-white sportsmen and women to the colour of their skin. The treatment of Arthur Wharton, the first black professional footballer, is a clear example. Phil Vasili, in researching his case, affirmed that

> [s]porting contests between Black and White were anything but equal. The opportunity for most White athletes to develop their skill and talent was far in excess of that to Blacks. The operation of the colour bar, official and unofficial, whether in Britain, its empire or indeed any part of the globe dominated by Europeans, sustained inequalities across the board.[30]

Race was used in Wharton's era to divide working class peoples and deflect attention from building consciousness and affirmative political goals. Indigenous sportspeople in Australia not only suffered racist attitudes and institutionalized racism like Wharton, but lacked the most basic and rudimentary of sporting resources. The few successes, such as Cathy Freeman, Lionel Rose and Graham 'Polly' Farmer, shield a far wider prejudice. When indigenous men and women are accepted as sporting heroes, they are rarely accorded the full rights of Australian citizens. Respect comes from sporting ability, denying and underdeveloping other possible successes in the law, art, music or literature.

Four of the eight indigenous fast bowlers before the modern era have been no-balled by umpires, and termed a chucker. This ultimate attack in cricket is a simple way to keep indigenous men out of the game. Indigenous men are heavily over-represented in working class sports, such as boxing, rugby league and Australian Rules football, but under-recognized in golf, sailing and gymnastics. Because of cricket's liminal positioning in national popular culture, the indigenous role in this sport is more complex to determine. Attention to Australia's indigenous cricketing history opens out the contradictions in identity, to determine the social function of whiteness and blackness.

## (E)Race

Australia was England's first and oldest enemy in cricket. That is not surprising considering none of the black cricketing nations had a national team before the twentieth century. Since that time, and with the success of India, Pakistan, the West Indies and Sri Lanka, cricket has transformed into an aspirational game. However, Australia has a black history – literally and metaphorically. There is, as Henry Reynolds has argued, an 'indelible stain' on sport and life.[31] In his book, he reasoned that if Australia's colonization was as brutal as it appears then genocide is an accurate description.

Racial consciousness develops through time. An awareness emerges that physical differences are aligned with behavioural traits, and are immutable. Race in Australia passed through distinct phases, from dispossession through the control of citizenship and immigration rights, legislative restriction of movement and marriage and finally leading to the Racial Discrimination Act of 1975. This Act outlawed any exclusion based on race, colour or national/ethnic origin. But structural and institutional racism survived as racist policies were integral to the historical formulation of the nation. The difficulty is that there was no language to create a bridge of experience between settler populations and Aboriginal and Torres Strait Islander populations. Henry Reynolds has shown how, between 1900 and 1960, indigenous populations were written out of Australian history. Frontier conflict was unmentionable, as was Aboriginal resistance. The reasons for this silence are clear. There could be no treaty between colonizer and colonized if there had never been a war:

> The racist past still weighs heavily on the present and might yet destroy any hope of reconciliation in this generation. Black-armband history is

often distressing, but it does enable us to know and understand the incubus which burdens us all.[32]

A judgement of 'terra nullius' declared the Australian continent vacant upon the settlers' arrival. It has been difficult to summon alternative narratives since that time. Australian society was founded on a racialized interpretation of value, land, identity and ownership. Therefore, it is necessary to place any understanding of Australian cricket in this context.

Writing about sport – particularly in a colonized nation – can never be a neutral presentation of run rates, scores and wickets. Australia is not Yorkshire, which maintained a 'born in the county' ruling which excluded many prospective black and British Asian players. This birth qualification even blocked the legendary Antiguan Sir Vivian Richards from county selection. Chris Searle demonstrates the deep feelings this decision summoned:

> In a post-imperial era, where much of the chauvinism of Empire and nation has been transferred to a regional or city jingoism – which itself has been fanned through the parochial fervour of football team worship – the notion of Yorkshire 'birthright', far from withering away, has grown stronger. In 1987, the rumour that the Yorkshire club was considering 'signing' West Indian captain Viv Richards to play for the county side was greeted by aghast ex-Yorkshire cricketers like Fred Trueman as a crime. Trueman later threatened to tear up his membership card of the county club if an 'overseas' cricketer ever played for Yorkshire.[33]

Not surprisingly, black players based in Leeds have formed their own Quaid-e-Azam League, which plays on Sundays. The white rose of Yorkshire has often remained pure, but at an enormous cost. The red rose across the border, Lancashire, has frequently included black players, including Patrick Patterson, Wasim Akram and Clive Lloyd, who was the captain for many years. Australia's racial history, tempered by a complex colonial dialogue, is not as precisely determined as the Yorkshire/Lancashire border.

The racism that remains in Australian society is debilitating and deep. Mick Dodson, a controversial but remarkable indigenous rights campaigner, has investigated how black men in particular have internalized second class status. He has stated that 'Aboriginal and Torres Strait Islander men – and, with us, our families and communities – are the basket cases of Australia'.[34] He desires honesty in acknowledging violence and family difficulties. The intergenerational legacy of dispossession, and the loss of pride, respect and family structures, damage men and women in the present. The loss of self-determination through such a practice only reinforced the loss of lands and family. Dodson also asked that indigenous men should 'seek to draw inspiration from our past … Yagan, Pemulwuy, William Cooper, William

Ferguson, Eddie Gilbert, Vincent Lingiari, David Unaipon, Rob Riley and Charlie Perkins'.[35] Sport becomes important to the making of new meanings and finding a positive and proactive way forward. Indigenous men are believed by Dodson to have systematic problems with violence. The only way in which colonial truths can be established after settlement/invasion is through the imposition of force and control. Then these practices become internalized and naturalized, so that the (formerly) colonized continue to colonize themselves.

Aboriginal histories will always use hot, intense sources. The searing inequalities never slot cleanly into a conventional historical narrative. A homogenized singular Aboriginality has been imposed on diverse groups, collectives and communities who, prior to colonization, regarded themselves as separate and distinct. By focusing on black and white, the key is not to stress domination and subordination, oppressors and oppressed, but to focus on dynamic power relationships, so that change is possible. In this way indigenous discourses are not only a state-imposed formation, but a creative force. Reconciliation in Australian society – if assumed as a project – means that different stories will need to be told, with new goals and audiences. This will be the challenge. As Peter Read has shown, 'Australia has a very bad record indeed of clandestine and administrative violence'.[36] There is a need to re-evaluate the meanings of land, identity, nation, competition and sport. Racial vilification in sport has too often been downplayed because of the masculine notion that what is said on the field should be left on the field. Sledging, or verbally ridiculing the sporting opposition, is neither innocent nor socially distinct from the rest of life. While Eddie Gilbert managed racism on and off the field, it was his quiet acceptance of reduced expectations and hopes that perpetuated the worst violence of all: a violence to the self.

## Nature's gentleman

To rewrite Andy Warhol's cliché, Eddie Gilbert had six balls of fame. The rest of his life is more difficult to fathom. His date of birth was never recorded, but could be anywhere between 1903 and 1912. The record of his life and death, like his birth, is crowded with misinformation and confusion. The Aboriginal Protection Act caused the movement of Anderson and Alice Gilbert, Eddie's parents, to far North Queensland, entering the mission of Barambah, which was later renamed Cherbourg. This meant that at the age of 3, Gilbert was forcibly taken from his home. Children such as Eddie Gilbert were placed in dormitories away from their parents, to be taught the English language, brought up as Christians and taught 'useful' skills to serve the new colonial society. These children knew little but life within an institution. It was in this context that Gilbert started to play cricket. For mission officials, sport was a way to discipline and control young people in the colonizer's system. Gilbert still continued to throw a boomerang rather than a cricket ball, and that practice created his remarkable action. He famously was able to take a seven-step run in and deliver the ball at such pace that it was unreadable out of the hand and cramped the batsmen with pace at the crease. While Gilbert stood alone in this action during the 1930s, Jeff Thomson – also a Queensland fast bowler who would have the chance of representing Australia – similarly displayed a short run and delivered an unreadable seam.

Gilbert's bowling average in the 1929–30 country competition was five runs for each wicket taken. His success brought him to the attention of Queensland cricketing officials, who assessed his potential. Because of his lifelong institutionalism, he was 'perceived as a "good black" – Christian, educated and raised in the white system'.[37] Knowing his place, he was not a 'troublemaker'. It was difficult for him to misbehave: he had to be granted written permission from authorities whenever he wanted to travel. He had married Edith Owens in 1927, in an Anglican church no less. The conditions in the missions created a culture of oppression, and formed an open wound of memories from Australia's colonial history. It also created a docile and disciplined sporting body.

He represented his state well, playing 19 Sheffield Shield matches. He played in four other matches for Queensland, against the West Indies and South Africa in 1931, England in 1933 and the MCC in 1935. It was only after Don Bradman was dismissed for a duck that, in November 1931, A.L. Rose, the New South Wales manager, charged that Gilbert had 'thrown' the ball in Brisbane. The chucking laws have always been ambiguous. Much attention is placed on the straightening of the arm and elbow from the shoulder. The photographs of Gilbert's action show a rigid arm. His wrist did bend in a flicking action, but this should not constitute a throw. If it did, then every wrist spinner would be no-balled in every over they bowled. The Queensland Cricket Association had filmed his action and demonstrated its legality. Unfortunately, Bradman's response to his dismissal in a short newsreel interview after the match did the great man a disservice. The segment featured an interview between Bradman and the former Test player and journalist Arthur Mailey. An article of the time reported the content of the footage.

> In this talkie Mailey draws a sketch of Bradman and by easy stages the conversation veers round to the duck that Don achieved when he met Gilbert. 'And what do you really think of Eddie Gilbert?' asks Mailey. Looking round him, as if to see that no one can over-hear, Bradman whispers something in Mailey's ear and they both break into a hearty chuckle as the picture fades out.[38]

As always with Bradman, it is the silences – the fade-out – that are interesting and disturbing. Only later, when Ken Edwards wrote to Bradman, did the batsman remove the intrigue from the case: 'the few balls he sent down to me in that fateful over were the fastest ever bowled to me'.[39]

Unfortunately, he did not make this statement at the time. The no-balling controversy that emerged after Gilbert had dismissed Bradman inevitably led to the calling of a no ball in a subsequent match. In his first 'southern' tour, for a match against Victoria, the intrigue commenced. On the fourth ball of his first over, umpire A.N. Barlow ruled no ball, as he did for the subsequent three deliveries. The ratio-nale for this decision was 'for jerking the wrist'.[40] When Gilbert moved to the other end for a bowling stint, the other umpire, Moore, did not censure, but from square-leg Barlow no-balled him four more times. The next morning, he again bowled. Barlow no-balled four deliveries in the over.[41] At this point he was taken off, and did not bowl for the remainder of the game. When he next bowled, against South Australia at Adelaide Oval, neither umpire questioned his action. The rest of the season passed without incident.

The second time that Bradman and Gilbert met, this time at the Adelaide Oval, Bradman scored 233 runs. Bradman certainly won that encounter. The third and last time was at the Gabba. Bradman, perhaps seeing Gilbert's form, lowered himself down the order so that Gilbert – who bowled short and sharp spells – would be taken off. On 10 January 1936, Bradman made 31 runs. Only four of these runs were taken off seven Gilbert balls. On the seventh ball, Bradman was dismissed by Gilbert's bowling, with a catch at gully.

After this no-balling incident, Gilbert's bowling became more incon-sistent, and charges of alcohol abuse and promiscuity surfaced. By the early 1940s, with erratic behaviour, inconsistent bowling and little support from the authorities, the cricketing establishment turned away from Gilbert. Of all the tragedies of this story, the most disturbing event revolved around his Queensland blazer. It is clear that he was proud of his accomplishments in the state team. Whenever an 'official' photo-graph was taken at Barambah, inside or outside the sporting context, Gilbert wore the blazer. After the no-balling controversy, and with no further 'use' for the fast bowler, the Queensland Cricket Association sent Gilbert back to the settlement. The tragedy is that the Association asked J.W. Bleakely, the Protector of Aborigines, for the return of the cricketer's clothes. A letter to the appropriately Dickensesque-named Bleakely stated, 'with regard to the cricketing clothes bought for Gilbert, it is asked that arrangements be made for these to be laun-dered at the Association's expense, and delivery of the laundered clothes to be made in this office'.[42] For a man who had owned so little but seen so much, we – as history's onlookers – will never know what the loss of that blazer meant to Gilbert. His photographed self, so proud and tall in the jacket, is silent to the pain. But perhaps not.

In 1947, he was arrested for public drunkenness. A son was conceived outside his marriage.[43] On 8 December 1949, Gilbert was admitted to a mental hospital in Brisbane. He was believed to be suffering from ter-tiary syphilis, which caused his mental instability. Receiving electric shock treatments, he tried to escape three times. In 1960, after being moved to a new ward, he was found standing on the hospital's cricket pitch. Remarkably, through all this turmoil and sickness, he did not die until 9 January 1978, by which time he was confined to bed and refused to eat. Throughout much of this period, he was in obscurity. When 'rediscovered' by a journalist in 1972, he was unable to speak.

The Gilbert autopsy revealed that it was not syphilis that had caused his mental instability and death. That was treated with penicillin early in his stay in the mental hospital. Actually, he suffered from Alzheimer's disease, which explains much of his long-term instability. It was not diagnosed until after his death. His body was taken back to Cherbourg by train. Neither Bradman nor Gilbert's son was present at the burial. The cost of the funeral was $325. The Queensland Cricket Association paid this bill. The other social debts – for pain and suffering – would remain unpaid.

## Howard's way

Australia has elected two prominent conservative Prime Ministers after World War II. One ruled through the 1950s and the other wanted to. Robert Menzies and John Howard, as historical figures, cast a shadow over Australian history. The two men are linked in many ways, but the most symbolically important connection is their love of cricket. This sport also captures the beliefs that Howard inherited from 1950s Australia: free enterprise, family values, monarchism, individual responsibility and anti-collectivism. Such ideologies have also expressed a denial, not simply an ambivalence, of multiculturalism and indigenous rights. For Howard, the deep – and quite real – passion for cricket is not the usual political love fest for sporting figures. As has been argued throughout this chapter, the 'tradition' of cricket expresses a nostalgia for a simpler rendering of the Australian nation. The team itself is a snapshot of an earlier period in history, without the troubled concerns of multiculturalism or reconciliation to pepper the competition. John Howard's enthusiasm is more than a fan's joy for a sport. It holds a political function, and requires subtle attention.

Howard often expresses his public enthusiasm for men's cricket. He toured London in 1997, corresponding with the Second Ashes Test. He visited the cricket on four days of his seven-day tour. No doubt, Howard has a detailed knowledge of its history. His affiliation with Mark Taylor was strong, Howard making him the 1999 Australian of the Year. Steve Waugh was given the same honour in 2004. Yet it is Donald Bradman that is the focus for his public celebrations of the nation.[44] Brett Hutchins described this affiliation as 'nostalgia for middle-class values consistent with a British-derived, Anglo-Saxon, pro-imperial Australian past in which Bradman was the national hero, and Menzies the indomitable leader'.[45] Yet Howard not only has restated the Menzies platform, but has grafted to it the Thatcherite neo-liberal agenda. Indeed – considering the scale of social, economic and ideological changes to the population and industrial infrastructure of the nation, Menzies' policies are completely inappropriate to contemporary Australia, except in generalities. All that can be transplanted is a popular memory of Don Bradman.

Cricket is Australia's unquestioned national sport not only because it is socially conservative, but also because it is safe. The Australian Cricket Board's history on women in sport, multiculturalism, race and South Africa during the apartheid era is not commendable. Also, because Don Bradman was reclusive through much of his post-playing and particularly post-administrative career, his persona and biography could be mobilized and shaped at will by political figures. The publicly expressed Bradman commitments to the monarchy,[46] business, private enterprise and Protestantism fitted the Howard agenda.

Bradman's stance on indigenous issues and the White Australia Policy is more difficult to determine, particularly in the earlier stages of his career.

Throughout his life, he did acknowledge Eddie Gilbert's fast bowling, but never placed this bowling in its appropriate context. While Bradman could make a life, business and family with his wife, Gilbert was under the rule of the 'Protector of Aboriginals', having to return to the Barambah Aboriginal Settlement at the conclusion of each season. Perhaps there is little reason why he should have known this. Between 1850 and 1987, of the 7,076 male Australian first class cricketers, only seven were indigenous.[47] Jason Gillespie became the first Australian Test player who acknowledged indigenous ancestry. He only announced this identity after gaining Test selection. His decision is an interesting one, but understandable. Until Jason Gillespie, no indigenous men and only one woman – Faith Thomas – were selected to play for Australia. At its most basic and brutal, Australian cricket is a game for Anglo-Saxon men, and, considering the changes to society through multiculturalism, feminism and reconciliation policies, an unmitigated political celebration of the game should be monitored carefully. It remains the national sport – a game for everyone – that has throughout its history either structurally excluded or socially inhibited women, indigenous citizens and ethnic communities. To place this remarkable affiliation between politics and popular culture, John Howard and cricket, into context requires an appreciation of what happened in Australian society in the five-year period before the turn of the twenty-first century.

On 16 September 1996, John Howard spoke to a group of Indonesian officials, stating that Australia was not part of Asia. He was continuing a suspicious distance from the region that has existed as long as European settlement of Australia. David Walker recognized that 'one of the remarkable features of Australian history is the periodic rediscovery of our proximity to Asia'.[48] Australia arrived at nationhood at the time of expanding Asian development and power, which created the invasion narratives best captured by the phrase 'yellow peril'. Howard's affirmation of distance from Asia established a distinction from the prime ministership of Paul Keating, who courted the relationship with Indonesia and the Asian/Pacific region.

At the time of Howard's speech in Indonesia, a new Australia was emerging from within. Australia has been built by immigrants. The extraordinary diversity of new citizens who entered the country in the post-war period has meant that a 1950s vision of Australia is no longer realistic or possible. However, to look at the faces of politicians, sporting leaders and media presenters, it is as if mass immigration never happened. The only caveats to this statement are the two public broadcasters – the Australian Broadcasting Corporation and Special Broadcasting Services – and pay television sporting channels, where a diversity of accents, experiences and faces are seen. Because soccer in Australia has strong ethnic support, to the point where it has been termed 'wogball' through much of its history, the expert commentators are frequently immigrants or the sons and daughters of immigrants. Association football and its media coverage are an important rupture in the Anglocentric media and political system. With the growing interest in and knowledge of football in Australia, this multicultural intervention is important. Football is the future: cricket is the past. The difficulty is that cricket commentary in the country, although outstanding, relies on former players for 'expert' discussion of play. Obviously, former players have been Anglo-Celtic and male in origin. What is required is an alignment of population changes in the last 60 years with movements in communication strategies and media services.[49]

Power in Australia presents a white face. Every few years, a scare campaign emerges where 'the yellow peril' becomes an issue. The late 1980s, like the late 1990s, was such a period. Monitor this published view from one-time radio commentator Ron Casey:

> I suppose it's too much to ask Australians to use words like 'bonzer'. In another ten years, with all the blinking Japs and slopes we've got coming into this country, it'll be 'Bonzai, Bonzai'. Wait until the white-born Australian becomes the minority, mate, the world will be ours. We'll be able to get housing commission flats, we'll be able to do anything we like, but first of all we've got to get enough slopes in here so that we become the minority.[50]

This is one man's view, but it does provide insight into the complex relationship between Australia and the Asian and Pacific region. This racial vilification is pointed, but also terrifying. Multiculturalism, as a policy, has not silenced this type of critique. Hage reached the point in 1994 where he termed multiculturalism 'Anglocentric and racist'.[51] There is verification for this judgement. The voice and face of power have not changed in Australia. Multiculturalism has become a battering ram for the forces on the political right to attack what they perceive as a loss of rights, position and dominance. In difficult times, of xenophobia and fear against non-Christian religions and peoples, multiculturalism – as a word and policy – provides a refuge, affirmation and hope for change. There is a need to reconcile the governmental application of multiculturalism with the lived experience of diversity in contemporary Australia.

Australia, as a post-colonial, industrialized nation, is not composed of a single race or ethnic group. For any mode of multiculturalism in Australia to work, there is a desire to establish unity from diversity, or cohesion out of plurality. The difficulty for the national project is that immigrants bring into the country their own models of socialization and solidarity. The drive to national unity serves to revalidate Anglocentric power structures, sports and languages. Only when a policy agenda is able to acknowledge the daily experience of diversity and dismiss a singular and desperate desire for an imaginary 'unity', will multiculturalism be successful. There is a productive instability and anxiety in Australia that is not well served by the representational politics of national leaders or the national sport.

During the late 1990s, Pauline Hanson rose to public prominence. Australia's 'problems' with difference did not commence with Hanson and have not evaporated since she left public prominence. She ran a political party based on such terms as reverse racism, silent majority, mainstream Australia and racial ghettos. (Only) 10 per cent of the Australian population voted for Pauline Hanson's One Nation in the 1998 Australian Federal election. She defended assimilation, desired a reduction of Asian immigration, and confirmed the reverse racism against indigenous Australians:

> I am fed up with being told, 'this is our land'. Well, where the hell do I go? I was born here, and so were my parents and children. I will work beside anyone and they will be my equal but I draw the line when told I must pay and continue paying for something that happened over 200 years ago.
> I and most Australians want our immigration policy radically reviewed and that of multiculturalism abolished. I believe we are in danger of being swamped by Asians.[52]

All the pressure points of Australian history are pressed: the guilt or dismissal of indigenous dispossession, fear of Asia and disgust with multiculturalism. It is important to remember that Pauline Hanson was elected into office with these views, but only lasted for one term. She lost office when a general fear of foreigners spilled into phrases like border protection and mainstream political parties. Both the Australian Liberals and Labor expressed concern with the arrival of refugees, captured by the *Tampa* crisis, and the fear of 'invasion' from the north. September 11 and the Bali bombings did not ease this fear of difference.

To claim Donald Bradman as a national hero at this point of Australian history requires some pause and a pensive assessment. The affirmation of the 'The Don' is a politicized and pointed nostalgia requiring a selection of one version of Australian national history over others. It is no surprise that Don Bradman has entered popular memory, but his current role in popular culture is not necessarily as a cricketer. He has been stripped of sporting meaning to represent a better and simpler time in Australia. Bradman has a function for the nation, in a way that Eddie Gilbert or any indigenous cricketer could not. Every commemoration of a white man confirms a contestation of meaning won by the powerful. Popular memory studies must serve as a reminder that other public representations are possible.

Two significant interventions in this celebration of Bradman have required active forgetting. While the celebration of the Invincibles remains a significant moment in cricket history and a 'return to normalcy' after the war, this acknowledgement has meant that recognition of another team has been washed away. There was actually an earlier Australian cricket team that brought the game back to the English. From April 1944 until January 1946, an Australian Services Cricket Team played 64 matches throughout England, India and the Australian states, all on servicemen's pay. The team was quickly forgotten in the celebration of the Invincibles.[53] Similarly, Richie Benaud made his debut in the year of Bradman's retirement. His era has been decentred because of attention to Bradman's 1930s and 1940s, and Chappell's 1970s. Besides the tied Test with the West Indies, scholarship and popular publications have been limited on the era of Benaud's captaincy. It was an era of falling spectators and bubbling controversies about apartheid. Importantly, it was also the era of West Indian Tests. Gideon Haigh, in his remarkable revisionist history *The summer game*, acknowledged the paradox of the tour of 1951/52:

> It was not an unhappy tour, and the West Indies were well liked. Australians might have barely acknowledged their own black population, denied them the vote and broken up their families, but they saw nothing incongruous about applauding a coloured cricket team.[54]

Politics and sport, indigenous policies and cricket, are enmeshed. The contradiction of applauding a West Indian team while dispossessing and denying citizenship to indigenous citizens remains a paradox that only the 1950s political environment could reconcile. Instead of probing these paradoxes, it is easier to celebrate 'Our Don', instead of 'their Eddie'. Much later – in 2001 – when a physical education teacher, Greg Locke, tried to encourage his indigenous pupils to play cricket rather than Australian Rules football, he showed them footage of the West Indies team, not Waugh's men. He justified this decision with the realization that 'you really need them to have role models to get them interested'.[55]

## And in the end

Upon the death of public figures, the path of popular memory can be monitored with precision. Contradictions and paradoxes suddenly emerge from the authenticating autobiographical record that slipped through the crevices of a great sporting career. In the later stages of Bradman's life, it became clear that he reconsidered many of the assumptions of his youth. One of the most remarkable intervention in the Bradman aura emerged in 2002, when Margaret Geddes assembled a collection of oral histories on 'The Don'. One interview showed remarkable historical revisions. Meredith Burgmann, who went on to be President of the New South Wales Legislative Council, was a member of the Anti-Apartheid Movement in Sydney during the early 1970s. At 20 years of age, she received a letter from Don Bradman, asking her why she campaigned against the Springboks rugby tour of Australia in 1971. At that time, he was on the Australian Cricket Board and making a decision about the South African tour of Australia in 1971/72. That first letter asked her why she was mixing sport and politics. She replied to his question, and the cricketing legend and 20-year-old campaigner exchanged letters about the issue. For Burgmann, it was clear that he was considering her argument and shifting his opinion. In September 1971, an ACB announcement was made. They could have called off the tour for 'safety concerns'. Donald Bradman, however, went further in his comments to the *Sydney Morning Herald*:

> Sir Donald said that his board has faced every aspect of the unenviable problem and had weighed carefully the views expressed by responsible authorities including churchmen and policies. It had decided with great regret that it would have to advise the South Africans that in the present atmosphere earlier invitations would have to be withdrawn ... the Board said it hoped that the South African government would in the near future so relax its apartheid laws that cricketers of South Africa would once again take their place as full participants in the international field.[56]

This response was more than simply a concern with crowds or player 'safety'. Bradman had made a political judgement about sport. Another remarkable moment emerged in the Burgmann letters where Bradman actually connected South African policies with Australian indigenous history. He probed the complexity of the young woman's politics:

> And if you'll pardon me for saying so – how did you come to get a chance of a university education? It was made possible because your forebears and mine plundered this country, murdered Aborigines etc. etc. and took over the land. Our ancestors evidently did things as bad or worse than the South African whites have done.[57]

This incredible, accurate and socially just rendering of Australian history emerged at the very time when Australia and other Commonwealth countries were attempting to grasp the scale, violence and consequences of apartheid. There are so many banal Bradman books that restate the same stories – invariably in the same way. There are indeed a few of these stories restated in the Geddes book. But the interview which reported on the letters of Bradman to a then 20-year-old Meredith Burgmann offers incredible insight, beyond the endless 'yarns' about innings, strokes and scores.

To even more unsettle the comfortable relationship Australian politicians have established with the aura, rather than the person, of Don Bradman, Alan Jones recalled his attitude towards the future Prime Minister in his monthly lunches with 'the Don'.

> The interesting point was his overarching political interest, even though obviously he was not in any way either capable of influencing politics or desirous of influencing politics, but he wanted to know, you know. Who's going to win? What do you think of Fraser? What about Hawke? What about this Keating? He was always the local bloke. 'Howard? Howard's no good, how will he win?' And you'd have these very earthy discussions.[58]

It is remarkable how rarely these statements critical of John Howard or apartheid bleed through the bland narrative of Bradman. To complete this frequently unwritten history of his race-base interest is his support of Sri Lankan cricket. The first time Bradman played cricket outside of Australia was in Sri Lanka in March 1930. Actually, he only ever played cricket in Australia, England, the United States and Sri Lanka. Harold de Andrado, on the death of Bradman, recalled his correspondence with the batsman, recording that 'he was a great friend of Sri Lanka and most Sri Lankans mutually loved him as I did . . . He supported Sri Lanka's entry into the ICC regrettably vetoed by England and South Africa'.[59] Again, in the celebratory histories of Bradman, this 'fact' is rarely reported.

Don Bradman protected his privacy. He stated that 'I have lived a life where I have been subjected to the most intense publicity imaginable and now that I've retired, I would really prefer to be left alone.'[60] But Eddie Gilbert's privacy – and his redundancy in Australian cricket history – became a curse that locked him in sickness, a mental institution and a solitary death. The Howard government so wanted to 'protect' the name of Bradman that, after an approach from the

family, it made an amendment to the Companies Act. Such a decision controlled the rights to the name for the family and the Bradman
Trust. No such intervention was necessary for Eddie Gilbert, but his
name has been summoned to support – free of charge – other indigenous sportspeople facing difficulties.

Bradman's death in 2001 created national mourning. Mentioned in
the British and Australian parliaments, it appeared as if a part of
Australia died with him. His ashes, and those of his wife, Jessie, to
whom he was married for 65 years, were spread over the town oval of
Bowral, where he had played in his youth, and adjacent to the Bradman
museum. The ashes were scattered in multiple sites of the oval, so that
no shrine could be formed.[61]

Like Bradman, Eddie Gilbert has no headstone. Instead, he has a
grave marked with a cross and number, 217. Eddie Gilbert's death has
suffered as much falsehood and reinscription as his life. His supposedly
incurable syphilis masked attention being placed on his Alzheimer's
disease, which he had been suffering undiagnosed for 20 years.

Denied a name in death, he has survived in memory far better than
the earlier indigenous players. This recognition has remained because
his name has been tethered to Bradman's. Everything and everyone
with which Bradman was affiliated became significant. Some of that
inflence has stabilized Gilbert's role in history. He has even been commodified in the burgeoning commercial bat business:

> The bat features laser burnt in signature of Eddie Gilbert and his
> bowling action. An original hand painting of a lizard by licensed
> authentic Aboriginal artist Michael Connolly. Limited Edition
> of 100 bats. Ideal Collectors or playing bat. Eddie Gilbert was a
> former Queensland Sheffield Shield opening bowler who was one of
> the few bowlers ever to take Sir Donald's wicket for a duck. Free
> poster of the first indigenous Australian cricket team to tour England
> in 1868 included with each fullsize bat. Replica mini is also
> available.[62]

All the elements are there: Bradman, the duck and even a mention
of the first indigenous cricket team. The irony is that that an 'authentic
Aboriginal artist' has hand-painted on the great symbol of English
sporting culture. There is something quite poignant in this paradox.

The sources for Gilbert's life and history are scattered. There are few documents outside of regional newspapers which detail results and scores. But the name and the commitment against the odds has survived. Mike Colman and Ken Edwards' remarkable book on Eddie Gilbert is well written, accessible and considered in its narrative. Based on seven years of research by Ken Edwards for his Ph.D., his research material was then crafted by Colman into book form. It is a brilliant intervention in making Gilbert more than one over, and more than a bowler to Don Bradman.

Other tributes have also surfaced. On 1 June 1999, Eddie Gilbert was acknowledged at the first inaugural Queensland indigenous sport recognition night. Coordinated by the Brisbane City Council, it was an opportunity to recognize many sports, men and women, and have a memory, impression and record codified and captured.[63] Further, the Queensland Cricket Association decided to establish a coaching programme named after Eddie Gilbert.[64] Through this initiative, cricket clubs have been set up in rural and regional areas, including the most northerly cricket club in Australia, at Thursday Island.[65]

A remarkable, but yet to be written, final chapter to the Eddie Gilbert story is continued by Jason Gillespie. He is described as possessing 'a distant Aboriginal heritage'.[66] To use such language as distant and close, part and full, is to restate nineteenth century truths about race. Importantly, Geoff Clark did not repeat this mode of differentiation:

> Jason Gillespie publicly confirmed that he is the first Aboriginal to play for the Australian team. I am hoping that with the support of our best-known cricket fan, Mr Howard, the tragedies of our past will begin to be offset by the dawning of a new era for all Australians – both on and off the field.[67]

Ashley Mallett, coach of the 2001 indigenous team, believed that 'I suspect quite a few Aboriginal players have actually played for Australia before Jason Gillespie but they never owned up to it because if they had, they wouldn't have played'.[68] What is odd is that the official website for Australian cricket, baggygreen.com, lists Eddie Gilbert as 'still Australia's most successful Aboriginal cricketer'.[69] Gillespie's representation in the Test team denies this claim, unless distinctions about race and identity are being made on a basis other than personal declaration and acceptance by indigenous leaders. Skin colour must never be a determinant of race.

There is a deep structural and symbolic difficulty with indigenous men representing the nation.[70] Recognizing that a structural inequality exists in Australian cricket, the ACB held a forum on Aborigines in Cricket in 2001. After the two-day seminar, a game was held between the Prime Minister's XI, captained by Steve Waugh, and an indigenous side, captained by Jason Gillespie. The symbolism is stark, and unfortunate. A superb exercise in increasing the visibility of indigenous cricketers was marred by the Prime Minister associating himself with the non-indigenous players. Why could the Prime Minister not name and claim the indigenous participants as 'his' XI? Only then would the identity of the non-indigenous team be clear: white Australia versus Indigenous Australia. For the Prime Minister to claim the white players as his chosen team masks racial inequality with nationalism.

Not only should Eddie Gilbert have been treated better as a cricketer, he should have been treated better as a person. Bradman – the most famous Australian who ever lived – bestowed an accidental gift on the greatest fast bowler that Australia never had. That one ball signified potential and opportunity – that just occasionally black could beat white. Through this symbolism, Gilbert would not fade into obscurity like Jack Marsh, Albert Henry or Dick-a-Dick. Although he is only remembered for one over, there is a potential to build a better memory for those supported by Gilbert's name and myth. At a press conference, John Bradman announced that the Bradman Trust would continue the social justice concerns that his father had discovered late in life. Besides assisting juniors, the Trust would also support indigenous cricket. In the conference, he stated, 'and then there was Eddie Gilbert, the Aboriginal fast bowler . . . He knocked the bat out of my father's hands. No-one ever did that. He never forgot it.'[71]

This chapter commenced with a remarkable over. Throughout his life, Eddie Gilbert would only be known as the man who removed Bradman for a duck. This selection of facts actually confirms the institutional racism that survives in Australia. Bradman was removed for a duck many times throughout his career, but this one scoreline is remembered. The reason is clearly revealed when we add one more 'cricketing fact' to the story. There are probably only two batsmen who equal Bradman in style, flair, footwork and technical proficiency, if not averages. Sachin Tendulkar and Brian Lara are batsmen who are iconographic in India and the West Indies respectively, but also have a remarkable capacity to sight the ball, and move with its flight. They could never 'be' Bradman – no one will ever be – but they are Bradmanesque.

Brian Lara, like Don Bradman, is also known for one ball. Zoe Goss, former Australian cricket captain and champion bowler (for the women's team, but this bracketed caveat should not be necessary),[72] bowled out Lara. Although she has had a remarkable career, she will be forever remembered for this single delivery. The reasons for this emphasis in popular memory are troubling. Both Eddie Gilbert and Zoe Goss were heavily disempowered in cricket, one through race and the other through gender. Both removed the best batsmen of their eras. Such an event was neither expected nor predictable. It is not expected that 'weak' players – that is, women or indigenous cricketers – could possibly have the talent of the 'great men' of the game. Nineteenth century hierarchies of power and domination continue to frame the wicket. The fame derived from this ball is that 'even' a woman or an Aboriginal could remove 'the great' Lara and Bradman. Such a dismissal did not renegotiate power relations, but confirmed them. It was not only unexpected, but almost funny. It has been remembered because it was so ridiculous that it shows that anything can happen in cricket. It is a shame that such bowling surprises do nothing to change the conditions of race and gender off the wicket.

The treatment of indigenous citizens remains a loose thread in the cloth of Australian culture. Sport is a significant strategy to reconnect indigenous concerns with the national popular. It appears that Australia is denying formal, constitutional change such as becoming a republic, but is instead renegotiating with public representations. Cricket has been part of nation building, but has also maintained the values and power of colonizing elites. These two social forces collide, adding density and disquiet to any Test match.

# Chapter 6

# Bending memories through Beckham

At first glance, *Bend it like Beckham* seems the conventional sporting tale of an underdog made good. That this underdog is a young British Asian woman, rather than a freckled-faced white boy from Millwall or a luckless lad from Liverpool, seems only to add spice to the story. But it is the bedrock – the underlying tragedy of racism, despair and prejudice – that transforms this 'feel-good' flick into significant cinema. It is an important film, but it is also a potent intervention in sporting history.

The story encircles Jess, a young woman who wishes to play football. She faces challenges from her family, friends and community. She is not alone in sporting ability: Jess's father used to play cricket. Because of prejudice against Indians in England, he left the game for a life of work, sacrifice and seething hatred for his youthful experience of prejudice. His turban became the symbol of all the costs and losses of immigration. The leaving is temporary, but the loss is permanent. Only when he realizes that his daughter is fighting – not accepting – prejudice is she granted the opportunity for a professional footballing future.

The finest touch to this polished film is the ending – the real ending, not the waving-goodbye-at-the-airport cliché. Jess's coach and soon-to-be love is an Irishman, a piquant touch. The notion of these two great global diasporas – the Irish and Indian – unifying in critiquing English prejudice is imaginative, and creatively political. The final scene features both the men in Jess's life – Irish boyfriend and Indian father – in cricketing whites. Once more, sport is a unifying force, but only when the English are removed from the pitch. Such an implicit message is hammered home when one realizes that Jess gained footballing opportunities in America, not her home (and the home of the game): England.

Film does not freeze histories of the present. It is the repository of popular memory. It does not shadow narratives of the political economy, but captures the spark of subjectivity and how individual experiences are collectivized. *Bend it like Beckham* is directed by Gurinder Chadha, who was able to build an audience for a film featuring the three great pariahs of American cinema: soccer, sportswomen and racism. By intertwining the three great unpopularities, a new popular cultural imagining space is created, making viewers ponder the nature of the nation, sport, loyalty and identity. Not surprisingly, the film was highly successful in diverse markets, including Britain, India, Australia and New Zealand.

While the decline of David Beckham's sporting celebrity is tracked by his movement from Manchester United to Real Madrid,[1] it is important that this great film not be forgotten through the changing fortunes of a man mentioned in the title. Beckham remains important as he captures a particular moment in celebrity culture, where fashion, gossip, music and football dialogued with energy and dynamism. That moment has now passed, with a current generation of celebrities famous for being famous. They do not play sport. They do not play a musical instrument with proficiency or skill. They have not achieved academic excellence. The less they do, the more time they have to be a celebrity. David and Victoria Beckham were pivotal translators, moving journalism and popular culture into this new celebrity stage. Beckham was a footballer who enjoyed fashion. Now celebrities simply wear fashion. This film plays off these changing discourses, but adds the incisive grafts of race and migration.

British Asian film makers confront many problems. Perhaps the most significant one is that filmic critics and academics wish to isolate them in boxes and categories. They 'represent' black cinema, social realism or multiculturalism. While all these boxes can be ticked for *Bend it like Beckham*, this film is more than a liberal rendering permits. Most importantly, the film confronts viewers with the complex and frequently conflictual reality of Britain. Chadha was continuing a project instigated in *Bhaji on the beach*: how to signify Asianness within – rather than outside – British iconography and ideologies. Like *My beautiful laundrette* and *Sammy and Rosie get laid*, the two great stories and films inspired by Hanif Kureishi, the assumed unity of the United Kingdom and Great Britain crumbles into dust. To understand the nation state now requires an appreciation of plurality. As Kureishi has stated, 'you couldn't get too caught up in issues of representation and continue to write'.[2] When cultural narratives mix, new approaches to identity, subjectivity and body politics merge into a positive and proactive vista. *Bend it like Beckham* is a film about women in sport and creates productive and dissociative representations. The greatest problem confronting women who play football, cricket, rugby union and league in particular is that there are so few images of competency, success and triumph.[3] This film is impressive because it constructs women footballers as strong, skilled and passionate about the game. Through the expert filming of on-field play – a very difficult task – sporting women are naturalized, rather than rendered freakish, butch or a joke.

This chapter plucks out four trajectories from the film: American soccer, women in sport, Indianness and Beckham. All these narratives dialogue to render *Bend it like Beckham* a pivotal filmic moment in feminism, postcolonialism and trans-national sport. It is visual culture at its most dynamic and intertextual, creating a space for speaking and silence, denial and consciousness. As the Beckham era of sports media is replaced by the (mis)demeanors of both Wayne Rooney[4] and José Mourinho,[5] it is necessary to recognize that Beckham's ambivalent summoning of both tradition and innovation created space for new masculinities and race-based discussions to emerge through film.

## Brandi's bra

The United States is the only country in the world where women's soccer is better known than the men's game.[6] Although the men's competition hosted the 1994 World Cup, the game continued to have grass-roots support but with little international success. While the men's team did qualify for the quarter-finals of the 2002 tournament in Japan and Korea, it was a televisual failure. The irony that no major US network holds the rights to soccer is remarkable, as it is probably the most visually effective of all sports. Many reasons have been suggested for the systematic decentring of football in the United States. First, the US is not globally dominant in the game. Also, there are national sports, such as gridiron and baseball, which take attention away from more global pastimes. There is also a gendered explanation. Women's football through its history has had a television deal, spectators, publicity and sponsors. The reason for this success has little to do with the permeation of feminism through American society, or a deep respect for sportswomen. As Stefano Hatfield realized, the men's competition remains hampered because 'there is no Brandi Chastain to take off her top as she did in the women's World Cup, thus revolutionizing the game'.[7] The social and sporting implications of this semiotic and literal stripping were wide-ranging.

The final of the 1999 World Cup was an exciting match between China and the United States held at the Rose Bowl. A crowd of 90,185 people witnessed the game. This was the largest attendance ever to view a woman's sporting event. After 90 minutes of regular play and two 15 minute periods of sudden death play-off, a penalty shootout decided the champions. The Chinese team only missed one opportunity. The five successful shots from the US team concluded with Brandi Chastain's penalty. After beating the goalkeeper, she removed her shirt, revealing a black crop top bra. To refer to this item of clothing as a 'bra' is a misnomer. It is a shell top in which thousands of women exercise every day without the cover of a shirt. Nothing is said in daily aerobics classes about this outfit. In the United States, though, this act was highly sexualized, in a way not seen through the regular shirt lifting in the men's game.

The press coverage drawn to Chastain's bra was enormous. She became one of *People Magazine*'s 25 most intriguing people of the year in 1999[8] and appeared on the David Letterman show, and on the covers of *Time*, *Newsweek*[9] and *Sports Illustrated*. It was a Nike executive's dream come true, and pervasive exposure for their sports bra range.[10] However – once again – there was concern that the team received attention because they were attractive, not for their athletic ability. In retrospect, such a judgement seems obvious. What has survived through the historical documents is not the details of the game, not even the ending, but the muscular image of a bra-clad Chastain yelping with success.[11] While she has been called 'the face of women's soccer',[12] actually she is the breasts of the game. Her face was not the basis of the publicity. A few weeks before the World Cup, she was also featured in a nude photograph for *Gear* magazine. Her actions do raise questions about women's bodily rights and the differing expectations and behaviour of male and female athletes. Within an individualist framework, it can rightly be argued that Chastain can do whatever she likes with her body. She is free to pose nude, remove her shirt or advertise Nike sportswear. She has said that 'the publicity has given me a chance to talk about soccer with more people than ever, and that is what is most important to me'.[13] The paradox is clear. Her 'talk' was only made possible because of her body, or more precisely a bra.

Do female athletes – to gain media 'exposure' – have any alternative but to present a stripped and thin image of femininity? Such images can reinforce hyper-conservative notions of appropriate women's bodies. All women have the right to remove their clothes and be paid for that action. Chastain confirmed her right to pose nude in *Gear*: 'I didn't do it on behalf of my teammates, or for soccer. It was my decision.'[14] The question is whether or not women can gain success and empowerment without displaying a very narrow rendering of an appropriate woman's body. One website even features Brandi Chastain as a Barbie Doll, only recognizable through the black sports bra.[15] It was no surprise that *Sports Illustrated*, certainly not a bastion of women's sport, named the soccer team as the 1999 'sports*men* of the year' (italics mine). Beyond the bra, the success of the team did something remarkable. As Michael Bamberger realized, the World Cup 'fused two often ignored elements of American sports, women and soccer, into one transformative moment, and held a nation in thrall'.[16] A *Business Week* reporter was more direct: 'speaking for the men . . . I can say confidently (if a bit sheepishly), the Kodak Moment of the day was the sight of Brandi Chastain – in all her muscular glory – doffing her shirt'.[17] Not surprisingly, Bill Clinton also weighed in to the media frenzy:

> The day after the game, a lot of us who aren't so young anymore were trying to search the whole cluttered attic of our memories to try to think if there was ever a time when there had been a more exciting climax to an athletic event that meant as much to so many. I'm not sure that in my lifetime there has been.[18]

Not surprisingly, the President did not mention the bra. He also did not mention that penalty shootouts are reasonably common in football competitions.[19] The moment was made memorable by Chastain's action after her shot. The question is one of intent. Tom Carson described it as 'the first time a woman took her top off on national TV without any idea of pleasing men'.[20] He even believed that historical time can be cut up for the female athletes using the bra as a temporal marker: the BBC referred to 'Before Brandi Chastain'.[21] Her muscularity created new ways to think about fitness, agility and femininity. It was an important intervention, and institutional changes would follow.

The United States Soccer Federation did oppress their women's team, with both the coaches and athletes paid far less than the men's coaches and athletes, even though the women were far more successful.[22] Triggered by the visibility of the World Cup victory, the Women's United Soccer Association (WUSA) began in 2001, with media support and reasonably strong attendances. There was also on-the-pitch success. The San Jose CyberRays won the inaugural WUSA competition in 2002, and went on to defeat Arsenal's women's team 2–1. This was no surprise.[23] The lack of support for women's football in Britain is remarkable. In *Bend it like Beckham*, 'America' is the sporting promised land:

*Jules:*   I want to play professionally.
*Jess:*    Wow, can you do that? I mean as a job like?
*Jules:*   Sure. Not here, but you can in America. There's a pro league with new stadiums and everything.

It is ironic that English football administrators and journalists, who so often stress their role as the origin or inventor of the game, have lost out to the Americans in the women's competition. Such an inequality demonstrates that while feminism may have had an impact in English workplaces and legislation, sport is the untouchable embodiment of masculine nationalism. The English media have been disgraceful in their coverage of the women's game. For example, the BBC and Sky Sports coverage of the FIFA Players of the Year ignored women's football.

It was incredible today to watch the BBC World television and Fox SportsWorld television insult the millions of women playing soccer in the world today and carefully ignoring the FIFA Women's Player of the Year Award to Hamm. They gave extensive coverage to Figa [*sic*] winning the men's award and even had stories on the men's fair play award, but as far as they were concerned women were still not part of the soccer (football) scene.

In terms of attitude to women in soccer and sports the English media again confirmed our previous comments, and can be safely grouped with the Italians with their Neanderthal views of women in sports.[24]

Mia Hamm is worthy of attention. She is a pioneer in moving women's football into the global media. She was selected for five consecutive years as the United States Soccer Female Athlete of the Year and was twice FIFA World Player of the year. She maintained a 17-year career with the National Team, totalling 158 career goals in 274 international matches. She is the all-time leading scorer and the second most-capped player in football history, men or women. She represented the United States in all four World Cups.[25] Considering this reputation, she probably did deserve a mention in the media report.

It is easy – very easy – to attack the British media's coverage of sporting women. Clearly, though, there were also embedded problems in the US media coverage of women's soccer. The WUSA signed a two-year agreement with Paxson Communications to broadcast the games on PAC cable stations. Paxson was also a sponsor of the league.[26] Beginning in April 2002, twenty-two games were broadcast live on Saturday afternoons. However, letters soon arrived at the website Women's Soccer World on the poor quality commentary, showing inexperience with the game.[27] Funding troubles started to emerge. While, in *Bend it like Beckham*, America was the promised land of women's football, the collapse of the league and institution so celebrated in the film came swiftly. On 15 September 2003, the WUSA folded after three years of financial difficulties. There were many causes for the closure, the most obvious being that the organization had spent $100 million during its first three years. Darren Rovell, reporter for ESPN, asked, 'how expensive could it be to run a professional soccer league?'[28] When the league started in 2001, investors had ceded $40 million that was supposed to last for five years, but was fully exhausted by the end of the first year. Three problems ended the league: low attendance at games, little significant television exposure and low levels of sponsorship. The PAX Network deal, reportedly worth $2 million, only attracted 100,000 per broadcast. The league averaged 8,000 fans in the stadium during the inaugural season, and only 6,667 fans in the final one.[29] Disturbingly, this failure of women's soccer in the United States, which offered so much promise, also confirmed the structural difficulty in the discussion, promotion and proliferation of women's sport more generally. Gary Cavalli, the former commissioner of the ABL, the failed women's basketball league, diagnosed the dilemma:

> Many people think that women's sports is a cause as much as it is entertainment . . . That you should show up at games to support the cause as much as you should show up because you enjoy the entertainment, I don't think that's fair.[30]

The irony is that the folding of the WUSA coincided with the successful third final of the Women's National Basketball Association (WNBA), where 22,000 people attended a game between Detroit and Los Angeles.

It is remarkable how quickly the saturating legacy, visibility and success of the American team in the 1999 Women's World Cup were thrown away and not mobilized to build long-lasting structural change. Mechelle Voepel confirmed that:

> The WUSA could have used more fans. But its most immediate need was sponsorship money. And that dried up. That is partly just the reality of business, which exists to make money. But it's also a particular reality of sports entertainment, which is an overall risky business.[31]

As a sporting media product, WUSA was unable to create a large enough audience to sustain sponsorship. The people who watched and celebrated the World Cup in 1999 showed there were consumers of women's football, but perhaps not enough for a weekly competition. This is a reality of women's sport that must be managed and discussed. Golf has managed this reality with greater clarity. The Ladies' Professional Golf Association (LPGA) was formed in 1950. It faced challenges, but survived. The most successful year for that competition was 2003, when Annika Sorenstam confronted polit-ical ambivalence and hostility to play a PGA tour event. It is disturbing that women have to play men to lift the publicity for female athletes. The strategic development of women's golf, particularly in terms of women's rights, has provided a model for other sports. Slow, methodical and precise planning is necessary for long-term success of women's sports in the media. The desire to relaunch WUSA through 2004 was strong, particularly with the profile of the US Olympic team.[32] This impetus resulted in Tonya Antonucci being named as the Chief Executive. It was a strong choice, and far-sighted. She was the former head of Yahoo! Sports, played soccer at Stanford, and was an assistant coach at Santa Clara University. She knows the value of the product, describing her goal as 'to build . . . a disciplined, long-term plan that will allow us to showcase these amazing athletes and this great sport'.[33] Clearly, webcasting and convergent media strategies will be developed.

Through the failures and disappointments of the post-1999 WUSA, women's football in the United States still has a great advantage, even over the men's team. Good women's soccer players attend college, whereas male juniors turn professional at 17 or 18 years of age. That means that the best female players are in the college tournaments, which lifts the calibre of that competition and acts as a pivotal feeder for the national team. Therefore, it was no surprise that it was American college scouts who were watching Jules and Jess in the final sequences of *Bend it like Beckham*. Even more significantly, it was Santa Clara University who signed them up with a full scholarship. The women's soccer programme has been fully funded at Santa Clara since 1998. Not only was it the college attended by Brandi Chastain, but she was also an assistant coach, supporting her husband, Jerry Smith, as coach. The fiction and film crossover reached a zenith when Fox Searchlight, the distributors of *Bend it like Beckham*, screened the film for the US Women's team.

> The name David Beckham is larger than life in the U.K., but can it open a movie in the U.S.? ... Last Thursday, Fox Searchlight held a private screening in Pasadena for 14 members of the US Women's National Team, including Brandi Chastain, Julie Foudy and Mia Hamm. Says Chastain, 'this was a great message of how you can be spiritual and true to your culture and still have athletics as part of your life'.[34]

Even though she has a degree in television and communications from Santa Clara, it is clear Chastain was not using her training in the post-filmic analysis. Her use of 'culture' is sloppy, easily translating into a slippery rendering of race. Christianity within American culture saturates her analysis, but without a 'Jesus figure' to peg on a belief structure. Non-Christian faiths become 'spiritual'. There is no mention of gender, women or feminism. This film is so much more than a superficial multicultural love fest. It demonstrates the struggles that women confront with their bodies – with Jess wanting to cover up rather than reveal her skin because of burn scars to her legs. It shows overt racism on the sports field, rather than symbolic unity of collective enterprise. Finally, it demonstrates the intense fight – the enormous barriers and prejudices that sportswomen must overcome to gain success. New age 'appreciation' of 'spirit' and 'culture' does this film no justice.

The protectionism of American sport meshes with the insular nationalism of the nation. Andrei Markovits and Steven Hellerman, for example, have argued that this 'nationalizing' imperative has provided a barrier for entry into other sports. They argued that if a sport was established between 1870 and 1930, then its long-term success was more likely:

> Early arrival does not guarantee late survival, but it most certainly helps, because choices are very rapidly narrowed once sport spaces become filled both quantitatively and spatially, and qualitatively in that any newcomer must exert a great deal of power and expend major resources to be given ... a seat at the restaurant's increasingly limited table from which few want to depart.[35]

The lack of masculine and working class interest in soccer in the US has been of advantage to women playing the game. The social problem for US soccer is that it is played by Hispanic immigrants and suburban, white, middle class young women. From this basis, ensuring major media coverage is difficult. Cable television has made the difference, but it was not enough to save the WUSA. The women's professional soccer league did not have to fight for media access at the start of the WUSA because it was partly funded by the major cable companies. However, when it could not pull a viewing audience above 100,000 a game, it was dropped.

There is no doubt that the single action of Chastain revealing a black bra granted women's sports more attention than almost any other single act. The impact was felt far beyond the United States. On the New Zealand Soccer website, her shirtless photograph was displayed, without comments or captions.[36] Ironically – but correctly – Brandi Chastain stated that 'the greatest impact we'll have is when boys see women athletes and don't think twice about them'.[37] The question is whether or not her actions assisted or hampered this sporting future. Perhaps more appropriately, 'The Matildas' website, the virtual home of the national Australian women's soccer team, featured a giveaway for the video of *Bend it like Beckham* through 2003.[38] It is ironic that the Antipodean neighbours have chosen different representations of women's sporting success.

Through these failures and confusion, the irony is that women's participation in American sports like soccer and basketball is being claimed as more 'authentic' than the men's game. The rationale for this judgement is that – because they are not paid high wages with saturating sponsorship – they are playing for the love of the game. This attitude is revealed in this letter to *Newsweek*, following the 1999 victory.

> It has been many years since a sporting event made me feel as proud of my country's athletes as I did during that game. The team exhibited sportsmanship, class and determination to win throughout the tournament, and it was wonderful to see these ladies rewarded with a victory. In this era of athletes' megabuck contracts and endorsements, it was refreshing that they made the team's objective of being the best their own priority.[39]

Such an attitude is condescending. The notion that female professional athletes – ladies – play for the love of the game while men require money attempts to put a positive spin on the poor funding of women's facilities and players. Even in the United States at the moment, when the women's game is more popular than the men's, the women's coaches and players are still paid far less. Is this for the love of the game, or a desire for profit from sponsors?

My words are not meant to discount Brandi Chastain. She has been a remarkable athlete and a credit to the sport. The problem is that football is a team game requiring a range of physiological, psychological and perceptual attributes to ensure a strong performance. The American media's lack of experience with football resulted in a major lapse of priorities. In normal play, the goalkeeper's role is to prevent the game from being lost, rather than actually winning it for the team. In a penalty shootout, these roles reverse, with the victory reliant on the dexterity and reflexes of the keeper.

In normal play, most penalties will hit the back of the net. The key in a shootout is to disrupt the striker's rhythm. Actually Brandi Chastain's successful penalty did not win the game for the United States. Briana Scurry's stop of the third penalty kick by Liu Ying of China created the victory. It was an incredible save, requiring a fully extended dive to the left. Yet little attention was focused on her remarkable effort.

Briana Scurry is African American, the only one in the winning team of 1999. There was one other African American in the squad, Saskia Webber, but she was the substitute keeper. Without Scurry's effort, the United States would not have won the World Cup. Yet after the game, she received fewer endorsements and interview requests than her white teammates. ABC, who televised the match, ignored Scurry completely even in their after-game coverage. A spokesman for the network later regretted this lapse, but denied that it was racially motivated.[40] Sidono Ferreira, father of an 8-year-old soccer player, was more telling in his judgements: 'I don't want to say it's racism, but I think White people just don't get it . . . For soccer, she is Jackie Robinson.'[41] The valorizing of Chastain in the World Cup also required the forgetting of her performance one week before she removed her shirt in the final. In the quarter-final win against Germany, Chastain knocked the ball past Scurry for an own goal in the 3–2 scoreline. Importantly, Scurry – unlike keepers within the Peter Schmeichel school of sporting retribution – did not become agitated with the defender. Therefore, Chastain nearly lost the World Cup for the United States, besides winning it. This event was lost from the popular memory of her actions.

The social pressures confronting Scurry are difficult to measure. Grant Wahl recognizes that 'she is the only African-American starter on a team that plays in stadiums filled with more WASPs than a mud dauber's nest'.[42] Ironically, she did not play in the 2000 Olympic squad because of supposed weight gain. Grant Wahl reported in response that 'she promptly lost her starting job'.[43] Chastain did play. However, being officially an underdog and missing the Olympics, Scurry trained, lost weight and was blisteringly successful in the 2001 WUSA season. She held opposition teams scoreless for 540 consecutive minutes.[44] By 2002, she had fought back to return for the national team, with a 4–0 win over Norway. Scurry went on to reclaim her place in the 2004 Olympic team. Yet even when recognizing such achievement against the odds, in 2005, when fans were remembering their favourite players of Olympic team, it took 'keeperqueen18' to ask the list celebrating Julie Foudy and Brandi Chastain, 'why are keepers always left out of the loop?'[45]

Racial questions are still uncomfortable with the US soccer discourse. Outstanding players do emerge, such as Danielle Slaton, who was the only university student to be picked for the women's Olympic soccer team in 2000 and is also African American. Drafted to Santa Clara and the number one draft pick in her debut WUSA season, she carries a huge representational burden. Richard Manning, the Assistant Coach at the university, believes that she will have an outstanding career in women's football:

> I'd like her to get into it. She would be a great role model . . . In the soccer community there are not that many African American role models. She's proud of her heritage. Here's someone who's bright and an exceptional player. She brings competitiveness, but there's not a selfish bone in her body.[46]

Slaton is having to 'represent' far more than herself. Such pressures do not confront the white players on the team. Chastain can 'represent' her own interests. Black sportsmen and women must always be far more. Her positioning as a minority in a minority sport is also a crucial factor in shaping the narrative of *Bend it like Beckham*. The gulf of media coverage between Scurry and Chastain raises the 'problem' of race. This film's narrative and iconography remain important because they write in the space between white-dominated soccer and black-inflected football.

## Indian girls

Indianness, like all nationalisms, is in the eye of the beholder and the pen of the writer. Cricket is a unique sport. It is a conflictual, composite flicker of images from the nineteenth and twentieth centuries that montage into the contemporary digi-scape. It is remarkable how strongly cricket has been claimed by India, Pakistan and Sri Lanka, particularly considering that English racism at worst, or condescension at best, still frames the playing of the game. For example, Mike Brearley was summoned by Wisden to ponder the nature of Indian cricket:

> But what is 'being Indian'? Being married to one I need to be careful what I say but most Indian cricketing cognoscenti would understand the question. They would take it to refer to Indians' allegedly characteristic and defining tendency to show flair and brilliance but lack the capacity to drive home an advantage. I have often been told by Indian journalists, for example, that Indian players have never worked hard enough to make themselves fully fit; that they lack an appropriate 'Western' ruthlessness and ambition; that they need an Australian coach.[47]

Hiding behind anonymous informants, an Orientalist discourse has been clearly established. Flair and brilliance are not enough: Indians require ruthlessness and ambition. All the archetypes of the childlike, lazy colonized subjects are revealed in this passage.[48] Identity is being organized here into a hierarchy of England and the Commonwealth, self and other, winner and loser. Ironically, Australian coaches become tougher and more ruthless than the English. This is no surprise. White Australians have often been the servants and translators for Empire. Australia's liminal positioning in the colonial equation has proved useful throughout colonial history in the nineteenth and twentieth centuries.[49] That this cultural translation is still being revealed so overtly in the twenty-first century is a testament to the survival of colonial truths through sport.

English cricket and football are tantalizing traces of shifts in power structures. The desire to claim football as the English game and to release cricket as a 'Commonwealth' sport is a pivotal differentiation. Colonization, in a supposedly post-colonial environment, is no longer about pinpointing negative or positive images or representations. Instead, we must work at understanding how subject identities are formed. The notion that Indians play cricket but not football, which is an undercurrent of *Bend it like Beckham*, conveys much information about English identity. In a remarkable scene, Jess's father explains to her Irish coach why he would not support his daughter's footballing career:

Mr Bhamra:   Young man, when I was a teenager in Nairobi, I was the best fast bowler in our school. Our team even won the East African Cup. But when I came to this country, nothing. I couldn't play in any of the teams . . . they made fun of my turban and sent me off packing.

Joe:   I'm sorry Mr Bhamra. But it's now –

Mr Bhamra:   It's now what? None of our boys are in any of the football leagues. Do you think they'll let our girls? I don't want you to build up Jessminda's hopes so she ends up disappointed like me.

Jess:   But it's all changing now. Look at Nasser Hussain. He's captain of the England cricket team and he's Asian.

Mrs Bhamra:   Hussain's a Muslim name. Their families are different.

Her father later witnessed Jess being racially abused on the field, being termed a 'Paki' by an opposition player. Racism requires such exclusionary practices to form a hierarchy of differences. Such name calling is a rapid, sharp and shocking way to establish a power structure and demean others. It also demonstrates the interdependence of nationalism and racism. While all the players were English, this racialization of Jess established a representational strategy to demean and discredit her ability. When Jess fought back, *she* was sent off the field, not the racist perpetrator. Jess's Irish coach responded to this taunt in an evocative fashion:

Jess:   She called me a Paki, but I guess you wouldn't know what that feels like, would you?

Joe:   Jess, I'm Irish. Of course I understand what that feels like.

The key intervention is that Jess not only was aware of how racism operates like her father, but was prepared to fight against it. She had a consciousness of difference, but an ability to fight for that difference. By the conclusion of the film, her father has realized that the times have changed, not for the racist society, but for his politically conscious daughter:

> Those bloody English cricket players threw me out of their club like a dog. I never complained. On the contrary, I vowed that I would never play again. Who suffered? Me. But I don't want Jess to suffer. I don't want her to make the same mistakes her father made, of accepting life, accepting situations. I want her to fight. And I want her to win, because I've seen her play. She's brilliant. I don't think anyone has the right to stop her.

Appropriately, at the end of the film, Mr Bhamra is again playing cricket in the park across from his house, against Jess's Irish coach. This colonial game can create cultural bridges, but only when the English are not involved in the match.

There is also the misconception throughout the film that Indians do not play football. The insularity of English soccer and the success of India in cricket has meant that the events in contemporary India, and the shifting passions of the population, are being ignored. In the updated edition of his evocative and landmark A history of Indian cricket, Mihir Bose tracked the changes in sporting allegiance:

> Cricket, and even more hockey, are fairly limited in their international appeal and in the last decade, through television, India is being exposed to the sport that can truly claim to be the most popular in the world: football . . . The problem has been the failure of Indian football administrators, a byword for incompetence, to harness this enthusiasm and translate it into a national team Indians could be proud of. The appetite for world class football is immense. Millions of Indians, through television, can watch, almost nightly, the deeds of David Beckham, Michael Owen and many other international stars . . . If Indian football could get its act together – and it is a big if – then it could become a major force.[50]

Bose's words provide an historical context for Bend it like Beckham. The cliché of Indian cricketers, who perform the required role of flair and passion in the international game, has masked the changing conditions in Indian sport, triggered through television. Indian 'girls' do play football, as do men. As in Australia, once administrative incompetence is finally remedied, the game will be released from the shackles that have limited its development.

Cricket was built in India not on unity, but on diversity. While cricket was brought to India in the mid-eighteenth century by British soldiers and sailors, the first Indians to play were the Parsis of Bombay. The Oriental Cricket Club was established in 1848. This educated and affluent group believed that supporting cricket would increase the ties with the colonizer. Then Hindus began to play, to perform their rivalry with the Parsis. The first Hindu club was formed in 1866. Muslim cricket then began in Bombay, with the Muslim Cricket Club created in 1883. Cricket in British India was therefore highly fragmented and sectionalized, based on ethnic group, race, caste and religion. Importantly, cricket divided the colonized, rather than unified them against the colonizer.[51]

The nation in a post-industrial society is not – and has never been – an homogeneous group. Multiculturalism, as a soft policy rather than a structural imperative, aims to create cohesion from the diversity. The difficulty is that for this 'unity in diversity' mantra to function, the diverse groups must appear equal. The only way this falsehood may be perpetuated is to use the word 'culture' in an ambiguous way. Equality is granted to religion, music, language, food and clothes as long as these practices occur in private and in 'leisure time'. For example, food provides local knowledge about identity. But in the globalizing, culinary culture, 'Indian food' is objectified. Indian cookery is not a singular formation: there are myriad regional cuisines. There is a colonial conceit of London being a site of world cuisine, where differences are homogenized on the plate.[52] 'Going for a curry' does not change the structural racism confronted by Indian citizens in education, employment or sport. As Rushdie has affirmed,

> On the whole it is now recognized that the word 'curry' is inappropriate and inadequate as a generic description of Indian/Pakistani/Bangladeshi food. It is difficult for me to use the word without hearing and being deeply offended by its racist connotations.[53]

In *Bend it like Beckham*, Jules' mother is the voice of English insularity, restating all the archetypes of 'Indianness': arranged marriages, respect of elders and curries. Jules could only reply to her unknowing mother, 'you're embarrassing yourself'. She did not change her views or language throughout the film. The 'normal' practices of eating fish and chips, speaking English and being a Christian, for example, are taken for granted in the structures of society, such as the workplace, the law and the educational system. This means that deep practices of racism and structural inequalities are masked so that acceptable differences can be affirmed only at the level of 'culture'.

The term 'culture', in any discussion of 'sporting cultures', should be assessed and critiqued with great care, as it can perpetuate the assumed standards of the white, the middle class and the male. If an anti-racism project is taken seriously, then interventions are necessary in the nationalist project. In an era when 'active' ethnic minority support for football clubs in England has been assessed at between 0 and 2 per cent of the crowd, while concurrently 33 per cent of the clubs themselves believe they have been 'successful' at attracting black and Asian fans to matches,[54] much progress is yet to be achieved. Obviously there have been changes. John Williams reported his attendance at a Liverpool match:

> On Wednesday night this week at half time on the Liverpool Kop – half way, in fact, through the Nicolas Anelka show – I began chatting to a small group of young Asian Kopites. When I was growing up on Merseyside you hardly ever saw black or brown faces at the match, but this new era of seats, and falling racism and hooliganism at grounds has opened up football to a whole new set of fans. So I was delighted to see these Asian Reds, and took the opportunity to share some Liverpool stories. These guys were not from Liverpool of course. They came from the West Midlands and had followed the club on TV when they were kids. Before recent changes they had been afraid to come to football matches but now they felt comfortable among other Kopites.[55]

'Local' allegiances for British Asian fans and players are difficult to establish. With television occupying such a pivotal, formative influence in determining loyalty, Manchester United, Chelsea and Liverpool may gain new Asian fans. Clubs such as Millwall, with racist form, will lose these fans and communities.

There is a special link between the nation, sport and film. *Bend it like Beckham* is important to representations of Indianness because it demonstrates the shifts from cricket to football, denial to awareness, and consciousness to struggle. This fight is rendered even more significant because it involves a young Indian woman. With India as an imagined 'origin' and America as the buoyant land of opportunity, England is revealed as backward, racist and insular. Yet this film not only fights a battle against race-based prejudice, but also fights feminist battles over sexuality and women's bodies. Importantly, these battles are intertwined through sport.

### Lesbians, Lebanese and Punjabi

In a humorous and disturbing subplot, Jules' mother Paula spends much of the film dealing with her daughter's homosexuality, even though Jules is actually a heterosexual. Paula had assumed that any woman active in sport and physical culture must be a lesbian. Expeditions into lingerie shops, in search of a pumped-up bra, betray a desire to make her daughter conform to a very precise shape of womanhood. Her daughter fought such limitations. As Jules remarks in exasperation, 'Just because I wear trackies and play sport does not make me a lesbian.' The film's characters continually deny sexual differences, while superficially welcoming sexual diversity. Paula confirms her support for Martina Navratilova and sorrowfully recounted that 'it was terrible what they did to that George Michael'. At its most evocative, Paula reminds her daughter that 'there is a reason why Sporty Spice is the only one without a fella'. Melanie Chisholm, the former Sporty Spice, actually appears on the soundtrack for the film, with the song 'Independence Day'.[56] For Paula, though, protecting her daughter from lesbianism became similar to protecting her from a life-threatening illness.

Within the Indian community featured in the film, lesbianism was not hinted at or suggested. The binary of straight and gay was not required to patrol the limits of womanhood. Jess's father merely stated that playing football is 'not nice. You must start behaving like a proper woman, OK?' The irony is that, because homosexuality is not even considered within the family, Jess's gay friend Tony is able to remain closeted. The consequence of this ability to hide sexual desire is that his identity is fragmented and torn – between Indianness and homosexuality – rather than integrated into a coherent sense of self. It is Jess and Tony who remain fascinating characters of the film. They are the most transgressive, one through sport and the other via sexuality.

Sport is one of the few sites that still builds overt obstacles of difference between masculinity and femininity. Such a division has been important historically. David Winner, in his discussion of Association football's origins in the nineteenth century, acknowledges that

> the game they created was rough and imbued with martial virtues. It was played by sturdy, lion-hearted men using heavy leather balls in thick, ankle-high boots in seas of mud. The Victorians preferred pluck and strength to sensuality and creativity. Their aim was to teach boys how to be 'manly'. This old English conception of football still underpins all that is best and worst in the English game. It accounts for the energy and drive that makes our game exciting. It also explains why the typical English footballer has always been a sturdy fighter rather than an artist. The interesting question is: why did the Victorians make football this way?[57]

The answer to Winner's question is that football was integral not only to the project of masculinity and nationalism, but also to the Empire. Through the 1990s, with the arrival of 'foreign' coaches and players, the British colonial rendering of masculinity – expansionist, staunch and dogged – was critiqued. The place of women in this narrative of change is more complex. In an era where women can fight in a war and men can take parental leave, sport remains one of the few places masculinity continually slams against feminine differences, pummelling feminine specificity into subservience. Women's role in sport – as mothers, girlfriends and wives – keeps the script of sporting success in a familiar patriarchal groove. Sportswomen make men (and some women) uncomfortable. A strong, resilient and flexible female body is capable of defence, challenge, critique and transgression. Sporting women literally dance through the categories of femininity and masculinity. The notion that heterosexual women are strong and self-aware is the last bit of news that the patriarchy requires at this time. To label straight women as lesbians demeans not only lesbians, but all women. Body competency and sporting success are not relevant to or reliant on sexual preference. Steve Redhead realized that 'the close and deep association between sport and maleness means that most critical attention is paid to actual or potential male homosexuality, but there is also evidence of strong antagonism towards signs of lesbianism in sport'.[58] Western dualisms pose unique challenges for women in sport, and unique challenges for male sports theorists:

> By arguing that they can compete with men in soccer, cricket and other games, women interested in substantial change are inadvertently doing a great deal to hold that reform back – they merely confirm the worst fears of Australian society at large.[59]

With Australian society – and its fears – reduced to either patriarchal or masculine panic, women appear to have no place in sport. That is why the language that encircles athletic women includes tomboys, butches and dykes.[60] The consequence of this terminology is that women in competitive physical activities excessively stress the accoutrements of heterosexual femininity, such as children or a husband.[61] The late Florence Griffith Joyner deployed extraordinary nail polish and fashion. Anna Kournikova maintained long blonde hair and short tennis skirts. Brandi Chastain, in displaying her bra, was continuing a long-term verification of feminine credentials from sportswomen. Beach volleyball actually regulated the bodily displays of its athletes. For the 1999 Pan Am Games in Winnipeg, women had to wear small sports bikinis, with a maximum – rather than a minimum – leg length on the briefs. Men could wear long shorts and tank tops.[62] The International Volleyball Federation had enforced what many sporting organizations implicitly believed: that women's sport only gleans attention when it is sexualized. The best example of this tendency was in the WUSA, where the media telecasts showed a greater number of player close-ups than for the men's game.[63]

Women can use sport to gain independence, self-awareness and self-knowledge. It offers a way to claim their body, and change the representational parameters of the sporting media. Fitness and sport are feminist issues. Unfortunately, too few sportswomen claim the feminist imperative of their actions. When asked if she was a feminist, Brandi Chastain replied that 'I'm not comfortable with that definition . . . Most people think that feminism is a negative word.'[64] Her reticence is understandable. The second wave of the feminist movement focused attention on social justice in the workplace and family. Recreation and leisure were rarely considered. Indeed, women's leisure time is spent allowing others to enjoy their leisure. It is clear that an evaluation of sport, fitness, health and exercise can offer new insights into feminism, and women's lives. Without feminism, though, Chastain would not have been able to participate in a well-funded sports programme at Santa Clara University. Title IX was a crucial intervention in women's lives at schools and universities. Passed through the US Congress in 1972, it proclaimed that no one could be excluded from participation in any educational programme or activity receiving government funding. This ruling meant that women finally received support and structures to assist their entry into sporting organizations.

Acceptance of sportswomen is only possible through visibility. For most women, school-based physical education is poorly funded, structured and administered. Because sport is a site of masculine success, young women in particular rarely experienced a safe environment in which to take risks, and to learn how to succeed and fail. Women are taught from an early age that they are fragile and unable to manage complex coordination and motor skills. While fathers play football, cricket or rugby with sons in the backyard, daughters frequently have their activities restricted to the house or the shopping centre. Therefore, young women rarely learn athletic skills in a safe environment. With women's representation in the sport media being low, there are few models of bodily competency to follow. If swimwear editions were discounted, women's sport would occupy an even smaller space in magazines and newspapers.

The difficulty is that particular sports are affiliated so strongly as masculine or feminine. Wider social practices and behaviours, with expectations about potency, flexibility, speed and power, are carried onto the sports field and the park. Masculinity is defined through highly ideological terms like aggressiveness, competitiveness, muscularity and strength. When women compete in sport, they dislodge expectations of appropriate behaviour. This instability has consequences for how their body is read and judged. The easiest way to guard 'appropriate' behaviour is through sexuality. In a homophobic culture, sport acts as a catcher of all the taunts, abuses and debasements of lesbians and gay men. As Cathy Young realized, 'right-wing broadsides against women's sports are explicitly based on a distaste for the transgression of traditional gender roles'.[65] If an athlete is transgressive in one realm of the body – the sporting – then it is assumed that there may be other transgressions in the realm of sexuality. Sportswomen are challenging. Patriarchs should be frightened of strong, resilient and competitive women. The key is that women should not be put off by sexualized labelling. Sexuality is not relevant to sporting performance, success or enjoyment. To allow such connections to be made – between athleticism and lesbianism – will allow women's sports to continually be attacked and patronized.

Sport is part of popular culture, and a method to socialize and initiate the player and spectators into the narratives of masculinity. While it will be a long-term project to dislodge the tight embrace between sport and masculinity, change is taking place. The Marylebone Cricket Club allowed young women into its cricketing programmes for the first time from 2003. Female members were granted entry to the all-male club in 1999. Finally, with this decision, young women will have access to outstanding facilities and coaching.[66] The cricketing establishment in Australia and England – like football – has great difficulty welcoming women into its numbers. Even sponsors have difficulty in knowing how to handle female cricketers. Joe Sillett, Managing Director of Woodworm, agreed to sponsor the Lancashire women's team:

> Cricket is growing in many areas, none more so than in the women's game. I am absolutely delighted that the Lancashire women's team will be using the Wand this summer. I am sure they will score lots of runs with the bat and in doing so enjoy hours of fun, as well as being at the cutting edge of the ladies' game.[67]

It is always a good guide to reverse the gender in these sorts of statements, to reveal the sexism. If a sponsor hoped that the men's team – representing the historic Lancashire County Cricket Club – would 'enjoy hours of fun', he probably would not be supplying bats for very long. Women play for pleasure and leisure, men play with aggression and competitiveness to win. Also, the demarcation of men and women – real cricket and the 'ladies' game' – ensures that dual standards separate the sport into two distinct trajectories that continually demean women and their successes. This is not only a northern English phenomenon. Women's cricket at the Western Australian Cricket Association (WACA) mobilizes similar language:

> Cricket is a fun, entertaining way of being involved in a team sport and can give girls who do not want to play the traditional women's sports of netball, hockey and softball the opportunity to expand their horizons.[68]

This statement is particularly ironic considering the team's name is the Western Fury, while the men's team is the Western Warriors. Women's sport can 'expand horizons', while men's sport is embedded in national competitiveness. Cricket and football are tests of masculinity, and as Richard Cashman and Amanda Weaver have suggested, 'those women who played the game achieved little recognition at best and ridicule at worse'.[69] Sport is changing, particularly at junior levels. In Australia, for example, the Kanga cricket programme includes both girls and boys, with an aim of developing specific cricketing skills, with all having an opportunity to bat, bowl, field and keep wicket.

British sport has left a legacy of masculine affiliations, allegiances, structures and standards throughout the world. This is a long-term consequence
of colonization. Between the dollybird and the butch, sportswomen negotiate a body image. When Jess looked for a role model for sporting success,
she invariably plastered David Beckham's image over the walls of her
bedroom. When she tried out for the Harriers, she wore his Manchester
United number seven jersey. She wanted to bend the ball like Beckham,
not kick a penalty like Chastain.

## That skinhead boy

It is no surprise that David Beckham at the time of the film's release was
the icon for a young Indian woman wanting to play football. She speaks to
his posters and buys his Manchester United kit. Garry Whannel provides
an explanation for this interest:

> Pictures of David Beckham have both expressed and challenged some
> of the dominant assumptions of masculinity and identity, and that is
> part of the fascination with his image.[70]

He is not a hard man of football, and actually undermines the masculine
baggage carried onto the football field. He certainly has talent, but, unlike
the life histories of George Best or Paul Gascoigne, has maintained a
groomed image of successful husband and father, alongside a professional
career. Best's multiple marriages, and Gascoigne's assault of his long-term
partner Sheryl three months after their marriage, confirmed a violent,
abusive and dangerous performance of working class masculinity.[71] It was
only the sensational claims of Beckham's infidelity in 2004 that finally
corroded his gleaming public profile of adoring husband and father.[72]

Unlike the majority of footballers, Beckham moved from the sports pages
through to women's magazines via his wife's success. He activated a hybrid
iconography, moving between working class masculinity and middle class
fashions. In deploying a mixture of masculine and feminine modalities,
he commodified a private life to build sports celebrity. When his safe
masculinity enclosed in a monogamous relationship was lost, so was his
marketing profile. John Williams has realized that he 'offers an interesting
– and mainly positive – alternative to the usual macho sports model'.[73]
Beckham revolutionized the visual culture of sport, connecting commodifi-
cation and nationalism in an easy, innovative and entwined fashion. Blond,
white, fit and muscular, he was able to capture a mode of Englishness that
was not available to either John Barnes or Ian Wright. There still remains
a 'problem' with black Englishness. Ben Carrington believed that we need
a new way of thinking about the nation, creating 'an expansive and inherently protean sense of black Englishness that could include the positionings

adopted by Wright *and* Barnes, and even Bruno'.[74] Such a troubled allegiance was not Beckham's concern. He occupied the position of 'golden
boy' throughout his English career.

Beckham, although admired through the late 1990s and early 2000s, suffered incredible hostility from terrace 'fans' and the press. His sending off
in the 1998 World Cup match against Argentina, and the subsequent blame
he carried for England's loss of the game, was only removed when he scored
against the same nation in the 2002 World Cup as captain.[75] Most of the
taunting from the terraces attacks Beckham's wife and children, attempting
to both feminize and demasculinize the footballer. Gary Whannel asserts
that

> The obsession with anal sex, which can signify both submission and
> humiliation, is suggestive of a working-class masculine culture disturbed
> by fears both of the feminine and of the homo-erotic. In this context,
> the supposedly emasculated Beckham offered a convenient symbol onto
> which such fears could be condensed.[76]

The intense masculinity of football fandom, and the incredible domination
of the stands by men, creates an artificial, pressure-cooker environment for
the playing of a game. Australian Rules football creates a distinct environment because of the more equitable distribution of women and men in
the crowd. New Zealand rugby again has a distinct modality. Julie Burchill
went so far as to state that 'there is something very gay indeed about football fans; not gay in a good, healthy, out-there kind of way, but gay in a
closeted, self-loathing, woman-hating sort of way'.[77] Such an attitude
explains why players' wives, and particularly Victoria Beckham, are so vili-
fied. Through the scandal of Beckham's infidelity, she was blamed for not
moving the family to Spain.

Beckham tracked a change in the English game, a shift in the ideologies
of class, masculinity and the nation. The flashiness of Best in the 1960s was
matched against the slick marketing of the 1990s, only to be replaced by
the home-based stability of the 2000s. Beckham's political, social and
cultural significance at the cusp of the millennium was captured though the
film carrying his name. There is no contradiction or paradox in a young
Indian woman finding support in his image at that time. Both were transgressive figures.

Beckham is a talented footballer. The bending of free kicks is Beckham's
gift and, like all special abilities, requires intense practice. It is so difficult
to accomplish because the trajectory of the ball is influenced by many variables in its path through the air, including wind flow, air speed and pressure.
The drag experienced by the ball influences its trajectory. The capacity
to weight a ball to the foot of a striker is the greatest gift of a footballer.
Yet his cultural significance is far more than his talent could explain.

Sport is superb fodder for cinema in particular: both are dramatological forms that feed on fear, desire, victory and loss. Through Beckham, sport advertised not only a new masculinity, but the potential for social movement and challenge. For Jess, David Beckham offered hope. In the privacy of her bedroom, with the Premier League on television and his posters encircling her, anything seemed possible. He showed that a game for English white men can be played by Britain's others, and even an Asian woman. She bent the game through Beckham. Wayne Rooney offers few such deviations in sporting masculinity.

# Chapter 7

# On the Blacks' back

There is a provocative tendency in current post-colonial theories to over-generalize the similarities between formerly colonized peoples. In Australia, Canada and Aotearoa/New Zealand in particular, there is an assumed similarity in the discovery and appropriation of land, and its long-term consequences. Significantly, though, Aotearoa/New Zealand is not a multicultural society, applying generic policy templates of diversity, difference and 'celebration' of many 'cultures'. Instead, the nation maintains a policy of biculturalism, marking and acknowledging two communities: the indigenous Maori and the (white) settler populations, the Pakeha. This policy has dense problems but also profound strengths. It serves to mark New Zealand differences, but also creates an important lens through which to understand sport.

There is no other equivalent study in this book that captures the rugby union domination in New Zealand. Australian cricket or English football cannot match its influence. Rugby has been present and an active player in the major moments and challenges throughout New Zealand's history. It has been summoned in both formal political structures and as part of popular culture. The affirmative differences between Maori and Pakeha, and the bicultural system itself, have constructed a network of cultural affiliations, symbolisms and history which, at their best, are complementary. At worst, Maoriness can seem to steady and reinforce Pakeha domination, while only offering an indigenous culture on the terms required by the colonizer.[1] Through rugby and its surrounding symbolism, Maoriness is a potent mechanism to create a national identity that is not inevitably and always an England in the South Seas.

Rugby, like all sports, is a point of tension where race, class, gender, generation, sexual and national differences are activated. The Englishness that travels to the periphery is cut up and resisted through its own alterity. The controversies surrounding Pakeha identity capture what happens to colonial power when stretched to the extremities of Empire. Pakeha, as a description, conveys many paradoxes. It can be a residual category – those who are not Maori. It can also signify those of European descent who colonized and continue to dominate the country. However, it also has a reparative function, a desire to claim and create a new identity in the Pacific, and distribute social justice and power in new ways. To retheorize the place and the role of a colonizer in society is a crucial intervention in creating a post-colonial state. This chapter investigates Maori and Pakeha identity, showing how this dynamic relationship has created not only a famous rugby team, but an overt translation of English rules for Pacific conditions.

## Back to the scrum

There are many specificities that transform a few islands in the Pacific into a fascinating site for sport studies and cultural history. A small population distanced from Europe makes New Zealand research a productive social scientific context for sporting experiments. The English tendency to colonize lands that were already occupied means that a characteristic of their imperial process was to force a dialogue between indigenous values and those of foreigners. Conflict and compromise are the two tropes emerging from New Zealand history. Jamie Belich, in his description of nineteenth century social conditions, stated that 'this was colonial New Zealand, and boring was the one thing it was not'.[2] Settlers are always unsettlers, naming and taming the landscape to gain 'sovereignty'. In New Zealand, unlike in Australia, this process was legally, socially and politically very complex, rather than the blanket, brutal judgement of terra nullius.

The origins of biculturalism are many, but there is a singular and obvious origin. The Treaty of Waitangi was signed on 6 February 1840 between the iwi chiefs of Aotearoa and the British Crown. The agreement created the nation state of New Zealand. While this Treaty may seem clear in its rights and determinations, there are believed to have been at least five different versions of the document in circulation.[3] In recognition of these differences, both the Maori and English texts are statutorily recognized. The pivotal distinction in meaning between the languages and treaties is between the two words *kawanatanga* (governance) and *mana* (pride).[4] In the Maori version, the former was used, suggesting that governance, rather than sovereignty, was being signed over to the Pakeha.

Three articles make up the Treaty of Waitangi (see table). In the years since the document was signed in 1840, grievances have erupted about land, language and self-determination. Soon after the document was signed, the Pakeha ignored article two, by asserting dominance over the territory, while the chiefs were abiding by the Treaty and continued making independent decisions. By 1862, the Native Land Act attempted to encourage Maori traditional owners to individualize land holdings, so that the purchase of land by settlers could be accelerated. Attempts by Maori to invoke the Treaty were frequently not successful. Only with the formation of the Waitangi Tribunal in 1975, and protests coinciding with the annual Waitangi Day celebrations, were Maori claims and disputes being addressed. The findings

|  | English version | Maori version |
|---|---|---|
| Article one | Maori gave sovereignty to the Queen | Maori granted governorship – *kawanatanga* – to the Queen |
| Article two | Guarantees Maori the possession of lands, estates, forests and fisheries | Concurs with the English version, but is less specific |
| Article three | Grants the Queen's protection and British citizenship to the Maori | Same as the English version |

of the Tribunal in favour of the Maori unwound the historical narrative of the colonizing power and signalled the arrival – at least with brackets – of the (post)colonial era.[5]

A treaty is designed as an evolutionary practice and is not unusual in the history of colonization. In fact there are 30 volumes of Britain's published treaties from 1820 to 1924. This collection, *Hertslet's commercial treaties*, placed the Treaty of Waitangi in Volume Six.[6] Treaties formed a way to undermine the cultural and spatial integrity of indigenous peoples, a tactic through which to claim land. What makes Aotearoa/New Zealand different in the history of colonial treaties is that the document has not been forgotten, and is actually increasing in its currency and importance. Biculturalism is an attitude and a framework of meaning, being a way to define and interpret the world.

While the terms and framing of the Treaty of Waitangi may suggest a colonial 'settlement', the Maori did not peacefully grasp the hand of their colonizer. Colonial wars were fought between 1845 and 1876. What made these wars distinct in British history is that the British failed to win any battles. The Maori won several and the rest were stalemated. To justify these military losses, the British developed the ideology of the noble Maori. The struggle for colonial domination became a gracious conquest between the superior British and the superior natives. As Keith Sinclair offered, 'although they [the settlers] instinctively assumed their inherent superiority to the Maori, the majority of the settlers themselves could not be regarded, by European standards, as highly civilized'.[7] Through this colonial gauze, by the end of World War I, a myth of the nation was played to its logical conclusion. New Zealand became one people forged on the battlefield. A Maori Battalion fought at Gallipoli. The nation became a partnership: Maori and Pakeha/British had become one people – New Zealanders. Rugby captured, exploited and performed this ideology.

Rugby is a tough, intense game with profound physical challenges. Enormous prop forwards stare intimidatingly at the other team's hooker. Jerseys are sullied with mud, blood and sweat. The singular focus by New

Zealand men on rugby suggests a social importance that must be carefully assessed. It is an agent of socialization, a team sport which encourages integration and social cohesiveness. This group solidarity requires both an intense physical commitment and a strong competitiveness, within a swathe of conformity. While sport has been used to separate colonizer and colonized, New Zealand rugby is different and distinctive. In the early years of settlement, there was little chance for leisure or recreation. As Scott Crawford has suggested, 'before 1900 there were few public events which drew as many people together as did rugby'.[8] The sport was introduced into New Zealand in 1870 by the colonial elite, but was played by a diversity of men, particularly in terms of class and race. By 1914, New Zealand national sides had played 123 Test matches against overseas teams, only losing seven. Perhaps most famous was the 1905 All Blacks tour of the United Kingdom. They lost only one game through a disallowed try scored by Bob Deans in the Welsh Test. The dominance and aura of the All Blacks have been compared to the Waugh/Ponting era for Australian cricket. Tom Dusevic argued that

> this team of intimidating, relentless and unromantic professionals is not unique to the South Pacific. The Australians are becoming in cricket what New Zealand's All Blacks are in rugby, inspiring awe but little affection, sometimes down but never out – the team to beat.[9]

Considering this dominance, it is not surprising that sport history, sport sociology and sport media studies are areas of growth in New Zealand universities. The University of Otago has a specialist Chair in Sport and Leisure Studies. The focus on rugby union means that it is far more than simply a national sport: it is a matrix through which history, race, culture and difference can pass.

The symbolism of rugby is remarkable. It can forge a link between early rural society and contemporary urban New Zealand. It can link amateur ideals within a corporate matrix. It is a tough sport with a lack of protective clothing, but requiring scrums, rucks and tackles. Collisions and dives are common. Rugby has been claimed as 'a dominant, if not hegemonic, New Zealand masculinity'.[10] It is a part of masculine socialization that encourages 'rugby values' of independence, aggression, emotional distance and dominance. Its confluence of rugby and masculinity means that women's sport and spectatorship are ridiculed or ignored. Similarly, women's domination of netball is rarely granted the stature of the (men's) rugby team. The New Zealand national women's rugby team have been world champions and there are more participants in this version of the sport than in Australia or England. Yet their success is distanced from national iconography and success. Ben Tune, a former winger for the Wallabies, remembers the complex convergences of masculinity, rugby and New Zealand:

It's another world, New Zealand . . . I remember when Tana Umaga had to miss a Super 12s game because he was attending the birth of one of his babies. The Kiwis were outraged that he would dare to do something so selfish – I just remember thinking at the time, 'are these people dreaming'.[11]

This ideology of personal sacrifice for the nation's rugby team has been best captured by Jonah Lomu's struggle to come back from nephritis, a rare form of kidney failure, and an organ transplant. His desire to again become an All Black was so strong that the normal kidney transplant procedure was changed. Instead of positioning the replacement organ in the lower abdomen and just below the skin, Auckland surgeons inserted the kidney inside the ribcage and behind other organs, so it would be cushioned in a rugby tackle. The memory of his seven tries in five matches for the All Blacks in the 1995 World Cup is sufficient to encourage any comeback.[12]

The tight embrace between rugby and New Zealand identity means that its symbolism is intensely political. The embodiment of this principle has been the long and complex relationship between the All Blacks and the South African Springboks during the years of apartheid. Through the 1970s and 1980s, New Zealand was one of the few countries that maintained any official sporting contact with white South Africa. There is a rationale for this connection. Rugby has a similar stature and cultural significance for New Zealanders and white South Africans. Maori players have often been restricted from touring South Africa. This racist exclusion tested the application and importance of biculturalism. Particularly, agitation emerged during the 1960 tour summoned by the slogan 'No Maori – no tour'. Norman Kirk, the Labour leader, required that the rugby union scheduled for the Springbok tour in 1973 be deferred so that the international backlash would not result in boycotting nations for the 1972 Christchurch Commonwealth Games. Similarly, the 1976 All Black tour of South Africa created a desire to exclude New Zealand from the Montreal Olympic Games. While this did not happen, 27 teams withdrew from those games in protest. The Springbok tour of 1981 caused a civil crisis in New Zealand history.[13] The disapproval against this tour split the nation, demonstrating more potently than any other event that sport not only confirms dominant ideologies, but is a node of intense resistance. The 1985 All Black tour was cancelled, only to be replaced by an unofficial Cavalier tour in 1986, of which most of the team were All Blacks. Despite this tour, no official matches were played from 1982 to 1992. In 1987, the first Rugby World Cup was held. The All Blacks won, and this team included some of the former Cavaliers.

The rugby relationship between Australia and New Zealand could never capture the intensity of the All Black–Springbok rivalry. In most areas of cultural life, the trans-Tasman neighbours are strong adversaries:

Why do Australians have accents?
So that even the blind can hate them.

Why do Australians have accents?
So that New Zealanders can hate them in the dark.

Australian rugby union is an odd formation. Never able to capture the playing or spectatorial popularity of Australian Rules football or rugby league, it is an elite – rather than a national – sport. The difficulty has been nationalizing the game beyond class and region. Ignoring these social distinctions, Spiro Zavos used gross readings of the landscape to explain the Wallabies' victory in the 1999 World Cup:

> A high-protein diet and the chance to play outdoors all year from early childhood creates the sociological explanation for the superior speed, energy and stamina of Australian rugby teams. The influence of the bush in toughening the Australian type, in mind and body, shouldn't be overlooked.[14]

Such dietary factors are masks for the social and regional exclusions of the game. Cultural narratives about middle class Anglo-Celtic men have been generalized to questions of landscape and a culinary obsession with meat. The bush myth and the changing Australian diet away from 'meat and veg' deny a movement towards urbanity, multiculturalism and Asian ingredients and cookery.

While Australia and New Zealand share colonizers and political customs, there is too often an over-stating of the similarities between the nations. The cultural policies are distinct, as is the place of feminism in the social system. These differences became far more serious in the debate over the 2003 Rugby World Cup. The trans-Tasman neighbours were meant to act as joint hosts of the competition. The New Zealand Rugby Football Union refused to agree to the conditions set out by the International Rugby Board with regard to stadium advertising. They could not afford all the corporate boxes – at all venues – being handed over to the Rugby World Cup Ltd. Australia abided by those conditions, and took over a sole hosting duty. As Daniel Williams suggested, 'Australians speak the language of the new rugby more fluently than New Zealanders do.'[15] Perhaps this has been caused because rugby has had to fight for positioning against other codes in Australia. Innovations such as garish jerseys, night tests and heavy sponsorship demonstrate these symbolic changes. In New Zealand, rugby confirms tradition, masculinity and the nation. Rugby union and Aotearoa/New Zealand configure a metaphoric relationship between sport and society that cannot be reduced to a simile. The All Blacks *are* New Zealand.

Beyond these Australian marketing innovations, traditions survive in the two major rugby-playing nations. New Zealand rugby contests against South Africa are of a distinct order. Williams expressed best the scale of commitment for the game:

> New Zealand is the only country where rugby is the national sport; that while the All Blacks aren't world champions, they are to rugby what Brazil is to football – the benchmark – and have been for 100 years. No one loves rugby more than New Zealanders.[16]

Before 1970, rugby union was the only winter sport in New Zealand schools. For white South Africans, it maintains a similar aura. Rugby, until recently, was compulsory for white boys in South African schools. Afrikaners transformed English ideas of rugby, adding a combative toughness to the game. In both countries, the dominant group has a passion for rugby. It is therefore not hypothetical or excessive to suggest that the cessation of rugby contact played a significant role in the dismantling of apartheid in South Africa. While New Zealand maintained contact, the two great rivals could continue competitive matches. Donald Woods made this affiliation clear:

> Springbok–All Black rugby was full of tradition and lore. For us it was the greatest of international rivalries, and during World War II whenever South African and New Zealand troops encountered each other, whether in a Cairo street or a London pub, they would scrum down on the spot.[17]

The great difference between these scrumming solders was the social system from which these teams emerged. Since the Treaty of Waitangi, Maori have been partners with Pakeha in the scrum and wider society. Conversely, pre-1990s South African teams were founded on both racial segregation and white domination. Maori were excluded from tours to South Africa before World War II. When the National Party assumed power in 1948, formal apartheid policies were instigated in South Africa. This overt stance is what started the questioning and then protests towards Springbok tours. South Africa was expelled from the Olympic movement in 1970. This loss of international competition meant that rugby tours became even more significant. In 1965, the Springboks' racial demands on the visiting All Blacks were severe. Prime Minister Hendrik Verwoerd stated that the visiting teams must abide by 'local customs'. It was at that point that the Prime Minister of New Zealand, Keith Holyoake, called off the 1967 tour, stating that teams could not be selected on the basis of race. After Verwoerd's assassination in 1966, John Vorster – a former rugby administrator – became Prime Minister. Recognizing the increasing importance of New Zealand tours, he allowed New Zealand to send a representative national team. The 1970 All Blacks included three Maori and one Samoan.

Australia took a clear stance against sporting contact with South Africa after 1971. New Zealand did not. Actually, throughout the 1960s, New Zealand voted against or abstained from every United Nations resolution that attacked South African policies. Once Robert Muldoon became Prime Minister, he made a resumption of rugby relations with South Africa a campaign issue in 1975. Even though he agreed with the Gleneagles agreement in principle, he had room to manoeuvre and rules to bend. It was only the crisis created by the tour of 1981 that caused an end to sporting contact. The test at Eden Park in Auckland on 12 September 1981 was a shambles, created by a relentless Cessna 172 aircraft that assailed the ground with flour bombs, and pink smoke flairs being thrown by protesters. This imagery will be tied to New Zealand rugby for the remainder of its history. It signalled an end to the myth of a unified, nationalized rugby. South Africa and New Zealand would no longer be bound by the scrum. Social changes would emerge. John Nauright and David Black confirmed that

> in the unexpectedly rapid erosion of white South Africa's will to resist exogenous pressure and the heightening of its longing to win re-acceptance into the international community, the impact of sport sanctions in general and rugby sanctions in particular was crucial.[18]

New Zealand rugby competitions with South Africa were enough to maintain apartheid policies. Once those final internationals were lost, the policies were finally put under pressure.

The complex and highly ambivalent relationship between South Africa and New Zealand requires much more theoretical attention. How a bicultural nation, which signed a treaty with its indigenous peoples, was prepared to contact a nation with a racial bar is a troubling social paradox. Scott Crawford asked, 'what would an in-depth analysis of Maori culture and rugby tell us about New Zealand society?'[19] Similarly, John Nauright admitted that 'we still do not understand Maori involvement with rugby very well'.[20] To understand something of this relationship, closer attention to the Maori role in New Zealand is required.

## No Maori – no tour

An odd transformation has occurred in New Zealand rugby within the last few years. For the first time in New Zealand history, more people are playing Association football than rugby. Even more interestingly, the Pakeha presence in rugby teams is declining. As Daniel Williams reported, 'Maoris and Pacific Islanders comprise 17 per cent of New Zealand's population, yet last winter they made up more than half the players in its four provincial sides – and four-fifths of those in Auckland's premier tournament'.[21] He argued that parents are placing their sons in 'gentler' sports, because Pakeha are unable to match the size and strength of Polynesian players. Termed 'white flight',[22] this view constructs a racially deterministic argument that repeats assumptions about the violent, powerful, but 'nobly savage' Maori. That such an argument arises now, after the resumption of sporting contact with the Springbok and an increasing interest in the Bledisloe Cup,[23] suggests that the critiques of the sport – in terms of gender and race – at the time of the 1981 tour may have been applied by parents more thoroughly than has been researched. It is clear that, for Maori and Pacific Islander populations such as Samoans and Tongans, rugby is the supreme sport, and enmeshed in the building of national and immigrant identities.

The confirmation of this argument is witnessed through the Maori immigrants who live in Australia. Rugby has provided a site of community building for Maori, and an avenue for mixing and acceptance with indigenous and settler Australians. While other immigrants celebrate and play soccer – and were placed in an 'ethnic ghetto' because of this allegiance – Maori have gained visibility, respect and economic advantages through the game. Maori women have also been active in sport, particularly in Sydney, playing netball in the winter and touch rugby in the summer. Paul Bergin has stated that 'the Maori contribution to the developing sport of women's rugby in Australia has . . . been significant'.[24] Using rugby, Maori have gained a distinctive status in Australia and have broadened out the support and player base for the game.

Such a cohesive function of rugby union may be decreasing in New Zealand. Mark Williams believed that 'biculturalism has clearly been advantageous in fashioning an acceptable national self-image in a world where colonialism and racism are bad for business'.[25] Biculturalism does imply that there are two 'monocultures' in one geographical entity, downplaying the diversity of iwis[26] and Pakeha origins without considering class, religion, age, gender and sexuality. Certainly, biculturalism has allowed the complex question of sovereignty to be addressed, which has also worried those desiring a singular nationalism. Glyn Clayton, who was editor of the *Christchurch Mail* for ten years, stated that 'I'm of the era where we grew up and thought we were New Zealanders. Now we are Pakeha and Maori. That's not good. Difference creates division.'[27] Difference also creates consciousness, identity politics, community affiliations and social justice. The concern is that a culture of grievance, guilt, retribution and blame is also assembled, with long-term consequences. The Treaty of Waitangi was not only an agreement, but a series of promises. Like all promises, it is in the eye of the beholder to determine whether or not they have been kept. Laws and regulations are a way to compel acceptance of indigenous rights. Whether this compliance is instigated with respect or is begrudged is difficult to determine. It is obvious that Maori have not been economically or socially successful through biculturalism. Chris Laidlaw, who was a Labour Member of Parliament for Wellington, recognized that 'it is now abundantly clear that the relationship has been severely distorted by history and that as a result the dangerous descent of Maori into a permanent underclass has threatened to become unstoppable unless there is some pretty bold political and social surgery'.[28] New Zealand is not composed of one 'people', or even two. Yet the duality of the iconography is stark.

The duality within New Zealand identity is best captured in a haka before a rugby match. The haka – and there are many, not only the singular war dance performed before the All Blacks' games – is a small part of the Maori dance repertoire. It is a way to express anger, threaten outsiders, welcome guests, pay respect or teach.[29] It is also an affirmation of difference. Utilizing the Maori language, it carries a history of struggle whenever it is performed. Such a distinction is important, particularly when pondering the broader media. As Ranginui Walker has affirmed, 'being Maori is . . . thinking there's something wrong with your television when it appears to be always hooked up to Great Britain'.[30] Maori men are strongly affiliated in rugby, but if it is a sign and vehicle of social change, then why are they not also well represented in the political or economic spheres?

The Treaty of Waitangi guaranteed Maori rights, and has also blocked the arrival of multicultural policies. It is argued that, to cite Richard Mulgan, 'for the Maori there is no other home than New Zealand and there is therefore a not unreasonable expectation that this home and its institutions should effect that fact for them'.[31] The flaw of this maxim is that when migrants leave 'the home', they can never go back, as the passage of both time and place itself alters their origin. The neglect of minority rights under biculturalism will be a challenge for the next generation of New Zealanders. Those groups who are neither Maori or Pakeha are 'frozen out of the debate on the identity and future of the country and disenfranchised with respect to the policies of multiculturalism'.[32] Is it right – is it reasonable – to allow immigrants into a country and deny them symbolic or representational rights in a nation? An obvious argument is that if migrants choose to enter a bicultural country, then they should not expect multicultural policies. However, a point will come when there will be an even larger collective of diasporic Indian or ethnic Chinese from Hong Kong, Singapore and Malaysia that can no longer be 'frozen out' of cultural debates. This will be a crucial moment in New Zealand, particularly considering the staunch refusal of the multicultural future witnessed in Chris Laidlaw's words:

> There are other ethnic communities who are deeply dissatisfied with the indifference of others to their cultural rights. They privately complain that the state is obsessed with pandering to Maori at the expense of 'multiculturalism'. They maintain, for instance, that the languages of minority ethnic groups should have the same status as Maori or English. They are mistaken. That would not only be a practical impossibility; it would be inconsistent with the status of our two mainstream cultures.[33]

Also, 'multiculturalism' signifies Australia: biculturalism signifies New Zealand differences from the larger trans-Tasman neighbour. The issue remains, though: if immigrants are outside the 'mainstream', then their citizenship status is indeterminate.

Silent throughout this discussion of migrants and Maori rights are the Pakeha. Politically, it is important that a Maori term was chosen to signify a new type of colonizing identity in New Zealand. It also signifies a connection with the land, but in a different way to the indigenous peoples. Paul Spoonley expressed this difference most significantly:

> I am not a European or even a European New Zealander. I am a product of New Zealand, not of Europe. I am not English, despite immediate family connections with that country. Nor am I Maori or one of the other ethnic groups that exist here.[34]

Colonizing Australians were never able to capture a similar level of distinction or centredness. The only option was to affirm a strident and frequently damaging nationalism. As was argued in the chapter on Bradman and Gilbert, the cultural battle was to change the connotations of the word 'Australia' from black to white. The extreme racism in the country, which continues to this day, is part of this project to give an identity to white colonizers. By using phrases like 'white Australians', 'black Australians' are implicitly critiqued or negated, because stages and grades of blackness are assembled. Colonizers are then able to ask who is black 'enough', feeding into such nineteenth century languages as half-caste or mixed blood. Therefore, 'Pakeha' as a word and description has had an important representational function, signifying a duality of Aotearoa/New Zealand, not a crushing, singular, xenophobic nationalism.

Obviously racism exists in New Zealand, and frequently in odd quarters. Winston Peters, long-term Member of Parliament and one-time deputy Prime Minister, has played 'the race card' better than most. That he is Maori has granted him a protection never accorded to Pauline Hanson. He was so popular at the start of the 1990s that he was featured on the cover of the national magazine *North and South* with the headline 'The man YOU want as Prime Minister'. Pat Booth believes that 'he talks the language of worried middle class New Zealand on issues like race, education and unemployment. He gives off an aura of conviction.'[35] He was able to capitalize on a fear of Asia in speeches, at one point renaming the Auckland suburb of Howick as 'Chowick':

> The rows of ostentatious houses in this very suburb, occupied in some cases by children whose parents have no ties to this country other than the price they paid for the house and who prefer to remain outside its shores.[36]

This unfortunate and inappropriate statement was able to capture and crystallize fear and hostility of outsiders. There have been waves of 'concern' about immigration in New Zealand, seen in the treatment of Dutch immigrants in the 1950s, Pacific Islanders in the 1970s, and Asian migrants in the 1990s. Nicola Legat justified this concern in a precise and convincing fashion:

> We are worried about a huge bundle of late-20th century changes: globalization, internationalization. Immigration is part of that bundle and it's easy to lash out at immigrants because they're closer than Wall Street whiz kids and university economists – a bit like kicking the cat.[37]

Biculturalism has created a culture of blame and retribution, but the 'mainstream' culture of Maori and Pakeha is displacing many dialogues about sovereignty and power through the shield of immigrants. Instead of recoiling in fear at 'Asia', a rethinking of New Zealand citizenship is required.[38] Further, there must be a decision as to whether immigrants are moving to New Zealand, Aotearoa, or a combination of the two. The problem in New Zealand is not the migrants, but a lack of social, institutional and educational support for them.

New Zealand biculturalism has served the nation's specificities. Made up of islands, facing few military dangers and not requiring a large population, it has been able to maintain a peculiar immigration history which has served Maori and Pakeha well. A future concern will be the role of non-Maori and non-Pakeha in the Aotearoa/New Zealand state and identity. Certainly, changes to the national iconography are emerging. With rugby becoming increasingly dominated by Maori and Pacific Islanders, Pakeha men are in search of a new dreaming.

## Innocent until proven male[39]

Rugby is a man's game, which means that the women who play it are frequently dismissed as foolish, a joke or butch. As discussed throughout this book, the closer a sport is to national ideologies, the more masculine its modality. That is why Association football in England, cricket in Australia and rugby in New Zealand possess such a marked status. But this function is changing. New Zealand has an embedded feminism in its structures that has been unseen in Australia. In New Zealand generally, national leaders, businesswomen and cultural institutions frequently betray a feminine face. The first international women's tournament in rugby was held in New Zealand in 1990. The Silver Ferns are a fully professional outfit, and in the last ten years have been far more successful than the All Blacks. Te Papa, the national museum of New Zealand, is one of the finest national museums in the world and was curated by a remarkable woman. Not surprisingly, Te Papa has been attacked, with an early, inaccurate and patri-archal review appearing in the *New Statesman*. Theodore Dalrymple has misconstrued and misrepresented the political importance of this museum, particularly in its presentation of sport:

> Political correctness is much in evidence. As is well known, the New Zealanders are keen on sport, and it is only natural, therefore, that in a museum dedicated to every part of national life there should be a representation of this activity. And since the sport in which the New Zealanders undoubtedly excel is rugby, it is also only natural that this should be the sport depicted. And so there is a photograph of a game of rugby in progress, played by a young, mixed-sex team. I watched the visitors as they looked at this photograph for any sign of amuse-ment, any sign of ironical detachment or intellectual rebellion, but no, they simply looked at it and moved on. And thus they accepted with sinister equanimity what amounted to a deliberate propagandist lie, that the most typical expression of New Zealand rugby is the mixed-sex team.[40]

Museums never present the past or the present as they exist(ed). They summon particular versions of a past for productive political purposes. Women will continue to play rugby. The bemusement of Dalrymple shows the disquiet that women playing a national sport can create.

One of the best-known works of New Zealand history is Jock Phillips' *A man's country*. Published in 1987, it is an investigation of national masculin-ities. While focusing on war and rugby, it is also a primary source to understand how Pakeha men gained identity after the signing of the Treaty of Waitangi. War and sport are, historically, all-male institutions offering cultural traditions of masculine bonding. What made the New Zealand experience unusual is that for the 40 years until World War I, there were only marginally more married men than bachelors, which meant that there was a large group of men without family responsibilities. Such a group provided the basis of a male culture, where men would be in the company of other men. As Phillips realized, 'if rugby . . . was an alternative to romantic love, love and domesticity in turn were seen as a betrayal of rugby'.[41] Men were therefore compartmentalized away from the realms of the feminine and the private. Social changes after 1945 led to a decline in 'bloke' ideologies, including less rugby success after 1971, a movement to the drinking of wine over beer, and the playing of other sports including soccer, rugby league and squash. The explosion of women working outside of the home also dislodged clear binaries of public and private life. Phillips stated that after World War II, 'as men settled in to their domestic niches and as the society became more bureaucratic, organized and urban, so men clung to images of exaggerated physical prowess'.[42] This frontier masculinity utilized rugby as a channel of communication of strength, resilience and modesty. The All Blacks, along with Edmund Hillary and Ernest Rutherford, remained national icons. Feminism, consumerism and gay rights intervened strongly in this ideology, altering the parameters of acceptable male behaviour. Masculine heterosexuality is reliant on the strength of structures and institutions. When they weaken, the dominance of men's stature is also weakened. A successful male performance has defined itself through a superiority to women. Feminism and radical sexual politics have shredded the ideology of the masculine.

The link between violence, masculinity and sport can be essentialized, and there is a danger in this mode of conceptualization. Instead, there needs to be a subtle investigation of the practices that link male bodies with masculine ideologies. Rugby is the most physically challenging of sports: participants survive it; they do not just win the match. Pain becomes an agent of masculinity. This statement does not suggest that women are intrinsically less violent: merely that women's aggression and anger must take different forms.[43] Both men and women can speak the language of anger and violence, but the modality and translation are distinct. If men are being oppressed, then it is other men who activate that oppression. Tom Morton maintained that 'men have received all sorts of benefits from their power over women and continue to do so'.[44] Both men and women do benefit from the exploration of multiple masculinities. The difficulty is that games like rugby encourage one mode of masculinity and reward particular types of competition, aggression and focus. In squash, conditions are distinct. Nikki Wedgwood conducted an analysis of Pennant Squash in Perth, and discovered that A grade women are allowed only to play against the B grade men's team. Such a system 'avoids placing the male hegemonic "system" at risk'.[45] She reported that men 'become extremely irate when being beaten by women',[46] because sport is based on the popular ideology that men's sport is intrinsically superior to women's competition. A confirmation of the preferred patriarchal role of women in rugby comes from Shona Thompson: 'Thank the ladies for the plates.'[47] This phrase encloses and limits women's role in sport, as a supporting, nurturing and feeding function for the men.

Sport in Australia and New Zealand has tested the athletic ability of the colony and also tested masculinity. It is a public, media-regulated performance that leaves women on the margins of the national imagining. Daryl Adair, John Nauright and Murray Phillips asserted that 'organized sport developed as an essentially male reaction to fears of "feminization"'.[48] There are consequences of a sex-specific physical culture. The greater violence of rugby union made it a more 'manly' sport. Roger Horricks realized that 'No woman could "take it" like a man can take it on the rugby field or the football field.'[49] Such an attitude expressed a desire for segregation from women. Horricks confirmed that 'male sport has always had violence built into it'.[50] Rugby intensifies that principle far more than other sports. The different stature of netball and rugby in national representational systems demonstrates how violence and masculinity are aligned.

Netball is as popular with New Zealand women as rugby is with the men. That it does not have the international recognition suggests much about the status of women's sport. John Nauright marked this distinction:

> While rugby has been the 'national' male sport, netball has held virtually the same status among women. Netball has not been given the same wider social significance as rugby by the male dominated hierarchy in the country, but it is widely popular as a participation sport and increasingly as a spectator sport on television.[51]

Although reinforcing femininity, it has also been a mechanism for social and political emancipation. While rugby is a game of scrums and strength, netball has minimal contact and agility. Therefore netball, like golf and tennis, can be 'suitable' for women because it encourages fitness and health, which is then deployed to satisfy others. Netball has critiqued established roles for women and Maori. For example, Meg Matangi was captain of the 1938 New Zealand netball team, the first Maori to captain a national team in any sport. This role provided a high-level position of visibility for a group doubly marginalized.

There is an argument to be made about the inclusiveness of New Zealand rugby. It appears to validate and embody the inclusiveness of biculturalism, and the colonial grit required to develop farms and agricultural industries in a tough environment. To view this ideology, ponder this statement from Spiro Zavos:

> The inclusive imperative of the New Zealand rugby ethic was so strong, even at its beginning, that there was never any hesitation or question about bringing Maori players into their game and encouraging them to take leading roles on the field as captains and tacticians and off the field as administrators.[52]

Maori players have been brought into the game on Pakeha terms, and have been excluded from the game when it suited the apartheid-led South African government. Most significantly, the role and place of women in sport – whether playing rugby or netball, or being spectators – have been written out of New Zealand history. Australia has had a long and difficult history of sporting exclusions. Feminism and multiculturalism have not assisted the process of inclusion. Between New Zealand and Aotearoa, there is a space for a new type of sporting memory, through a bicultural plaiting of black and white, masculinity and femininity.

# Conclusion
## Leaving the Boot Room

It seems appropriate in an era of accelerated or liquid modernity that the wide-ranging colonial trajectories of this book are sandwiched in the space between two English Premier League games separated by two years. On 15 February 2003, Arsenal beat Manchester United in the semi-final of the FA Cup. This result in itself was not unusual. The post-match fracas became the extraordinary part of the day's fixture. Manchester United's manager, Sir Alex Ferguson, entered the change room of Old Trafford so disgusted with the loss that he kicked a soccer boot, hard and fast, across the space. The only problem is that the boot connected with David Beckham's face, hitting the player one centimetre above his eye. That this old man of football was so out of control that he actually – even accidentally – injured one of his own players is enough to suggest that old modes of football and masculinity must be replaced with something different. The symbolism is resonant. Ferguson literally – and violently – passed the boot of masculinity from an older to a younger version, injuring Beckham in the process. One of the most valuable faces in world sport was hit and damaged by a manager of the old Shankly school. This sort of behaviour is no longer (was it ever?) necessary and should not be tolerated. Violence against objects too often spills into violence against people. Ironically in this battle over masculinity, when Beckham left the metaphoric boot room for Madrid he lost his iconographic status. Ferguson continues to rule Old Trafford.

South of Manchester, changes to masculinity were being overwritten by more xenophobic concerns. Two years after Beckham's booting, on Valentine's Day 2005, a fascinating London derby initiated remarkable commentary. Arsenal, still smarting from vitriolic and definitive defeats at the hands of Manchester United during the season, played Crystal Palace. Both teams were playing for their lives: Palace for survival in the Premier League for another season and Arsenal for direct qualification to Europe. This mismatched game resulted in a scoreline that reflected this disparity: 5–1 to Arsenal. It was a magisterial performance by Arsenal. They played focused, precise and grounded football. Martin Tyler, probably the greatest football commentator in the English language, relished this exemplary game.

At its conclusion, he offered an odd if apologetic corrective. While caveating his statements and aware of their xenophobia, he stated that the only flaw with this great match was that the Arsenal team did not feature a single English player. They were all 'foreigners'.[1] Indeed, not only the on-field players, but none of the entire 16-man squad were British.[2] In the capital of the old Empire, two London teams played the most English of games. The definitive winner in this match was a team bled of its English allegiance and origin. It took a world-class commentator to suggest – ambivalently perhaps – that this was a problem. The periphery was p(l)aying back.

Tyler's disquiet was echoed by the press. In the subsequent week, the *Guardian* asked, 'Are soccer's millionaires putting enough back into the game's grassroots?'[3] John O'Farrell recognized the humour amid the English tragedy:

> This week, another football landmark was reached when a Premiership team fielded an entire squad of foreign players. 'What is Arsene Wenger doing?' said the pundits. 'I mean, OK, so Arsenal are 4–1 up, but they completely lack the homegrown talent of their opponents . . . Oh, hang on, now they're 5–1 up.' In fact, it should have been six but we're stuck with these useless English referees. 'Where oh where are the top British players?' asked a fan at half time, sensing that he vaguely recognised the bloke serving him a reheated hotdog . . . Or perhaps the way to make it harder to bring foreign players into the Premiership would be to put Michael Howard in charge of the FA. Football stars wanting to come here from overseas would be detained for months in offshore prison ships, forced to undergo humiliating tests for HIV before being compelled to learn by rote the various triumphs of the British empire.[4]

Clearly the buttons about the loss of English footballing power were uncomfortably aligned with the decline of global influence. The desire for 1966's triumphs was punctuating the present (again). Culinary mediocrity was merely the sauce for the goose, and the hot dogs. All this disquiet was odd for 'the others' – 'those foreigners' – who watch English football beyond Calais. To me, viewing this live game via Sky Sports on the outer edges of Empire in Perth, Western Australia, where it was 4 a.m. on 15 February, the Arsenal team sheet seemed appropriate. This is international football, where the boundaries between centre and periphery are not only malleable, but permeable.

*Playing on the periphery* has tracked these movements in popular culture. This book has instigated a dialogue of difference between peripheral sports and sports played on the periphery. It commenced at the 'Homes of Football' in the Lake District in the north of England, and finished in a scrum deep in the South Pacific. Colonization has left a stark and frequently damaging legacy. From the dense and deep tragedies of Eddie Gilbert to the layerings of meaning carried on the backs of the All Blacks, English traditions have been accepted, resisted and changed. The social origins of cricket and rugby have been translated for antipodean conditions. These games have entered new societies, to shape different social orders in innovative ways. English games have become world games. New masculinities and femininities have looped back to challenge the old European order.

The study of sport is too often isolated from other scholarly practices. This is no surprise, as governments have perpetuated an economic neglect of sport, particularly in the direct aftermath of World War II. Only as there has been a realization that the health of the population is suffering through inactivity and a lack of physical culture are sport, leisure and fitness being considered in a less elitist and more productive fashion. But biases remain. Mark Latham, a former great Australian hope for Blair's 'third way', perpetuated the demarcation of sport from the more 'important' parts of life:

> At the Sydney Olympics, Australia continued its love affair with sport. The successful countries of the coming centuries will have a love affair with lifelong learning. Their national events will be based on innovation and technology, rather than tourism and sport.[5]

Latham, while critiquing the relationship between sport and Australia, retired from politics in his forties for health reasons. While I understand and concur with his passion for learning, I have always understood politics differently from Latham. It is more productive to talk to citizens where they are, rather than where I want them to be. Hoping that Australians will be more enthused by the opening of a new search engine than by the first day of an Ashes Test is delusional. More importantly, Latham did not recognize that actually there is no separation of education and sport, learning and tourism. Sport is part of education and critical thinking about the world. It is embedded in technological innovation and tourism. Throughout this book, I have shown how sport is a frequent vehicle for innovative interactive technologies, such as the National Football Museum in Preston, or monitoring social change, like the 'Homes of Football' in Ambleside. New histories can be tracked via the paradoxes of an individual year, such as 1966, or through the gauze of regionalism and isolation via the Perth-based WACA. The legacies and potentials of colonization and social justice initiatives can be viewed through startling films such as *Bend it like Beckham*, the narratives surrounding Don Bradman and Eddie Gilbert or the bicultural potentials of Aotearoa/New Zealand rugby. Politicians and academics can use sport to further post-colonialism, re-evaluate past injustices and create resistance to earlier modes of power and domination. Sport offers, to poach Tom Bentley's title, 'Learning beyond the classroom'.[6] Social and economic goals can be furthered through leisure. Ironically for Latham, his British third way colleagues have recognized the potential of sport for some time. The Blair Government's plan for sport was published in March 2001, and aimed to match funding for the elite with community-based initiatives. Termed *A sporting future for all*,[7] it stressed the significance of sport for health, relaxation, social cohesion and national iconography.

Sport has an agenda: it is movement with a memory. It is no surprise that Staffordshire University in April 2000 offered a sport course with a section on David Beckham. It is also no surprise that the forces on the political right continued their tirade against such a curriculum, linking it with the decline in literacy.[8] The key for sports theorists is not to celebrate the spectacles of imperial sport, but to demonstrate how cultural figures like David Beckham, José Mourinho or Wayne Rooney feed English identity after the loss of Empire. In moving beyond the boundaries of England, iconography and ideologies spill into Aberfan, Perth and Dunedin, being translated in its cultural passage. Sport is associated with a sense of place, revitalizing the local and the particular. Bland theories of globalization and interactive media cannot capture the complexity of this movement. There is a patchiness to supposedly globalized sports, as witnessed through the United States and soccer, or Australia and basketball.

David Beckham left Manchester United and England for Spain. The transfer has been jagged in its success. United has not been the same since his loss, but it has been rebuilt along more traditional lines. When compared to Chelsea and Arsenal, Manchester United remains the English team, with far fewer European or 'foreign' players than its London rivals. Yet ironically, the most English of English Premier League teams has the most international of audiences, branding and marketing. From this context, the Malcolm Glazer 'takeover' was no surprise.[9] Such a realization – of the worldwide marketing value of Englishness – demonstrates the odd and uneven nature of globalization. Sports history and historians face challenges catching the coat-tails of such cultural moments and movements, furore and failures.

Popular memory, as a phrase and project, is able to explain how and why sporting events are either remembered or forgotten. During the 1960s and 1970s, social history offered a radical reworking of the parameters for discussing the past. Reading 'against the grain' of evidence became a technique to resurrect those left out of historians' notebooks. The directives of feminism, sociology and gay activism were the major imperatives for this shifting understanding of history. Through the 1980s and 1990s, cultural studies furthered these interests in otherness, aligning a proactive paradigm with diverse disciplinary perspectives. Not surprisingly, by the turn of 2000 the framework had become a self-standing 'discipline' of its own, recognized and validated by research assessment exercises and academies for humanities and social sciences. This credibility and acknowledgement by 'the establishment' must – in the long term – blunt the political initiatives of the paradigm. Popular memory studies continues much of the 'dangerous' work of early cultural studies and social history, trolling the cultural surfaces for difference, inequalities and politics. It is not quantifiable, and its hypotheses are frequently not 'reasonable'. In an era when science has become the solution to social ills, popular memory studies can shift and challenge the relationship between nationalism and common sense. Through such a study, sport moves from the edges of the academy. The regional nature of many team sports, such as cricket, netball and rugby, undermines post-colonial critiques, while the focus of sports journalism on retelling stories of scores, players and matches blocks diachronic potential. Beyond metaphorical cartography, popular memory studies demonstrates that meaning is never instantaneous, and that the most interesting, controversial or passionate culture moves through time in unexpected ways.

This book has relentlessly probed the limits of English power. The old certainties of race and gender have been unravelled and problematized. The popular memory of sport has provided an avenue to question the role and place of taken-for-granted narratives. Post-colonial histories remain works in progress. In such a study, we forget about popular memory at our peril. Its collective aspect requires a wide-ranging interpretation of sounds, images, scents and feelings. The vivid nature of these recollections is context specific and non-sequential. The images, sounds and sensations live in the present, and wind our personal and community clocks. Sport is so important because it is able to jump-cut time and graft strong personal emotions onto an event that is shared by many. Therefore, it is the ideal site to explore personal, collective and popular memories. The key with all memory research is to find a way to 'handle' the silences in the historical record. Two such problems were confronted in this book, between the World Cup victory in 1966 and the Aberfan disaster, and the national celebration of Don Bradman and the colonial denial of Eddie Gilbert. The common bank of experience can frequently exclude the uncomfortable or the unjust. At its best, popular memory studies provides a strong reminder of who is left outside of consciousness, imagining and remembering.

In leaving Shankly's Boot Room, there is a realization that passion and emotion survive through popular culture generally, and sport more specifically. History is dominated by the visible, but many modes of remembering have been offered in these pages. There are the sounds, tastes and textures of a day at the cricket or an afternoon at the football or rugby, that are remembered long after the crowd has gone home, a dodgy hot dog has been digested, or the hard plastic seats folded away. We, as visitors to the past, move in and through the gauze of memory, threading and stitching their potentials into the cloth of identity. On the memory pitch of the world, we are bounced, caught and bowled.

# Notes

## Introduction

1 Perhaps the most ironic twist in the tale of football managers is Chelsea's José Mourinho. He not only has triggered his own chants from the fans, but is gaining aura and fame in wider popular culture. Manchester City fans at a Stamford Bridge away match in the 2004/05 season famously chanted, in recognizing his ill-shaven presence and poor-fitting overcoat, 'You got that coat at Matalan.' Matalan is a discount clothing store.

2 For example, during the 2005 British election, the then Conservative leader Michael Howard stressed his relationship with Liverpool Football Club. Guy Adams stated that 'in an effort to appeal to the common man, the Tory leader has been making much of his longstanding support for the (electorally crucial) city's highly successful club. The tactic is about to backfire. For in an interview in this week's *Time Out*, Howard owns up to receiving free tickets to home games in Anfield, where he's often seen in the director's box. Fellow fans won't be impressed by the fact that he isn't paying his dues. And neither will MPs, because Howard's entry in the House of Commons Register of Members' Interests makes no mention of his freebie tickets. With other MPs declaring all their sporting hospitality, the Tory leader's failure to mention Liverpool FC . . . appears to put him in breach of the strict rules governing MPs' conduct.' From 'Howard lifts the lid on his Liverpool footballing freebie', *Independent*, 7 April 2005, 10.

3 Also, such a project acknowledges the important shifts and changes in leisure research, best embodied by William P. Stewart's and Myron F. Floyd's special issue on visual leisure in the *Journal of Leisure Studies* 36, 1, Fall 2004. They were interested not in quantitative movements in their field, but in exploring visual literacy and the representations of leisure. They noted that while photographs are often used to capture 'a scene' in leisure, there was only one article in 15 years of the journal that presented visual images. This bias they discover towards 'the verbal and the numeric' also has a resonance in sports research more specifically, with sports science gaining credibility, funding and publicity ahead of critical and interpretative sport studies. Refer to W. Stewart and M. Floyd, 'Visualizing leisure', *Journal of Leisure Research* 36, 4, Fall 2004, 2. Further, their research in leisure studies is obviously part of a series of methodological movements in the social sciences post-postmodernism. For example, M. Banks, *Visual methods in social research*, Thousand Oaks: Sage, 2001; G. Bloustien, 'Envisioning ethnography: exploring the meanings of the visual in research', *Social Analysis* 47, 2003, 1–7; the second edition of N. Denzin and Y. Lincoln (eds), *Handbook of qualitative research*, Thousand Oaks: Sage, 2000; P. Gobster,

'Managing urban parks for a racially and ethnically diverse clientele', *Leisure Sciences* 24, 2, 143–59; R. Manning, W. Valliere and B. Wang, 'Crowding norms: alternative measurement approaches', *Leisure Sciences* 21, 1999, 97–115; D. Natharius, 'The more we know, the more we see: the role of visuality in media literacy', *American Behavioral Scientist* 48, 2004, 238–47; L. Pauwels, 'Taking the visual turn in research and scholarly communication: key issues in developing a more visually literate (social) science', *Visual Sociology* 15, 2000, 7–14; L. Richardson, 'Postmodern social theory: representational practices', *Sociological Theory* 9, 2, 2004, 173–79; and J. Ruby, *Picturing culture: explorations of film and anthropology*, Chicago: University of Chicago Press, 2000.

4 For example, the journalist Cheryl Stonehouse asked, 'Is Rooney turning into Gazza?' *Daily Express*, 13 April 2005, 28–29. The piece explored Rooney's relationship with Coleen McLoughlin and the rumours of violence in the relationship.

5 Blomgren and Sorensen stated that 'the regions in question are economically underdeveloped and geographically peripheral to the main centres of economic activity, with which they have a historically conditioned dependency relationship', from K. Blomgren and A. Sorensen, 'Peripherality – factor or feature?' *Progress in Tourism and Hospitality Research* 4, 1998, 321.

6 An outstanding edited collection that focuses on multiple sports is David Andrews and Steven Jackson's *Sport stars: the cultural politics of sporting celebrity*, London: Routledge, 2001.

7 N. Gingrich, *New York Times*, 19 April 1995, cited by I. Rogoff, 'Studying visual culture', in N. Mirzoeff (ed.), *The visual culture reader*, London: Routledge, 1998, p. 14.

## 1 We're not really here

1 J. Sugden, *Scum airways*, Edinburgh/London: Mainstream Press, 2003.

2 S. Clarke, 'Exhibitions > Book', email, 25 October 2002.

3 S. Redhead, *Football with attitude*, Manchester: Wordsmith, 1991, p. 153.

4 T. Blair, 'Prices and info', *The 'Homes of Football' at Ambleside*, email, 3 April 2002.

5 I. Rogoff, 'Studying visual culture', in N. Mirzoeff (ed.), *The visual culture reader*, London: Routledge, 1998, p. 16.

6 S. Clarke, 'Email – Interested parties', email correspondence, 13 September 2002.

7 These two transitions were presented by Patrick Loftman and Brendan Nevin in 'Going for growth: prestige projects in three British cities', *Urban Studies* 33, 6, 1996, 991–1019. Manchester was described as moving from 'Textiles' to the 'Olympic City'. Its Olympic bid was unsuccessful, the Games passing to Sydney in 2000, but the city hosted the Commonwealth Games in 2002. Obviously, sport is crucial to the regenerative strategy, particularly in east Manchester, and is promoted through the City of Manchester Stadium and the National Indoor Cycling Centre. The growth of museums has transformed Manchester into a place of cultural preservation and heritage management.

8 For a discussion of tourist marketing and its images, refer to Martina Gallarza, Irene Gil Saura and Haydee Calderon Garcia's 'Destination image: towards a conceptual framework', *Annals of Tourism Research* 29, 1, 2002, 56–78.

9 Stuart Clarke's website is mentioned in *When Saturday Comes*, 198, August 2003, <http://www.wsc.co.uk/webroundup/web198.html>: 'Although the site only contains a fraction of the 65,000 images archived by the museum, it still boasts an impressive pictorial map of the British game. The quality and range of the

pictures are superb and worth the wait of the less than lightning download times' (accessed 30 March 2005).

10 Some of these problems may be addressed by the professionalization of Sports Tourism. Refer to the website of Sports Tourism International Council, <http://www.sptourism.net/>.

11 While many new groups and journals have emerged in the field of tourism, sport has remained a minor consideration. *Current Issues in Tourism* featured a special volume on this topic in 2002, and *Journal of Sport Tourism* was originally available online. By 2003, the profile and importance of the journal was recognized when it was included in the suite of Routledge journals. For a more detailed presentation of the changes to research in sports tourism, particularly since 1995, refer to the 'Sports Tourism International Council Research Program', <http://www.sptourism.net/research.html> (accessed 30 March 2005).

12 For Stuart Clarke's journalist impressions of Euro 2004, refer to 'Looking back on Portugal', *The FA.com*, 4 July 2004, <http://www.thefa.com/Euro2004/News AndFeatures/Postings/2004/08/SClarke_Euro2> (accessed 30 April 2005).

13 J. Bkingre and A. Sorensen, 'Peripherality – factor or feature?' *Progress in Tourism and Hospitality Research* 4, 1998, 325.

14 E. Cohen, 'A phenomenology of tourist experiences', *Sociology* 13, 1979, 187.

15 J. Urry, *The tourist gaze: leisure and travel in contemporary societies*, London: Sage, 1990, p. 1.

16 B. Creed, 'Medusa in the Land of Oz', *Camera Obscura*, 21 and 22, 1989, 62.

17 M. Hansen, 'Pleasure, ambivalence, identification', *Cinema Journal* 25, 4, 1986, 10.

18 L. Gamman, 'Watching the detectives', from L. Gamman and M. Marchmant (ed.), *The female gaze*, London: Women's Press, 1988, p. 16.

19 J. Berger, 'Appearances', from J. Berger and J. Mohr, *Another way of telling*, Cambridge: Granta Books, 1989, p. 96.

20 For example, refer to I. Cook and P. Crang, 'The world on a plate', *Journal of Material Culture* 1, 3, 1996. In this piece, they show how geographical knowledge of food results in an objectification of cultural life through material culture. They also demonstrate how the positioning of London as a site to experience globalization actually results in a homogenization of food, and of material culture more generally.

21 J. Williams, 'Rangers is a black club', from R. Giulianotti and J. Williams (eds), *Game without frontiers: football, identity and modernity*, Aldershot: Ashgate Publishing Limited, 1994, p. 161.

22 *New Findings in FA Premier League 2001 National Fan Survey*, Sir Norman Chester Centre for Football Research, p. 6.

23 R. Moran, 'Racism in football: a victim's perspective', from J. Garland, D. Malcolm and M. Rowe (eds), *The future of football*, London: Frank Cass, 2000, p. 191.

24 J. Walvin, *The people's game: the social history of British Football*, London: Allen Lane, 1975, p. 4.

25 Lord Justice Taylor, *Final report into the Hillsborough Stadium Disaster*, London, HMSO, 1990, p. 44, section 255.

26 P. Kelso, 'Juve fans turn backs on peace move', *Guardian*, 6 April 2005, 30.

27 S. Barnes, 'Sound of fury breaks silence', *The Times*, 6 April 2005, 72.

28 T. Collins and W. Vamplew, *Mud, sweat and beers: a cultural history of sport and alcohol*, Oxford: Berg, 2002, p. 86.

29 S. Doson and J. Goddard, 'The demand for standing and seated viewing accommodation in the English Football League', *Applied Economics* 24, 1992, 1155.

30 'Ancient Monuments', *The Economist*, 17 April 1993, 53.
31 Ibid.
32 Southampton and Oxford United were clubs that had stadium projects blocked by local planners in the early 1990s.
33 Darlington took a major risk in the 2002/03 season, opening a new 25,000-seater stadium, while resident in the Third Division.
34 D.J. Taylor, 'Boots, boots, boots, boots', *Spectator* 290, 9085, 21 September 2002, 50.
35 Refer to S.M. Dobson and J.A. Goddard, 'The demand for football in the regions of England and Wales', *Regional Studies* 30, 5, 1996, 443–53.
36 Ibid., 451.
37 D. Campbell, 'Stars back fight to get the UK fit', *Observer*, 10 April 2005, 9.
38 T. Brooking, ibid.
39 V. Duke, 'The drive to modernization and the supermarket imperative: who needs a new football stadium?' from Giulianotti and Williams, p. 133.
40 Families of Hillsborough victims were so upset by the coverage of the events on television, endlessly watching their relatives being crushed to death, that they attempted to sue to be compensated for their grief. For a discussion of their case, refer to Richard Canning, 'The end of innocence: Britain in the time of Aids', *New Statesman and Society* 7, 331, 2 December 1994, 36.
41 Clarke, 'Exhibitions > Book', email, 25 October 2002.
42 S. Redhead, 'Always look on the bright side of life', from S. Redhead (ed.), *The passion and the fashion: football fandom in the New Europe*, Aldershot: Avebury, 1993, p. 5.
43 Old Trafford spokesman, in S. Mathieson, 'Reds axe for ladies', *Manchester Evening News*, 28 February 2005, 2.
44 A. Mackintosh, in C. Bailey, 'See elite women', *Manchester Evening News*, 28 February 2005, 2.
45 'Appeal from the National Football Museum for objects detailing women's football heritage', The National Football Museum, <http://www.nationalfootball museum.com/News/women%27s%20appeal.htm> (accessed 30 April 2005).
46 M. Bushell, ibid.
47 *New findings in FA Premier League 2001 national fan survey*, Sir Norman Chester Centre for Football Research, 2002, 2.
48 Ibid., 3.
49 J. Crinnion, 'A game of two sexes', *Guardian*, 13 August 1998, 16.
50 E. Soja, *Postmodern geographies*, London: Verso, 1990, p. 39.
51 E. Hopkins, *The rise and decline of the English working classes 1918–1990: a social history*, London: Weidenfeld and Nicolson, 1991, p. 227.
52 Clarke, 'Exhibitions > Book', email, 25 October 2002.
53 Urry, p. 140.
54 G. Kavanagh, *Dream spaces*, London: Leicester University Press, 2000, p. 148.
55 R. Hewison, *The heritage industry*, London: Methuen, 1987, p. 23.
56 To observe the difficulties involved in raising public awareness of local history, refer to Alison Gregg's 'Our heritage: the role of archives and local studies collection', *APLIS* 15, 3, September 2002, 126–32.
57 The Lake District is a popular cultural venue on its own, forming the basis of a successful mini-series named after the region. Many northern areas have a similar popular cultural resonance. The North Yorkshire Moors is '*Heartbeat* Country'. The region around Thirsk in North Yorkshire is where *All creatures great and small* was shot. Tourism provides opportunities for popular cultural encounters in unusual spaces. Sport is part of this rewriting of the landscape.

## 2 If Shearer plays for England, so can I

1 Similar divisions can be made about Manchester. The Reds – Manchester United – have often been labelled the Catholic team, with the Blues – Manchester City – as the Protestant team. Obviously such designations are historical and do change, but these origins are significant.

2 The best-known study of museums utilizing Foucault is Tony Bennett's 'The exhibitionary complex', *New Formations*, 4, Spring 1988. To witness how Foucault's theories of prisons have been used in museums, refer to Andrea Fraser's 'Museum highlights: a gallery talk', *October* 51, 1991. A fine book continuing this work is Tony Bennett's *Culture: a reformer's science*, St Leonards: Allen and Unwin, 1998.

3 The Latin 'museum' also conveyed the meanings of a library, study, gallery and temple. Also, as T.W. Adorno realized, the German word *museal* affiliates with necrology – the culture of death and mausolea, from 'Valery Proust Museum', *Prisms*, Cambridge: MIT Press, 1981, p. 175.

4 An outstanding history of the relationship between the museums of Alexandria and revolutionary France has been written by Paula Young Lee, 'The museum of Alexandria and the formation of the "Museum" in eighteenth-century France', *The Art Bulletin* 79, 3, September 1997, 385–413.

5 D. Maleuvre, *Museum memories: history, technology, art*, Stanford: Stanford University Press, 1999, p. 9.

6 Such a debate has dogged the early years of the Australian National Museum in Canberra. Opened for the Centenary of Federation in 2001, the controversy has been about the role, place and interpretation of indigenous history within the national framework. At times – critics have argued – indigenous questions have been granted greater attention than colonisers' achievements. Prime Minister of the time John Howard was outspoken in his critique of 'black armband' history. The question this controversy raises is the role of contemporary political leaders in determining the form and mode of history to be circulated in the present. To view an analysis of this debate, refer to Glenn Milne's 'Museum set for fight over who owns the past', *The Australian*, 30 December 2002, 11.

7 G. Kavanagh, 'Preface', from G. Kavanagh (ed.), *Making histories in museums*, London: Leicester University Press, 1996/1999, p. xv.

8 K. Moore, *Museums and popular culture*, London: Cassell, 1997, p. 104.

9 I am using strategy and tactic in a Gramscian sense here, and as mobilized by Michel de Certeau's *The practice of everyday life*, Berkeley: University of California Press, 1988.

10 S. Frith and J. Savage, 'Pearls and swine: the intellectuals and the mass media', *New Left Review* 198, March/April 1993, 114.

11 D. Wilson, *The British Museum: purpose and politics*, London: British Museum Publications, 1989, pp. 57–58.

12 J. Mordaunt Crook, *The British Museum*, London: Allen Lane, 1972, p. 32.

13 Sport offers a space for the fetishization of ephemera, rendering significant a single scoreline, programme, photograph or signature. The most evocative non-museum presentation of this material is the 'book' written and collated by David Walmsley with Stephen Done, *The treasures of Liverpool FC*, London: Carlton Books, 2004. It is part-monograph and part-photograph album, but extraordinarily many pages feature cut slots into which copied artefacts are placed. The reader can interact with the book, removing scorecards, photographs, player contracts, fan chants and facsimile tickets. As a presentation of the range and scope of not only sport media but sport visuality, it is an extraordinary 'book', encouraging myriad reading strategies.

14 S. Macdonald, 'Introduction', from S. Macdonald and G. Fyfe (eds), *Theorizing museums*, Oxford: Blackwell Publishing, 1996/1999, p. 1.

15 I. Karp and S. Levine, in *Exhibiting Cultures*, Washington: Institution Press, 1991, p. 16, stated that 'we could argue that the museum is a uniquely Western institution, that exotic objects displayed in museums are only there because of the history of Western imperialism and colonial appropriation, and that the only story such objects can tell us is the history of their status as trophies of imperial conquest'.

16 Maleuvre, p. 9.

17 Such a problem was discussed by J. Lewis in 'Build a museum and they will come', *The Public Historian* 22, 4, Fall 2000. She explored the problems involved in creating an Arkansas-based museum exploring 'what happened' at Little Rock High School in September 1957. She found that material evidence such as photographs was discounted by the 'individual experiences' and memories of the time. Lewis stressed the need to move beyond the experience of participants, while being sensitive to the expectations of those present at the event.

18 K. Moore, *Museums and popular culture*, London: Cassell, 1997.

19 Ibid., p. 77.

20 The International Football Institute (IFI) was launched at the National Football Museum Hall of Fame Dinner on 30 November 2003. It was a partnership between the University of Central Lancashire and the National Football Museum. Its aim is to encourage and develop the study of football through research and teaching. Refer to 'International Football Institute – University of Central Lancashire', <http://www.uclan.ac.uk/host/ifi/index.htm> (accessed 30 April 2005).

21 G. Kavanagh, *Dream spaces: memory and the museum*, London: Leicester University Press, 2000, p. 1.

22 H.F. Moorhouse, 'One state, several countries: soccer and nationality in a "United" Kingdom', from J.A. Mangan (ed.), *Tribal identities: nationalism, Europe, sport*, London: Frank Cass, 1996, p. 56.

23 The exception is Maribel Dominguez, the first woman signed to a (male) professional football club. In a packed press conference, she stated, 'I'm not frightened of anything . . . I want to thank all those who believe in me and ask those who don't to give me the chance to try. Maybe I will fail, but at least I will have tried', M. Dominguez, from J. Tuckman, 'Mexican football club signs woman', *Guardian*, 18 December 2004, <http://football.guardian.co.uk/News_Story/0,1563,1376493,00.html> (accessed 18 December 2004).

24 One of the reasons why Association football does not appear to have the popularity in Australia when compared to other codes is that the form of the game is highly fragmented. Not only is the national team – the Socceroos – disengaged from the National Soccer League (NSL), which morphed into the Australian Football Association (ASA) in 2004/05, but women's football and youth football are splayed in diverse directions. To gain Australian Association football the stature it deserves, the many modes of the game need to be aligned. The game has so many advantages in Australia: more young people play Association football than any other sport. Yet the administrative structures have been so poor that this enthusiasm has not continued into adulthood. The appointment of Frank Lowy as the chairman of Australian Football Association in 2003 has overcome some of these structural difficulties. In April 2005, Lowy finally orchestrated the movement of Australia from the Oceania to the Asian pool of qualification for the World Cup. This opportunity to be part of the World Cup finals will be important to the development of football in Australia. In the United States, similar structural problems emerged, with huge participation in

numbers, but (until recently) lacking an elite, successful team. The World Cup in the United States went a long way to building a unified competition. For a discussion of football in the US, refer to John Williams and Richard Giulianotti, 'Stillborn in the USA', from R. Giulianotti and J. Williams (eds), *Game without frontiers: football, identity and modernity*, Aldershot: Ashgate Publishing Limited, 1994. To monitor the changes to Australian Association football in the 2000s, refer to Ross Solly's *Shoot out: the passion and the politics of soccer's fight for survival in Australia*, Milton: John Wiley & Sons, 2004.

25 In 2005, the National Football Museum opened a 'Culture Clash' exhibition to commemorate the tenth anniversary of the 'Let's kick racism out of football' group. This exhibition focuses on black footballers in England, with attention to the 2002 World Cup in Asia and the life story of Pelé.

26 P. Lanfranchi, 'Exporting football: notes on the development of football in Europe', from Giulianotti and Williams (eds), *Game without frontiers*, pp. 36–37.

27 E. Hooper-Greenhill, 'Cultural diversity: attitudes of ethnic minority populations towards museums and galleries', commissioned by the Museums and Galleries Commission, <http://www.gem.org.uk/culture.html> (accessed 10 December 2003).

28 Moore, p. 15.

29 R. Hewison, *The heritage industry*, London: Methuen, 1987, p. 83.

30 P. Wright, *On living in an old country*, London: Verso, 1985, p. 33.

31 J. Frow, 'Tourism and the semiotics of nostalgia', *October* 57, Summer 1991, 133–34.

32 S. Stewart, *On Longing: narratives of the miniature, the gigantic, the souvenir, the collection*, Baltimore: Johns Hopkins University Press, 1984, p. 23.

33 'Hall of fame: the National Football Museum', <http://www.nationalfootball museum.com/News/support_a_united_legend.htm> (accessed 30 April 2005).

34 Ibid.

35 Ibid.

36 N. Klein, *No logo*, London: Flamingo, 2001.

37 The official site presents the difficulties they have faced: 'The National Football Museum is home to the world's greatest football archive. It is the Museum's intention to open up this archive for academic research in the near future. The facility will enable the many individuals and organizations with an interest in the history of football to benefit from this resource. Researchers, under the guidance of our invigilators, will enjoy accessing this unique and comprehensive archive. Currently, due to limited funding in this area, the research facility is unavailable but it is hoped that it will be fully operational in the near future', from the National Football Museum, <http://www.nationalfootballmuseum.com/research.htm> (accessed 30 April 2005).

38 B. Lomax, 'Democracy and fandom: developing a supporters' trust at Northampton Town FC', from J. Garland, D. Malcolm and M. Rowe (eds), *The future of football: challenges for the twenty-first century*, London: Frank Cass, 2000, p. 79.

39 One exception is Port Vale, which is one of the six regions in Stoke.

40 N. Hornby, 'The Arsenal story', in M. Wade (ed.), *Museums in Britain*, Macclesfield: McMillan, 1994, pp. 43–44.

41 The deployment of oral testimony in the National Football Museum is so successful because pictures are used as a memory prompt, then oral history is able to flesh out the context and meaning of the images.

42 MOMI was not only part of the British Film Institute, but a sister organization of the National Film Theatre, and shared the South Bank site. MOMI cost £12 million to build, and received no government subsidy. It opened in September 1988.

43  M. Roth, 'Face value: objects of industry and the visitor experience', *The Public Historian* 22, 3, Summer 2000, 48.

44  Evelyn Fox Keller and Christine Grontkowski extended this argument, believing that 'the notion that vision is a peculiarly phallic sense, and touch a woman's sense, is, of course, not new. Indeed, it accords all too well with the belief in vision as a "higher" and touch a "lower" sense', from 'The mind's eye', in S. Harding and M.B. Hintikka (eds), *Discovering reality*, Dordrecht: Reidel, 1983, p. 207.

45  For example, hypertext theory is a booming area, focusing on how the clicking interface of hypertext is changing methods of reading, away from linearity and towards different shapes of movement. Reading, in and of itself, becomes an act of production and design. To see a concise rendering of these ideas, refer to Belinda Barnet's 'Storming the interface: hypertext, desire and technonarcism', *Continuum* 13, 2, July 1999, 187–203.

46  G. Hawkins and J. Thomas, 'Museums and new media', *Media International Australia*, 89, November 1998, 8.

47  The outstanding media educator Len Masterman posed this problem about print and visual communication years before the World Wide Web. Refer to his book *Teaching the media*, London: Routledge, 1985, particularly pp. 1–13 and 235.

48  G. Warner, interviewed by R. Gibson, 'Ecologies of meaning', *Media International Australia* 89, November 1998, 14.

49  S. Cubitt, *Timeshift*, London: Routledge, 1991, p. 1.

50  'Take a trip to football heaven', National Football Museum, pamphlet, 2002.

51  'Final whistle?' *Lancashire Evening Post*, 14 October 2002, 1.

52  K. Howlett, 'Soccer museum chiefs' fury at closure claims', *Lancashire Evening Post*, 14 October 2002, 2.

53  There are a great number of educational programmes targeted at schoolchildren in the museum. They produce a National Football Museum education newsletter. During the World Cup in 2002, for example, the museum promoted an 'Understanding Asia' activity. Refer to 'Understanding Asia', *National Football Museum Education Newsletter*, Autumn Term, 2002, 1.

54  S. Karlsen and G. Baybutt, 'Roaring success', *Lancashire Evening Post*, 28 April 2003, 3.

55  The 100,000th visitor to the museum in 2004/05 visited on 22 March 2005. Importantly, considering the stress on north-west development and sports tourism in the north of England, the visitor was Kath Townsend from Chorley, Lancashire. She had brought her two children to the museum. They were given an opportunity to be photographed with the FA Cup, the European Champions League trophy, the UEFA Cup and the ball from the 1966 World Cup final. Refer to 'The National Football Museum welcomes 100,000 visitors in less than a year', National Football Museum, <http://www.nationalfootballmuseum.com/News/100,000%20Visitor.htm> (accessed 30 April 2005).

56  M. Bushell, quoted in Howlett, 'Soccer museum chiefs'; fury', 2.

57  'MP points finger at "shadowy figures" who want to take museum to London', *Lancashire Evening Post*, 17 December 2002, 2.

58  H. Davis, 'The fan', *New Statesman*, 23 September 2002, 57.

59  Ibid., 57.

60  N. Carr, 'The young tourist', *Progress in Tourism and Hospitality Research* 4, 1998, 309.

61  Cover subheading, *The Quays*, Salford City Council and Trafford Metropolitan Borough Council, 2002, 1.

62  Ibid., 3.

63 This was a significant tourist project, created through an initiative not only by the Salford City Council and the Trafford Metropolitan Borough Council, but also with private sector businesses including the Lowry, Imperial War Museum North, Manchester United Football Club, the Lowry Designer Outlet, Daytona Manchester, Golden Tulip and the Copthorne Hotel.

64 D. Crouch, L. Aronsson and L. Wahlstrom, 'Tourist encounters', *Tourist Studies* 1, 3, 2001, 264.

65 Refer to Sarah Kelly's article 'More to do in Indianapolis', *Information Outlook* 2, 3, March 1998, 33. She shows the multiple attractions of Indianapolis for the 'active' tourist.

66 A fine example of how many museums build into a portfolio of tourist visits is the 'Explore seven wonders: Lancashire county museums'. Seven very different museums are bundled up into a package to 'discover, enjoy, experience'. These museums are the Judges' Lodgings, Fleetwood Museum, Museum of Lancashire, Gawthorpe Hall, Queen Street Mill, Textile Museums and Turton Tower. Refer to the brochure 'Explore Seven Wonders', Lancashire County Council, July 2002. The website <http://www.bringinghistoryalive.co.uk> also provides information about the multiple museum destinations in Lancashire.

67 To view these characteristics of 'new tourists' in an Australian context, refer to 'Multidestination travel patterns of international visitors to Queensland', *Journal of Travel Research* 37. 4, May 1999 [fulltext].

68 'New findings in FA Premier League 2001 National Fan Survey', Sir Norman Chester Centre for Football Research, 2002.

69 Ibid., 3.

70 Ibid., 6.

71 For example, New Zealand has an Office of Tourism and Sport, which was established to take advantage of the hosting of the America's Cup. Refer to 'New Zealand found to have made millions out of America's Cup', *Xinhua News Agency*, 26 October 2000 [fulltext].

72 The Commonwealth Government of Australia released a *Towards a National Sports Tourism Strategy*, Department of Industry, Science and Resources, Canberra: 2000.

73 B. Ritchie and D. Adair, 'The growing recognition of sport tourism', *Current Issues in Tourism* 5, 1, 2002, 2.

74 B. Ritchie, L. Mosedale and J. King, 'Profiling sport tourists: the case of Super 12 Rugby Union in the Australian Capital Territory, Australia', *Current Issues in Tourism* 5, 1, 2002, 34.

75 Manchester City supporters are a clear example of fans who left much in the economy of the streets surrounding Maine Road. The businesses run by the British Asian community in Moss Side flourished on match nights. The domination of Indian restaurants and takeaways, and the laser blue shirts that filled these establishments before and after a game, showed that there was an economic benefit to be gained in a business spatially close to sporting venues. Having an Indian meal became part of the Maine Road experience. The difference was markedly seen when Manchester City moved from Maine Road at the conclusion of 2002, to be relocated in the City of Manchester Stadium, the venue for the Commonwealth Games' opening and closing ceremonies. Around this stadium, however, there are few eateries and pubs. Therefore, the experience of attending the football, which is always much more than being at the game, changes and those businesses near Maine Road reliant on a form of internal 'sports tourism' lose part of their business.

76 Once more, though, a 'multidestination' factor comes into play here. There are – of course – two Old Traffords. The Lancashire County Cricket Club is within

close walking distance of the Theatre of Dreams. As I will argue in Chapter 4 on the WACA, no strategy is in place to recognize the potential of sports tourism by linking these two Old Traffords. Visitors do recognize the connection, by utilizing the accommodation at the LCCC in preparation for a Manchester United game. For Manchester United, though, there is no record or mention that one of the centres of world cricket is within one kilometre of the ground. Also – and again this might be a factor working against the Preston museum – the transportation to Old Trafford on the metro from central Manchester ensures a convenient and quick passage to the site.

77  K. Worpole, 'The age of leisure', from J. Corner and S. Harvey (eds), *Enterprise and heritage: crosscurrents of national culture*, London: Routledge, 1991.
78  Moore, p. 128.
79  Moore, p. 128.
80  To monitor the relationship between oral history and popular culture, refer to the early article by Carl Ryant, 'Oral history as popular culture', *Journal of Popular Culture* 15, 4, Spring 1982, 1504–60.
81  Moore, p. 15.
82  D. Chakrabarty, 'Museums in late democracies', *Humanities Research* 9, 1, 2002, 9.

## 3  They think it's all over, but it isn't

1  P. Fussell, *The Great War and modern memory*, Oxford: Oxford University Press, 1975, p. 335.
2  R. Samuel, *Theatres of memory*, London: Verso, 1994, p. 3.
3  K. Jenkins, *Re-thinking history*, London: Routledge, 1991, p. 70.
4  G. Eley, 'Distant voices, still lives', from R. Rosenstone (ed.), *Revisioning history: film and the construction of a new past*, Chichester: Princeton University Press, 1995, p. 41.
5  A. Sked, *Britain's decline: problems and perspectives*, Oxford: Basil Blackwell, 1987, p. 1.
6  Robert Hewison demonstrated the application of this authenticity in his discussion of the Wigan Pier Heritage Centre, which was opened in 1984. The exhibition explored Wigan in the 1900s, not Orwell's Wigan from the 1930s. Yet even its rendering of the 1900s had gaps, including the removal of the Maypole Pit Disaster of 1908 where 76 miners died. Refer to Robert Hewison, *The heritage industry: Britain in a climate of decline*, London: Methuen, 1987, p. 21.
7  W. Van Deburg, 'The battleground of historical memory: creating alternative culture heroes in postbellum America', *Journal of Popular Culture* 20, 1, Summer 1986, 50.
8  Considering his remarkable success in the World Cup final, it is ironic to realize that Geoff Hurst was not the first choice as striker. Jimmy Greaves had been injured earlier in the tournament, and was left out of the side in the final.
9  To view a fascinating review of the refereeing of this controversial match, refer to Denis Howell's (the UK's first sports minister) text 'Soccer refereeing', <http://dialspace.dial.pipex.com/bob.dunning/howell.htm> (accessed 25 January 2005). This text was originally published by Pelham Books in 1968.
10  'Champions of the world', BBC Sport, 30 July 1966, <http://news.bbc.co.uk/sport1/hi/in_depth/2000/wembley/948302.stm> (accessed 25 January 2003).
11  The 1966 World Cup was a bad one for South American countries. Of the three South American teams in the 1966 championships, Brazil failed to qualify in their group, and Uruguay and Argentina were knocked out in the quarter-finals.

12  M. Johnes, 'Play up! Play up! And play the game!' *History Review*, September 2001, 26.

13  G. Madgewick, *Aberfan: struggling out of the darkness*, Blaengarw: Valley & Valem, 1996, p. 23.

14  Pupil, Pantglas Junior School, from 'The last day before half-term', <http://www.nuff.ox.ac.uk/politics/aberfan/chap1.htm>, 1999 (accessed 18 January 2003).

15  For an outstanding presentation of events in the Tribunal, refer to Iain McLean and Martin Johnes, 'The Tribunal of Inquiry into the Aberfan disaster', <http://www.nuff.ox.ac.uk/politics/aberfan/tri.htm> (accessed 18 January 2003).

16  Martin Johnes and Iain McLean reported that 'in the past months relatives of those who died in the Hillsborough disaster have been in court in a private prosecution against the two police officers in charge of that fateful football match years earlier. In bringing that prosecution they had to overcome numerous official obstacles. Like the people of Aberfan, they question who the state is there to serve', from 'Echoes of injustice', *History Today*, December 2000, p. 30.

17  'The Aberfan Disaster Fund', <http://www.nuff.ox.ac.uk/politics/aberfan/adf.htm> (accessed 18 January 2003).

18  Bereaved parent, 'The last day before half-term', compiled by Iain McLean and Martin Johnes, <http://www.nuff.ox.ac.uk/politics/aberfan/chap1.htm> (accessed 18 January 2003).

19  Ron Davies, the Secretary of State for Wales, paid £150,000 back into the fund. Importantly, Professor Iain McLean's role in raising the awareness of the Blair Government to this injustice is a pivotal reason for the returning of these funds.

20  Bereaved mother, 'The last day before half-term'.

21  The National Coal Board's mistake in its tipping procedure continued to have devastating effects on the Aberfan community. Sixty properties were flooded in October 1998 at Pantglas Fawr, where the rain caused the level of the River Taff to rise. The flood was made worse through the dumped spoil from the since-removed tips. In 1999, the flood embankment was raised.

22  The trophy itself has a story; it was stolen before the World Cup commenced, and later found by a dog – Pickles – under a bush in south London.

23  M. Johnes, 'Play up! Play up! And play the game!' p. 26.

24  K. Moore, *Museums and popular culture*, London: Cassell, 1997, p. 40.

25  Ibid., p. 50.

26  Cultural studies also has another advantage beyond working with popular culture throughout much of its history. It has also dealt with audiences, spectatorship and fandom – a necessary intervention to understand sports history. Without this work, too much of sport would be about match results, professional organizations and players. The reasons why people are passionate about a sport can rarely be revealed from such statistics or structures.

27  Moore, p. 121.

28  The ball was given to Jürgen Hemut by his father on his fifth birthday.

29  Pelé had a difficult World Cup in 1966, receiving incredible physical attention in the opening games, with Brazil not passing beyond the group stage.

30  Moore, p. 133.

31  In 'FM: The National Football Museum, Preston', the small brochure publicizing the museum, the ball is one of only six photographs featured.

32  This innovation resulted in the Infusion Soccer Ball being shortlisted for the 2002 Sports Edge Sports Production of the Year. An inflatable micropump was the key innovation. The award was eventually granted to TrailSkate, an inline skate that works on multiple terrain, becoming the mountain bike of the inline

skate market. To read a short article on this award, refer to Dianne Lofshult, 'Top sports product named', *IDEA Health and Fitness Source*, 2002.

33  An outstanding article on the engineering of footballs is Matt Youson's 'Golden balls', *Engineering*, June 2002, 28–29.

34  H. Wolf, *Visual thinking: methods for making images memorable*, New York: American Showcase, 1988, p. 11.

35  P. Young, 'Following English football from afar', England Football Online, 23 January 2002, <http://www.englandfootballonline.com/Features/FeatAfar.html> (accessed 25 January 2003).

36  Johnes and McLean, 'Echoes of injustice', 30.

37  Rescue worker, 'The last day before half-term'.

38  Bereaved father, 'The last day before half-term'.

39  D.J. Taylor, 'Turned off at last', *The Spectator*, 7 July 2001, p. 18.

40  D. MacCannell, *Empty meeting grounds*, London: Routledge, 1992, p. 23.

41  Bereaved father, 'The last day before half-term'.

42  To view the mode of this research, refer to Albert Tortorella, 'Crisis communication: if it had a precedent, it wouldn't be a crisis', *Communication World* 6, 7, June 1989, 42–44.

43  D. Kinchin, 'What is post traumatic stress disorder?' <http://www.burnsurvivors ttw.org/ptsd1.html> (accessed 18 January 2003).

44  C. Minett, from B. Summerskill, N. Randall and H. McDonald, 'Can wounds heal?' *Observer*, 25 August 2002, <http://www.observer.co.uk>/focus/ story/0,6903,780346,00.html> (accessed 18 January 2003).

45  P. Hodson, ibid.

46  A. Brien, 'Pornography of violence', *New Statesman* 76, 28 October 1966, 621.

47  Ibid., 622.

48  Ibid., 622.

49  F. Engels, 'The condition of the working-class in England', from K. Marx and F. Engels, *Collected Works 1844–45*, Volume 4, London: Lawrence and Wishart, 1975, p. 349.

50  I. McLean and M. Johnes, 'Remembering Aberfan', <http://www.nuff.ox.ac.uk/ politics/aberfan/remem.htm> (accessed 18 January 2003).

51  Taylor, p. 19.

52  'World Cup commentator Kenneth Wolstenholme has died in Torquay', Devon Sport – BBC, <http://www.bbc.co.uk/devon/sport/032002/26/kenneth.shtml> (accessed 25 January 2003).

53  Ibid. Such a realization is quite odd for those of us brought up with Australian Rules football and Australian cricketing commentary. It is common to have two or three commentators, with constant chatter about statistics, replays and history. For Australian audiences, the sparse commentary of Premier League matches is unusual to our taken-for-granted expectations of sport journalists.

54  Ibid.

55  *Great Football Moments from the '50s & '60s*, BBC Enterprises, 1993. This video is a re-release, which carried the earlier title of *They think it's all over . . . it is now*, thereby repeating the famous line from Wolstenholme's commentary.

56  P. Lanfranchi, 'Exporting football: notes on the development of football in Europe', from R. Giulianotti and J. Williams (eds) *Games without frontiers: football, identity and modernity*, Aldershot: Ashgate Publishing Limited, 1994, p. 23.

57  J. Sugden and A. Tomlinson, 'Soccer culture, national identity and the World Cup', from J. Sugden and A. Tomlinson (ed), *Hosts and champions: soccer cultures, national identities and the USA soccer World Cup*, Aldershot: Ashgate Publishing Limited, 1994, p. 3.

58 C. Critcher, 'England and the World Cup', from Sugden and Tomlinson (eds), p. 87.

59 Ibid., p. 79.

60 This internal colonization is also enacted and performed through football. H.F. Moorehouse showed that 'overall, a major element in the symbolism produced by the routines of football in the United Kingdom is a resentment of English power and pretensions, an element which echoes in many other places in the world', from 'One state, several countries', in J.A. Mangan (ed.), *Tribal identities: nationalism, Europe, sport*, London: Frank Cass, 1996, p. 58.

61 'Just Williams: the business of England', *Leicester Mercury*, 6 September 2001, <http://www.le.ac.uk/fo/publications/mercurycolumns/jw2.html> (accessed 3 December 2002).

62 I. Winstanley, 'Alphabetical list of mining disasters in Great Britain', <http://www.cmhrc.pwp.blueyonder.co.u/lodisalp.htm> (accessed 18 January 2003).

63 To explore how the Thatcherite decade 'managed' this transformation, refer to Sean Glynn, *No alternative? Unemployment in Britain*, London: Faber, 1991.

64 'World war, national decline and the English football team', *The Economist* 339, 7969, 8 June 1996, 91.

65 S. Glover, 'Why I hope England will be knocked out in the first round', *The Spectator*, 1 June 2002, 10.

66 D. Bull, 'More balls than most', *New Statesman and Society*, 1 March 1996, 24–25.

67 Glover, 10.

68 J. Coghlan with I. Webb, *Sport and British politics since 1960*, London: Falmer Press, 1990, p. 5.

69 Following the Australian example, an English cricketing academy has been established, with Rodney Marsh – Australia's big-hitting wicket keeper – at its head. In May 2003, Marsh went on to be a member of the English board of selectors, replacing Hussain, the captain of the English Test side. He left this post at the end of 2004 and returned to Australia, with English cricket in a far more successful position within international competition. His role in internationalizing cricket is clear. The success of the English team in the 2005 Ashes series demonstrates the ability of the ECB to transform the team by changing the coaching structure.

70 J. Cowley, 'Still haunted by the ghosts of '66', *New Statesman*, 3 July 2000, 15.

71 A powerful revisionist history of the role and impact of Richie Benaud on the post-Bradman Australian team is Gideon Haigh's *The summer game: Australian Test cricket 1949–71*, Melbourne: Text Publishing, 1999.

72 Andrew Ramsey named the Ricky Ponting-led Australian team 'New-age invincibles'. He stated that 'The greatness of this Australian team was further emphasised yesterday when it pulled off a stunning Test victory, the likes of which was last achieved by Donald Bradman's legendary Invincibles.' Ramsey was describing the victory over New Zealand at Christchurch in March 2005. The victory was made more extraordinary because Ponting misread the pitch and sent New Zealand in to bat. The Kiwis made an enormous score in the first innings, and the Australians were playing comeback cricket throughout much of the game. Adam Gilchrist was man of the match, hitting 121 runs from 126 balls, and being part of a 212-run seventh wicket partnership with Simon Katich, who went on to score 118 runs. Refer to 'New-age invincibles march on', *The Australian*, 14 March 2005, 17.

73 Cowley, 15.

74 Bobby Moore was not only England's captain, but also the captain of West Ham.

75 Refer to Patrick Carter's *English national stadium review*, Interim Report, 19 December 2001, House of Commons, London: HMSO, 2001, p. 13.
76 Carter, p. 7.
77 Cowley, 15.
78 The Wimbledon Men's Tennis Championship has not been won by an Englishman since Fred Perry was successful in 1934, 1935 and 1936.
79 Cowley, 16.
80 E. Yeager, S. Foster and J. Greer, 'How eighth graders in England and the United States view historical significance', *The Elementary School Journal* 103, 2, 2002.
81 Cowley, 15.
82 Johnes and McLean, 'Echoes of injustice', 29.
83 An intermediary stage between collective and popular memory is termed social memory. James Fentress and Chris Wickham believe that the characteristic of this formation is that it is 'capable of being transmitted'. Refer to J. Fentress and C. Wickham, *Social Memory*, Oxford: Blackwell, 1992, p. 47.
84 Pupil, Pantglas Junior School, 'The last day before half-term'.
85 'The Aberfan Tragedy', <http://www.webspawner.com/users/aberfan/> (accessed 18 January 2003).
86 I. McLean and M. Johnes, 'Corporatism and regulatory failure: government response to the Aberfan disaster', <http://nuff.ox.ac.uk/politics/aberfan/esrc. html> (accessed 18 January 2003).
87 I. McLean and M. Johnes, 'Summary of research results', <http://www. nuff.ox.ac.uk/politics/aberfan/eoafinal.htm> (accessed 18 January 2003).
88 V. Bogdanor and R. Skidelsky, *The age of affluence: 1951–1964*, London: Macmillan, 1970, p. 10.
89 I. McLean and M. Johnes, 'Remembering Aberfan'.

## 4 You've just been bounced at the WACA

1 Rahul Dravid's Indian team was well beaten at the WACA in 2004. Dravid described the WACA as 'definitely . . . one of the bounciest pitches I have come across . . . It's not the easiest of wickets to get used to. We played only two one days here so it can get tough. But once you are set, you can play your shots here', from 'India will carry no scars, says Dravid', *The Tribune*, 3 February 2004, <http://www.tribuneindia.com/2004/20040204/sports.html> (accessed 1 May 2005).
2 Merv Hughes – years after his retirement in 2005 – maintains the record at the WACA of 39 dismissals from 6 matches. At the conclusion of the 2004/05 summer, Glenn McGrath was only two wickets short of this record.
3 Brett Lee was quoted as saying, 'I'd love to go out there with a spade now and dig it up and take it home in my bag, but I don't think the WACA would appreciate that . . . I do love playing here – I enjoy the crowd, I enjoy the atmosphere', from 'Lee shares his WACA appreciation', *Sportal*, 3 January 2005, retexted on *BrettLee.Net – The Official Brett Lee Site*, <http://www.brettlee.net/articles/appreciation030105.php> (accessed 1 May 2005).
4 Glenn McGrath's inclusion in this list is not taken for granted. His form at the WACA has been uneven. It has seen his greatest triumphs but, for much of his career, it was the pitch with the highest runs scored off his bowling per wicket. On 19 December 2004, in spite of this track record, he captured the second-best figures in Australian Test history. In the victory over Pakistan, he recorded 8 wickets for 24 runs, the best Test figures of his career. Refer to Trevor Marshallsea, 'Sheep to lion at the WACA', *Sydney Morning Herald*, 20 December 2004, <http://www.smh.com.au/articles/2004/12/19/1103391638457.html?one click=true> (accessed 1 May 2005).

5 Rodney Marsh played 97 matches for Western Australia from 1968/69 until the 1983/84 season. He also played in 96 Tests. At the conclusion of his career – and like Dennis Lillee – he was awarded an MBE for services to cricket.

6 A discussion of Hayden's innings is found in Malcolm Conn's 'The spirit of Australia', *The Weekend Australian*, 11–12 October 2003, 1 and John Townsend's 'World beater', *The West Australian*, 11 October 2003, 192. It is also significant to note that the batsman at the other end of the crease during much of Hayden's innings was the Western Australian wicketkeeper Adam Gilchrist, who also went on to a stellar innings, scoring 113 runs.

7 E. Probyn, *Outside Belongings*, New York: Routledge, 1996, p. 9.

8 M. Coward, 'Nasser, it's a technical knockout', *The Weekend Australian*, 30 November–1 December 2002, 47.

9 T. Marshallsea, 'And it's a marvellous fighting comeback by the Poms – just kidding', *The Sydney Morning Herald*, 11 November 2002, 1. This heading was a response to England's second innings total of 79 – all out. The Australians took just under two hours to enact these dismissals.

10 S. Perera, '"Cricket with a plot": nationalism, cricket and diasporic identities', *Journal of Australian Studies*, 65, 2000, 22.

11 Of the 32 finalists in the FIFA World Cup of 2002, only England and South Africa play Test cricket.

12 S. Berry, 'Spreading the gospel', *Wisden Cricket Monthly*, October 2002, 50–53.

13 S. Fay, 'It's time for cricket to go global', *Wisden Cricket Monthly*, July 2002, 5.

14 Berry, 50.

15 For example, in the first 18 competitive games of county cricket in the 1998 season, no more than 1,000 supporters attended. Refer to Darcus Howe, 'It's that time of the year again', *New Statesman*, 24 April 1998, 13.

16 For a discussion of these conditions, refer to Jack Simmons, 'New committee set up', *Spin*, Summer 2002, 5.

17 To monitor the significance of cricket in India and Pakistan, refer to Ramachandra Guha's 'Batting for the nation', *UNESCO Courier*, April 1999, 30.

18 M. Fatkin, from Emma John's 'No coloured caps here', *Wisden Cricket Monthly*, July 2002, p. 16.

19 H. Bhabha, 'The other question', in R. Fergus, M. Geer, T. Minh-ha and C. West (eds), *Out there: marginalization and contemporary cultures*, Cambridge: MIT Press, 1990, p. 72.

20 B. Wilson, 'Padding up', *New Statesman* 129, 4439, 7 June 1999, 48.

21 E. Hobsbawm, 'Identity politics and the left', *New Left Review*, 217, May/June 1996, 46.

22 F. Keating, 'What treasures lie buried beneath the hallowed turf at Trent Bridge?' *New Statesman*, 15 August 1997, 25.

23 'Bowled over by tradition', *The Economist*, 14 June 1997, 94.

24 A remarkable story about the difference between English coaching and 'the others' was told by Christopher Martin-Jenkins. He stated that 'Clive Lloyd, another left-hander with a high backlift and mighty bat, hailed from across the sea in Georgetown, Guyana. He once attended a class for advanced coaches in England. All of them were asked to demonstrate the stroke they would play to a fast-rising, short ball on the off stump. To a man, the English coaches put their back foot across the imaginary wicket and played back-foot defensive strokes. Lloyd essayed a vivid hook over square-leg', from 'Foreword' to A. Hignell, *Rain stops play*, London: Frank Cass, 2002, p. xiii.

25 T. Greig, interviewed by C. Ryan, 'Tippexed out of history', *Wisden Cricket Monthly*, July 2002, 30.

26  S. Caterson, 'Towards a cricket history of Australia', *Quadrant*, November 2001, 26–27.
27  Coward, 47.
28  In the 2003/04 season, the WACA was the host for a Test between Australia and Zimbabwe. An Australian–India Test was not part of the fixture list. Therefore Tests are being systematically removed from the venue.
29  This title, besides being in clichéd usage, was also deployed by Jonathan Rice, *One hundred Lord's Tests: a celebration of the home of cricket*, London: Methuen, 2001.
30  Ibid., p. xi.
31  A. Hignell, *Rain stops play*, London: Frank Cass, 2002.
32  A. Barker, *The WACA: an Australian cricket success story*, St Leonards: Allen and Unwin, 1998, p. 196.
33  A. Gilchrist, from Kim Hagdorn, 'Angel knocks up another ton', *Warrior News*, 5 February 2003, <http://www1.vivid-design.com.au/WACA/publicpages/news. asp> (accessed 8 February 2005).
34  Another significant footnote to Western Australian cricket is Kim Hughes, born on Australia Day 1954. His cricket developed at the WACA, and he eventually played 70 tests for Australia (28 as captain). His achievements included nine Test centuries and 26 first class centuries from 216 matches, and in 1981 he was honoured as the Wisden Cricketer of the Year.
35  This site was granted to the Western Australian Cricket Association by Governor Broome in 1889.
36  J. Cumbes, 'Old Trafford and pop concerts', *Spin*, Summer 2002, 6.
37  Robert Mills, in his 'Field of dreams: Headingley 1890–2001', *Yorkshire Post*, 2001, p. 1, stated that 'in terms of creature comforts, the ground has been bottom of most people's list of Test and even of county venues for years, both for members and for the general public'.
38  N. Aisbett, 'On a good wicket', *The West Australian*, 27 July 2002, 4.
39  I. Carpenter, ibid., p. 5.
40  'The best bowling in Test cricket', <http://www.cricketworld.com.au/r0025301. htm> (accessed 8 February 2005).
41  For an excellent review of Indian sports tourism, refer to 'Now, sports tourism packages for you!' *rediff.com*, 13 April 2005, <http://in.redif.com/getahead/2005/ april/13sport.htm> (accessed 30 April 2005).
42  The changes of 1985 were also of a great scale. Twenty thousand tonnes of soil was removed and new soil was laid, along with a good draining system and new wickets.
43  The WACA website features views of its grounds. Refer to 'WACA ground 3D panoramic tours: general information', <http://www/waca.com.au/waca/ground. htm> (accessed 8 February 2005).
44  N. Bell, 'The WACA – a West Australian icon', *Australian Turfgrass Management* 1.1, February/March 1999.
45  Richard Winter left his appointment at the WACA in 2005 to become the Arena Operations Manager at the Melbourne Cricket Ground. He stated that 'The M.C.G. is the Mecca as far as venues go in my line of work and a place you strive to work at', from 'WACA curator secures MCG management role', <http://www.waca.com.au/news/news-detail.asp>?ID=460> (accessed 1 May 2005).
46  R. Winter, 'What a class act', <http://www.agcsa.com.au/atm/articles/vol42/ waca.htm> (accessed 8 February 2005).
47  'Dennis Lillee to develop WA's future fast bowlers', Media Release 92136806, Department of Sport and Recreation, 11 June 2002, <http://www.surfcam.dsr.

wa.gov.au/pubs/mediarelease/dennis%20lillee%20minister.asp> (accessed 8 February 2005).

48 'The Dennis Lillee fast bowling academy: introduction', <http://www.waca. com.au/cricket/dlfba.htm> (accessed 8 February 2005).

49 Ken Piesse particularly focused on the 'bad boy' image of Dennis Lillee in *Cricket's greatest scandals*, Ringwood: Penguin, 2000. Dennis Lillee is also known for the moment when umpires prohibited his use of an 'aluminium' bat. He hurled it away in disgust. This moment was remembered when Ricky Ponting attempted to introduce a reinforced carbon graphite bat. Refer to 'ICC to discuss Ponting's bat', ABC Online, <http://www.abc.net.au/cgi-bin/common/print friendly.pl?http://www.abc.net.au/sport/> (accessed 16 May 2005).

50 B. Ligman, 'D.K. Lillee', *Mead Living Magazine*, 5, 2005, 26.

51 Lillee, ibid., 26.

52 An example of this event management early in Dennis Lillee's tenure in leadership was the WACA ground hosting the Ford V8 Superbreakfast in the first week of May. This breakfast was an event linked with round three of the V8 Supercar Series in Australia, held at the Barbagello Raceway from 6 to 8 May 2005. Refer to 'WACA to host Ford Superbreakfast', WACA, <http://www. waca.com.au/news/news-detail.asp>?ID=457> (accessed 1 May 2005). This event was also an example of brand sponsorship, with Ford being both the official car supplier for the WACA and the sponsor for Dennis Lillee's Fast Bowling Academy.

53 On 27 September 2002, the WACA appointed Vivid to partner their online initiatives. The aim is to roll out online membership and e-commerce services. Refer to 'Vivid interactive and design', <http://www1.vivid-design.com.au/pages/ newsView.asp>?article=55> (accessed 8 February 2005).

54 To view the 'Sitemap', refer to <http://www.waca.com.au/sitemap/sitemap.htm> (accessed 8 February 2005).

55 The significance of information technology to cultural tourism was evaluated by Meral Korzay and Jinhyung Chon, 'Impact of information technology on cultural tourism', *Annals of Tourism Research* 29, 1, 2002, 264–66.

56 R. Hotten, 'How Melbourne broke away from the norm', *The Times*, 16 November 2002, 52.

57 The Australian Capital Territory has been able to create a sports tourism strategy, particularly centred around the Super 12 Rugby Union. For a discussion of this initiative, refer to Brent Ritchie, Lisa Mosedale and Jill King, 'Profiling sport tourists', *Current Issues in Tourism* 5, 1, 2002, 33–44.

58 Importantly, the aligning of sport, tourism and localism has been recognized at both an institutional and a cultural level in Ireland and Canada. The Irish Department of Arts, Sport and Tourism focuses particularly on the sustainability of sport tourism. Refer to The Department of Arts, Sport and Tourism, <http:// www.arts-sport-tourism.gov.ie/> (accessed 30 April 2005). Of particular strength is the Canadian Sport Tourism Alliance, <http://www.canadiansport tourism.com> (accessed 30 April 2005). Their focus on planning and the development of industry tools to both create and assess sport tourism is particularly advanced, being influenced by the more general palette of event management.

59 Intriguingly, the recognition of the WACA museum and tour as a site of tourism has come from Perth-based hotels informing guests of attractions. Refer to 'Regal Apartments – Western Australian Cricket Ground (WACA)', <http://www. regalapartments.com.au/index.site.attractions.attraction.568.html> (accessed 1 May 2005) and 'Quest Apartments – WACA Ground', <http://www.westend. property.questwa.com.au/index.site.attractions.attraction.708.html> (accessed 1 May 2005).

60 An excellent article on the social consequences of this suburbanization is Deborah Stevenson's 'Community views: women and the politics of neighbourhood in an Australian suburb', *Journal of Sociology* 35, 2, August 1999, 213–59.

61 J. Rajchman, 'Foucault's art of seeing', *October*, 44, 1988, 103.

62 'About the WACA museum, <http://www.waca.com.au/museum/about.htm>, (accessed 8 February 2002).

63 'Students clean bowl museum', <http://www.imm.uwa.edu.au/imm/waca.htm> (accessed 8 February 2002).

64 It is important to note that the virtual display of memorabilia and goods on the WACA website is improving. Refer to 'WACA museum gift shop', WACA, <http://www.waca.com.au/waca/waca-museumshop.html> (accessed 1 May 2005).

65 S. Macdonald, 'Introduction', in S. Macdonald and G. Fyfe (eds), *Theorizing museums*, Oxford: Blackwell Publishing, 1996/1999.

66 Peter Lalor wrote a six-page article on Adam Gilchrist with 'The Family Man' as his title, *The Weekend Australian*, 5–6 March 2005.

67 At the conclusion of Australia's domestic season in March 2005, Gilchrist had attained 280 dismissals from 65 tests. The three players above him on the rankings are Mark Boucher from South Africa, with 298 dismissals from 78 tests, Rod Marsh, with 355 dismissals from 96 tests, and Ian Healy, 396 dismissals from 116 tests.

**5 Our Don and their Eddie**

1 This event is still seen as so important that it was listed as one of the significant events of the twentieth century in Brisbane's history. Refer to 'Timeline – Greater Brisbane 1914–1932', <http://static.thecouriermail.com.au/federation/Timelines/CMFedTimelineBris2.htm> (accessed 8 February 2005).

2 T. Miller, 'Exporting truth from Aboriginal Australia', *Media Information Australia* 76, May 1995, 7.

3 Ibid., 8.

4 P. Mollon, 'Don Bradman', <http://www.freud.org.uk/bradman.html> (accessed 8 February 2005).

5 Australian history is also dominated by the 'larrikin', continuing the bush myth of a tough man overcoming a difficult environment. A strong article on how the Australian cricketing scandals fed into national iconography is Douglas McQueen-Thomson's 'The corruption of heroism', *Arena Magazine*, 39, February–March 1999, 5–6.

6 M. Knox, 'Wake up Australia, racism is a problem', *Guardian*, 20 January 2003, <http://sport.guardian.co.uk/cricket/story/0,10069,878108,00.html>.

7 J. Langer, 'Foreword', from W. Powell, *The Australians in England*, Stroud: Tempus Publishing Limited, 2001, p. 7.

8 P. Kell, *Good sports: Australian sport and the myth of the fair go*, Sydney: Pluto Press, 2000, pp. 10–11.

9 Steve Waugh demonstrated this reputation most clearly when playing in the first innings of the final Ashes Test in the 2002/03 season. He was playing for his captaincy, which was under threat, and the continuance of his professional career. On 3 January 2003, he scored 100, reaching that mark on the last ball of the day with a four. Mike Coward, the cricket writer with *The Australian*, was so impressed by this innings that he utilized the title 'Cometh the hour, cometh the Iceman', *The Weekend Australian*, 4–5 January 2003, 33.

10 An outstanding investigation of this colonial relationship in cricket is Grant Farred's 'The maple man: how cricket made a post-colonial intellectual', in G. Farred (ed.), *Rethinking C.L.R. James*, Cambridge, MA: Blackwell, 1996, p. 170.

11 A. Appadurai, 'Playing with modernity', in C. Breckenridge (ed.), *Consuming modernity: public culture in a South Asian world*, Minneapolis: University of Minnesota Press, 1995, p. 23.

12 M. Marqusee, *Anyone but England: cricket and the national malaise*, London: Verso, 1994.

13 Under Mark Taylor's captaincy, the Australian side won nine consecutive series without defeat. It was Taylor's team who transformed the 1990s into the decade of Australian international success, particularly when compared with the mixed fortunes of Alan Border's team, especially in the Ashes series. To view a history of this period, refer to Ken Piesse, *The Taylor Years*, Harmondsworth: Penguin, 2000.

14 P. Mewett, 'Fragments of a composite identity: aspects of Australian nationalism in a sports setting', *The Australian Journal of Anthropology* 10, 3, 1999, 358.

15 N. Wedgwood, '"Spewin', Mate!" – a day at the cricket', *Social Alternatives* 16, 3, July 1997, 29.

16 D. Birley, *A social history of English cricket*, London: Aurum Press, 1999, p. 135.

17 A. Mallett, *Bradman's band*, St Lucia: University of Queensland Press, 2000, p. 62.

18 G. Clark, 'Passport to nowhere', *Online Opinion*, <http://www.onlineopinion. com.au/Feb00/Clark.htm> (accessed 8 February 2005).

19 Remarkably, after the success of this outstanding team, indigenous cricket has been downplayed and ignored for much of the twentieth century. Ashley Mallett took a second indigenous team on tour, 130 years after the first.

20 M. Colman and K. Edwards, *Eddie Gilbert: the true story of an Aboriginal cricketing legend*, Sydney: Australian Broadcasting Corporation, 2002, p. 26.

21 On 18 January 1933, during the third Test match of the 1932–33 England–Australia cricket series, the Australian Cricket Board of Control dispatched a telegraph from Adelaide to the Marylebone Cricket Club in London. It was in this telegraph that bodyline was referred to as unsportsmanlike. For a discussion of this event, refer to Brian Stoddart's 'Cricket's imperial crisis: the 1932–33 MCC Tour of Australia', from R. Cashman and M. McKernan (eds), *Sport in History*, Brisbane: University of Queensland Press, 1979.

22 A. Mallett, 'Back on tour, 133 years on', *The Age*, 20 August 2001, <http://www. theage.com.au/sport/2001/08/20/FFXM6ARPJQCV.html> (accessed 8 February 2005).

23 For a detailed statistical analysis of his career, refer to Donald George Bradman, <http://www-aus.cricket.org/link_to_database/PLAYERS/.../BRADMAN_ DG_02000492 (accessed 8 February 2005).

24 Lord Desborough, *The Times*, 13 October 1927, cited by J. Williams, *Cricket and England: a cultural and social history of the inter-war years*, London: Frank Cass, 1999, p. 89.

25 R. Wilkinson, 'Ashes to ashes', *History Today*, February 2002, 36.

26 E. Bedser, in M. Geddes, *Remembering Bradman*, London: Penguin, 2002.

27 An outstanding book investigating the role of cricket in the West Indies is Keith Sandiford's *Cricket nurseries of colonial Barbados*, Barbados: University of West Indies, The Press, 1998. He expresses an excellent argument about Gary Sobers' role in creating a new nation.

28 Controversy surrounds Bradman's Freemasonry. Charles Williams interviewed Bradman for his biography. He recalled that 'I mentioned Freemasonry and he said, "Oh well, I only joined that because the Captain of St George said you

should become a Freemason." And gave up "the craft", as he said, when he went to Adelaide. To use the expression "the craft" shows that you're a bit more into Freemasonry than having joined it just for the fun of things, so I suspect he was probably a bit more involved. He didn't want to talk about it at all', in Geddes, p. 463.

29  There is also an important history to be written about the role and place of religion in Australian cricket. Alongside the famous anti-Irish and anti-Catholic charges levelled against Bradman, only one Jewish man has been chosen to play for Australia. Julian Wiener made his debut for Australia in Perth. His parents escaped the Nazi concentration camps, with his father derived from Austria and his mother from Poland. For a discussion of his career and the context of his selection, refer to John Harms' 'The Opener', *The Age*, 19 December 2004, <http://www.theage.com.au/news/Cricket/The-opener/2004/12/19/11033127 91530.htm> (accessed 16 May 2005).

30  P. Vasili, *The first black footballer: Arthur Wharton 1865–1930 – an absence of memory*, London: Frank Cass, 1998, p. 187.

31  H. Reynolds, *An indelible stain?* Ringwood: Viking, 2001.

32  H. Reynolds, *Why weren't we told?* Ringwood: Viking, 1999.

33  C. Searle, *Pitch of life: writings on cricket*, Manchester: Parrs Wood Press, 2001, p. 14.

34  M. Dodson, 'Healing body, mind and spirit – it's about time we took a stand', Queensland Centre for the Prevention of Domestic Family Violence, <http://brampton.cqu.edu.au/noviolence/speechesmickd.html> (accessed 8 February 2005).

35  Ibid.

36  P. Read, 'Reconciliation, trauma and the native born', *Humanities Research 9*, 1, 2002, 33.

37  Colman and Edwards, p. 62.

38  'Bowler is hurt by Bradman's talkie crack', *Smith's Weekly*, 7 February 1932, cited in Colman and Edwards, p. 137.

39  D. Bradman, 'Reserve judgement, let the Dogs play, with a tighter cap', *Sydney Morning Herald*, 24 August 2002, <http://www.smh.com.au/articles/2002/08/23/1030052974638.html> (accessed 8 February 2005).

40  Colman and Edwards, p. 152.

41  There was a fifth no ball in this over – the eleventh ball – which was a wide delivery.

42  This letter is reproduced in the plate section of Colman and Edwards.

43  This son, Eddie Barney, would go on to represent Australia as a boxer at the Perth Empire Games in 1962.

44  John Howard named two Australians and two Englishmen as his heroes: Sir Robert Menzies, Sir Donald Bradman, Sir Winston Churchill and Louis Mountbatten. Refer to G. Henderson, *Menzies' child: the Liberal Party of Australia*, Sydney: Allen and Unwin, 1998.

45  B. Hutchins, 'Social conservatism, Australian politics and cricket', *Journal of Australian Studies 67*, 2001, p. 57.

46  Don Bradman made frequent references to the 'mother country' in *Farewell to cricket*, Sydney: Hodder and Stoughton, 1950/1994.

47  B. Whimpress, *Passport to nowhere*, Sydney: Walla Walla Press, 2000.

48  D. Walker, *Anxious nation: Australia and the rise of Asia 1850–1939*, St Lucia: University of Queensland Press, 1999, p. 1.

49  One of the best analyses of immigration and media flows is the Stuart Cunningham and John Sinclair edited collection *Floating lives: the media and Asian diasporas*, Nathan: University of Queensland Press, 2000. In particular,

John Sinclair and Stuart Cunningham's 'Diasporas and the media', pp. 1–34, provides an excellent mechanism to move beyond a centre/periphery model of difference, marginality and diaspora.

50 R. Casey, *Confessions of a Larrikin*, Paddington: Lester-Townsend Publishing, 1989, p. 12.

51 G. Hage, 'Anglo-Celtics today', *Communal/plural* 4, 1994, 44.

52 P. Hanson, 'Appropriation Bill – first speech', Australian House of Representatives, *Hansard*, 10 September 1996, 2.

53 In a superb example of historical excavation, Ed Jaggard has established much information about the team. Refer to 'Forgotten heroes: the 1945 Australian Services Cricket Team', *Sporting Traditions*, 12, 2, May 1996, 61–79.

54 G. Haigh, *The summer game: Australian Test cricket 1949–71*, Melbourne: Text Publishing, 1999, p. 43.

55 G. Locke, 'Another innings opens', Kowanyama community – March 2001', <http://www.whichway.accq.org.au/projects/kow/cricket.html> (accessed 8 February 2005).

56 Geddes., pp. 338–39.

57 D. Bradman, Geddes, p. 340.

58 A. Jones, Geddes, p. 463.

59 H. de Andrado, 'Sir Don Bradman is dead! And world cricket is a widow', *The Wicket.com, the online cricket magazine*, <http://www.thewicket.com/2001_06_25/sub_story2.asp> (accessed 8 February 2005).

60 D. Bradman to Garry Barnsley, Geddes, p. 417.

61 For a discussion of this ceremony, refer to 'The boy from Bowral has come home at last', Bradman Museum, <http://www.bradman.org.au/ashes.html> (accessed 8 February 2005).

62 'Eddie Gilbert', Outdoor Cricket Catalogue, BATS/Handcrafted, <http://www.kdsport.com.au/outd/bats/Gilbert.htm> (accessed 8 February 2005).

63 'Queensland indigenous sports recognition night', Indigenous Sport and Recreation, <http://www.brisbane.qld.gov.au/council_at_work/supportcomm.../sport_rec_night.shtm> (2001) (accessed 8 February 2005).

64 'Another innings opens', Kowanyama Community – March 2001, <http://www.whichway.accq.org.au/projects/kow/cricket.html> (accessed 8 February 2005).

65 'The Bull Pen – news from around the state', *Cover Point*, Issue 4, 2 September 2002, 1.

66 K. Taylor and M. Fuller, 'Aborigines may get Treaty vote', *The Age*, 4 January 2001, <http://www.theage.com.au/news/national/2001/01/04/FFXWFGGVHHC.html> (accessed 8 February 2005).

67 Clark, 'Passport to nowhere'.

68 A. Mallett, 'Back on tour'.

69 'Eddie Gilbert', <http://www-aus.cricket.org/link_to_database/PLAYERS/AU.../GILBERT_E_02007444> (accessed 8 February 2005).

70 A discussion of Gilbert's symbolic importance is presented in 'Australia's shame', *ABC of cricket*, <http://www.abcofcricket.com/Article_library/art1/art1.htm> (accessed 8 February 2005).

71 J. Bradman, cited in Colman and Edwards, p. 263.

72 Lisa Keightley, top order batter for the Australian cricket team, expressed her views about the differences between the male and female national teams. She argues that 'she is not particularly upset by the disparity in standing and sponsorship between men's and women's cricket and points to the strides already gained in her lifetime. When the world-beating women's side returned to Australia from India in 1997, each player was presented with an invoice for

$15,000 to cover the costs of the tour. Now touring expenses are covered by Cricket Australia. The only thing that really bothers her is the lack of television coverage of women's cricket at home. "We've been on TV in every country we've visited, but not in Australia," she bemoans.' From Anne Lim, 'Hello', *The Weekend Australian Magazine*, 19–20 March 2005, 11.

## 6 Bending memories through Beckham

1 An incisive review of David Beckham's first season playing for Real, before the sex scandals dented his celebrity value, is Phil Ball's *An Englishman abroad: Beckham's Spanish adventure*, London: Ebury, 2004. At the conclusion of the book, he offered a strangely prophetic challenge to the footballer. Ball stated, 'Because there is something oddly endearing about the man, I found myself wanting Madrid to win. I didn't want him to fail – not because he was English but because I know what it's like to be in a situation where you suddenly cannot communicate what you feel, where you are visited by the abrupt sensation that you may have made a mistake, and that there is no turning back. I hope he does well in his second season, and that the club can concentrate a little more on doing what they do best. I hope he learns the language, and gets to spend more time with his kids. More than anything else, I hope he can begin to understand Spain. It's not easy, but it's well worth the effort', p. 271. In his recommendations for Beckham, Ball had predicted the seeds of future failure.

2 H. Kureishi, from N. Yousaf's *Hanif Kureishi's The buddha of suburbia: a reader's guide*, New York: Continuum, 2002, p. 10.

3 A major problem in recent years in Australia has been a specific decline in young women's involvement in sport. While there has yet to be a systematic study of this shift, which appears to be a rapid widening of participation between young men and women, the dilemma has been tracked by Sue Headley. She has suggested that 'the reasons behind the decline in young women's involvement in sport must also be addressed. Anecdotal evidence suggests that sport is considered unfeminine and female athletes as unattractive to boys . . . Some young women also appear to be socialised to accept a role in adolescence as spectators and admirers of boys' sport rather than participants in girls' or mixed sport. It has been argued that Australian sport, in general, has a patriarchal structure . . . While sport continues to privilege certain members of society over others, it will not provide equal opportunities nor will it appeal to all young people as an essential and positive activity.' From 'Local initiatives: background notes on obesity and sport in young Australians', *Youth Studies Australia* 23, 1, 2004, 45.

4 One of the most insightful analyses of Wayne Rooney was written by David Aaronovitch for the *Observer*. He explores why the press have shown such interest in Wayne and Coleen's fashion, interior design choices and public fights, particularly in the run-up to a British election. In a 17 April 2005 article titled 'Are we just jealous of Wayne's world?' he explored why Wayne and Coleen in particular receive this treatment. Aaronovitch asks, 'why does this matter? We have more important things to think about in the run-up to 5 May, you could argue, than one very young footballer's rather savage treatment at the hands of the press. But this is an election where, so far, one of the main issues has (for God's sake) been immigration – the issue without a problem. And I just wonder, given the facts, what this says about us. We seem to have become jealous of those with more, fearful of those with less', p. 5.

5 For example, UEFA's disciplinary committee accused José Mourinho of 'poisoning' football after claiming that the referee Anders Frisk had spoken at

half time to the Barcelona manager Frank Rijkaard at the Camp Nou in February 2005. UEFA charged that 'by further disseminating these wrong and unfounded statements, Chelsea allowed its technical staff to deliberately create a poisoned and negative ambience amongst the teams and to put pressure on the refereeing officials'. Refer to Matt Scott's 'UEFA rages at Mourinho "poison"', *Guardian*, 22 March 2005, <http://football.guardian.co.uk>/News_Story/0,1563,1443121, 00.html> (accessed 22 March 2005). The consequences of his actions resulted in a touchline ban, which only served to add to his aura. Matt Dickinson reported that 'the absence of Jose Mourinho from the dugout did wonders for the cult of Europe's most talked-about manager. The legend grew at Stamford Bridge as Mourinho triumphed not only against a formidable German outfit but also against UEFA, the media and whoever else the Portuguese was mysteriously alluding to last week when he talked about his struggles against "the under-world"', from 'Mourinho's "hat-trick" magic', *The Times*, 7 April 2005, 80.

6  Jerry Smith, the women's soccer coach at Santa Clara, stated that 'I'd have to say that right now women's soccer is probably at least equal in popularity to men's soccer. It may even have a better following than men's soccer.' Interview by Kevin Newell, 'Mr Smith goes to Santa Clara', *Coach and Athletic Director*, December 2002, 47.

7  S. Hatfield, 'It's the world's "beautiful game" except for here in the US', *Advertising Age*, 2002 [fulltext article].

8  'Brandi Chastain', <http://www.paralumun.com/celebchastain.htm> (accessed 5 February 2003).

9  The *Newsweek* cover is particularly interesting. Featuring a photograph of Chastain with knees in the green turf and shirt in hands, the title reads 'Girls rule'. It is ironic how women's sporting success is reduced to 'Girl power'. At the time this photograph was taken, Chastain was 30, and a veteran in the sport. For a discussion of language in women's sport, refer to the excellent article by Joli Sandoz, 'Victory? New language for sportswomen', *Women and Language* 23, Spring 2000, 33–36.

10  There was publicity at the time that Nike orchestrated Brandi Chastain's shirt removal at the World Cup, to grant exposure to their brand. Nike's intervention in women's soccer is an important one, as Adidas is the international brand for soccer. Therefore, by emphasizing women's soccer, they were able to create a differentiation in the market. Refer to Hilary Cassidy's 'Playing with a new attitude', *Brandweek*, 30 July 2001.

11  This image was reproduced in the 'Cool and Nasty Gallery' on the *Muscles at work* website, <http://muscles_at_work.tripod.com/html/cool_and_nasty02.html> (accessed 5 February 2003).

12  M. Evans, 'Catching up with Brandi Chastain', <http://studentssports.thein siders.com/2/50797.html> (13 June 2002) (accessed 5 February 2003).

13  '10 burning questions for Brandi Chastain', <http://www.espn.go.com/page2/s/ questions/chastain010618.html> (accessed 5 February 2003).

14  Ibid.

15  'Brandi Chastain', <http://www.oceansiderevolution.com/BrandiChastain.htm> (accessed 5 February 2003).

16  M. Bamberger, 'Dream come true', *Sports Illustrated* 91, 24, 20 December 1999 [fulltext article].

17  'The "Babe factor" in women's soccer', *Business Week*, 3639, 26 July 1999, 118.

18  B. Clinton, 'Remarks honoring the 1999 Women's World Cup Champion United States Soccer Team', *Weekly compilation of presidential documents* 35, 29, 26 July 1999, 1405.

19  For example, the 2005 FA Cup between Manchester United and Arsenal was decided through a penalty shootout.

20  T. Carson, 'The feminine physique', *Esquire* 134, 1, July 2000, 40.

21  Ibid.

22  An outstanding analysis of the World Cup victory, and the inequalities in infrastructure confronting the women's team, is Jere Longman's *The girls of summer: the US women's soccer team and how it changed the world*, New York: Harper-Collins Publishers, 2001.

23  Roger Le Grove Rogers reported that 'in an interview with the head of the women's section of Arsenal Football club, after they had won the triple (FA Cup, League, and League Cup) but barely beat Fulham in the Cup Final, he was asked if he thought that there should be a women's professional league. His answer was that it was not time yet . . . and he did not think that it would be for a few years. No one asked him why a rich Arsenal club, that was supported by women's money as well as men, could not supply financial backing for a talented women's team. Fulham has obviously been successful with its men's team and we predict that their women's team will soon shake up the establishment.' From 'Commentary', Womens [sic] soccer world, <http://www.womensoccer.com/refs/comment_refs/comm-england_3august01.html> (accessed 25 January 2003).

24  'Commentary', 17 December 2001, <http://www.womensoccer.com/refs/comment_refs/comm-eng_17dec01.html> (accessed 25 January 2003).

25  For a review of her career, refer to 'News: farewell game for Mia, Julie and Joy', *WUSA*, 20 November 2004, <http://www.wusa.com/news/?id=1716> (accessed 20 April 2005).

26  For information about this agreement between Paxson Communications and the WUSA, refer to 'Women's soccer to be broadcast on PAX', *Marketing to Women*, January 2002, 9.

27  'Commentary', 29 October 2002, <http://www.womensoccer.com/refs/comment_refs/com-tvcom_29oct02.html> (accessed 25 January 2003).

28  D. Rovell, 'Still a business, not a cause', *ESPN.com*, 15 September 2003, <http://espn.go.com/sportsbusiness/s/2003/0915/1616775.html> (accessed 20 April 2005).

29  These figures are derived from Rovell, ibid.

30  G. Cavalli in Rovell.

31  M. Voepel, 'From the valley to the peak in 24 hours', *ESPN.com*, 16 September 2003, <http://espn.go.com/wnba/columns/voepel/1617900.html> (accessed 20 April 2005).

32  To monitor the profile of this team, refer to 'Fab Five look for a golden ending', *Newsobserver.com*, 25 August 2004, <http://www.newsobserver.com/24hour/olympic/soccer/v-printer/story/1599967p-924 (accessed 8 May 2005).

33  T. Antonucci, quoted in 'News: women's soccer initiative WSII to steer WUSA re-launch', *WUSA*, 7 December 2004, <http://www.wusa.com/news/?id=1723, accessed 20 April 2005.

34  K. Kennedy and R. Deitsch, 'Sports beat', *Sports Illustrated* 97, 20, 18 November 2002, 36.

35  A. Markovits and S. Hellerman, *Offside: soccer and American exceptionalism*, Princeton: Princeton University Press, 2001, p. 15.

36  'The Ultimate New Zealand Soccer website', <http://www.ultimatenzsoccer.com/id823_cf.htm> (accessed 5 February 2003).

37  B. Chastain, 'A whole new ball game', *Newsweek* 134, 17, 25 October 1999, 76.

38 'The Matildas', <http://www.matildas.org.au/frmain.htm> (accessed 25 January 2003).
39 A. Yatzus, 'It's a GOOAAALLLL!!!!', *Newsweek* 134, 6, 9 August 1999, 15.
40 'Team USA star goalkeeper Briana Scurry's greatness ignored by media in World Cup soccer victory', *Jet*, 2 August 1997, <http://www.memofix.ca/usa-soccer-cup.html> (accessed 6 May 2005).
41 Ibid.
42 G. Wahl, 'She's a keeper', *Sports Illustrated* 91, 2, 12 July 1999, 36.
43 G. Wahl, 'Question 5: why isn't the US women's soccer team smiling?' *Sports Illustrated* 93, 10, 11 September 2000, 94.
44 J. Wyllie, 'Still the one', <http://www.findarticles.com/p/articles/mi_m0FCN/is_1_26/ai_98922383/print> (2003) (accessed 8 May 2005).
45 'Keeperqueen18', 'Forums > Women's national team players / United soccer athletes', 25 April 2005, *USA message board forums – favorite player form 2004*, <http://forums.unitedsoccerathletes.com/messageview.cfm?catid=3&threadid=1 0561&> (accessed 8 May 2005).
46 R. Manning, quoted in E. Yates, 'Reaching goals on and off the field', *Black Issues in Higher Education*, 26 April 2001, 30.
47 M. Brearley, 'Indian or what?' *Wisden Cricket Monthly*, October 2002, 32. Fascinatingly, Brearley's prediction became true, with Greg Chappell appointed the Indian national coach in May 2005.
48 Unfortunately, such representational logics dominate sports writing. For example, in an article (ironically) titled 'Cultivating cultural sensitivity', *Idea*, October 2002, Ingrid Knight-Cohee attempted to explain how fitness professionals can handle diverse cultural and ethnic backgrounds. Quoting an 'expert', he stated, 'Americans continue to view India as a Third World country, says Hoffman, yet many Indians are highly informed and very perceptive,' p. 58. A great method to see if a racist ideology has been perpetuated is to invert the nationalities in this statement. Ponder this: '*Indians* continue to view *America* as a Third World country, yet many *Americans* are highly informed and very perceptive'. The question is that if 'many' Indians are well informed and perceptive, what adjectives would describe the remainder of the population?
49 This issue is discussed more overtly in chapters 4 on the WACA and 5 on Bradman. However, Australia and New Zealand in particular occupy the sphere termed 'the colonial margin' by Homi Bhabha. He believed that in this zone, 'the West' reveals its differences and limitations. Refer to 'The other question: difference, discrimination and the discourse of colonialism', in R. Fergus, M. Gever, T. Minh-ha and C. West, *Out there: marginalization and contemporary cultures*, New York: MIT Press and the New Museum of Contemporary Art, 1990, p 71.
50 M. Bose, *A history of Indian cricket*, London: André Deutsch Limited, 1990/2002, p. 476.
51 Indian cricket history has been favoured with outstanding scholars. A remarkable history of 'British India' and sport has been written by Ramachandra Guha. Refer to his 'Cricket and politics in colonial India', *Past and Present* 161, November 1998 [fulltext article].
52 To explore the consequences of 'world cuisine' in London, refer to I. Cook and P. Crang, 'The world on a plate', *Journal of Material Culture* 1, 2, 1996.
53 S. Rushdie, *Indian Cookery*, London: Arrow Books, 1991, p. 12.
54 Steven Bradbury, 'Executive summary', *The New Football Communities*, Sir Norman Chester Centre for Football Research, University of Leicester, 2002, p. 1.

55  J. Williams, 'Just Williams: the new generation', *Leicester Mercury*, 8 March 2002, <http://www.le.ac.uk/fo/publications/mercurycolumns/jw14.html> (accessed 3 December 2002).

56  *Bend it like Beckham – music from the motion picture*, Cube Soundtracks, 2002. Mel C's track is number 16. Victoria Beckham also has a song on the soundtrack, 'I wish', track 6.

57  D. Winner, 'The hands-off approach to a man's game', *The Times*, 28 March 2005, 12.

58  S. Redhead, *Football with attitude*, Manchester: Wordsmith, 1991, p. 141.

59  B. Stoddart, *Saturday afternoon fever: sport in the Australian culture*, Sydney: Angus and Roberson, 1986, p. 156.

60  M. Burton Nelson showed how these terms were deployed through the interventions of feminism in her book *The stronger women get the more men love football: sexism and the American culture of sports*, New York: Harcourt Brace & Company, 1994.

61  Patricia Clasen asked why 'female' athletes need to subscribe to narrow 'feminine' practices in 'The female athlete: dualisms and paradox in practice', *Women in Language* 24, 2, 2001.

62  Marnie Ko investigated this decision in 'How to play the game', *The Report*, 7 February 2000.

63  For a discussion of the coverage on cable television, refer to R. Thomas Umstead's 'Women's soccer league kicks off in high gear', *Multichannel News* 22, 15, 9 April 2001, 46.

64  B. Chastain, 'She-Male Nation', *National Journal*, 2 October 1999, 2831.

65  C. Young, 'Good sports?' *Reason*, November 2001, 23.

66  The Women's Sports Foundation in the United Kingdom has provided both an advocacy and a monitoring function. It is the only organization in the United Kingdom that has as its sole purpose to improve and promote the chances for women and girls in sport. They discussed the nature of this MCC decision in 'Women's Sports Foundation – the voice of women's sport', <http://www.wsf.org.uk/>, 3 December 2002 (accessed 7 December 2002).

67  J. Sillett, 'Woodworm to give the Lancashire Women's team an extra edge', *LCB News*, Lancashire Cricket Board, Summer 2002, 1.

68  'Womens [sic] cricket', <http://www.waca.com.au/cricket/womenc.htm> (accessed 8 February 2005).

69  R. Cashman and A. Weaver, *Wicket women: cricket and women in Australia*, Kensington: New South Wales University Press, 1991, p. vii.

70  G. Whannel, 'David Beckham, identity and masculinity', *Sociology Review*, February 2002, 2.

71  Julie Burchill stated that 'Boxing is a sport where men beat up men; football is a sport where men beat up women'. From *Burchill on Beckham*, London: Yellow Jersey Press, 2001, p. 96.

72  The cover of *Who* on 2 May 2005 featured the headline 'Posh and Becks crisis point'. This story was triggered by the statements made by their former nanny Abbie Gibson in *News of the World*. One of her claims was that 'It was all about Brand Beckham. Their fortune is based on them having a successful marriage. If there wasn't a commercial interest holding them together they would be finished', from 'Scoop!' *Who*, 2 May 2005, 28.

73  J. Williams, 'Just Williams: Beckham's brand', *Leicester Mercury*, 14 December 2001, <http://www.le.ac.uk/fo/publications/mercurycolumns/jw8.html> (accessed 3 December 2002).

74 B. Carrington, 'Postmodern blackness and the celebrity sports star: Ian Wright, "race" and English identity', from D. Andrews and S. Jackson (eds), *Sporting stars: the cultural politics of sporting celebrity*, London: Routledge, 2001, p. 118.

75 The highly publicized injury suffered by Beckham prior to the World Cup in 2002 resulted not only in front page news, but also a website, 'Help Beckham get fit, England 2002', <http://www11.brinkster.com/todchats/beckham.htm> (accessed 25 January 2003). This website features an animated figure of 'Beckham', which the viewer can make move into a jog, stretch or jump.

76 G. Whannel, 'Punishment, redemption and celebration in the popular press: the case of David Beckham', from Andrews and Jackson, p. 142.

77 Burchill, p. 90.

### 7 On the Blacks' back

1 Nicholas Thomas described this more negative rendering of biculturalism as to 'partake . . . of a cultural essentialism that construes Maoriness primarily in terms of its difference from pakeha identity and this reduces it to terms that complement white society's absences', *Colonialism's culture: anthropology, travel and government*, Princeton: Princeton University Press, 1994, p. 185.

2 J. Belich, *Making peoples: a history of New Zealanders*, Auckland: Penguin, 1996, p. 450.

3 *Treaty of Waitangi and Social Policy*, The Royal Commission on Social Policy, Te Komihana a te Karauna Mo Nga Ahuatanga-a-iwi, Discussion Booklet No. 1, Wellington, July 1986, 4.

4 It is important to recognize that there is no effective English equivalent to words like tapu or mana. For a discussion of the way in which Maori and English languages worked within the Treaty and te Tiriti, refer to Bruce Biggs, 'Humpty-Dumpty and the Treaty of Waitangi', in I.H. Kawharu (ed.), *Waitangi: Maori and Pakeha perspectives of the Treaty of Waitangi*, Auckland: Oxford University Press, 1989, pp. 300–12.

5 The Treaty was deployed in many parliamentary decisions in the 1980s. More precisely, the Treaty of Waitangi was mentioned in the Environment Act 1986 and the Conservation Act 1987. For a further evaluation of the Labour Government's recognition of the Treaty, refer to Jane Kelsey's *A question of honour? Labour and the Treaty*, Wellington: Allen and Unwin, 1990, particularly pp. 72–77.

6 'Treaty of Waitangi', *Hertslet's commercial treaties*, London: Foreign Office, 1845, VI, pp. 576–81.

7 K. Sinclair, *The origins of the Maori wars*, Auckland: Auckland University Press, 1957, p. 19.

8 S. Crawford, 'Rugby and the forging of national identity', *Sport, power and society in New Zealand*, ASSH Studies, 11, 1995, 8.

9 T. Dusevic, 'Winners without mercy', *Time International* 153, 26, 5 July 1999, 10.

10 J. Park, 'The worst hassle is you can't play rugby', *Current Anthropology* 41, 3, June 2000, 446.

11 B. Tune, in C. Harvey, 'Is this man mad?' *The Weekend Australian Magazine*, 19–20 March 2005, 22.

12 For an outstanding review of Lomu's career and kidney transplant, refer to C. Harvey, pp. 20–23.

13 In 1981, All Black flanker Graham Mourie made himself unavailable for the series against the Springboks because of the apartheid policies. Similarly, All

Black winger John Kirwan refused to play in the 1986 Cavaliers tour of South Africa.

14 Spiro Zavos, *The golden Wallabies: the story of Australia's rugby world champions*, Ringwood: Penguin, 2000, p. 37.

15 D. Williams, 'All black and bruised', *Time International* 159, 5 April 2002, 40.

16 Ibid., 40.

17 D. Woods, *Black and white*, Dublin: Ward River Press, 1981, p. 43.

18 J. Nauright and D. Black, 'New Zealand and international sport: the case of All Black–Springbok rugby, sanctions and protest against apartheid 1959–1992', *Sport, power and society in New Zealand*, ASSH Studies, 11, 1995, 69.

19 Crawford, p. 15.

20 J. Nauright, 'Introduction', *Sport, power and society in New Zealand*' ASSH Studies, 11, 1995, 1.

21 D. Williams, 'Islanders: rugby's biggest winners', *Time* 158, 19, 12 November 2001, 16.

22 Ibid.

23 The Bledisloe Cup is the annual rugby union competition between the Australian Wallabies and the New Zealand All Blacks. The matches are played in different venues between the two nations.

24 P. Bergin, 'Maori sport and cultural identity in Australia', *The Australian Journal of Anthropology* 13, 3, 2002, 261. This outstanding article by Paul Bergin provides an excellent investigation of Maori immigration to Australia and the sporting consequences of this movement, to Australia but also to the new immigrants.

25 M. Williams, 'How many cultures make a culture?' *New Zealand Books*, October 1996, 12.

26 Loosely translated, 'iwi' refers to a tribal structure.

27 G. Clayton, in C. Archie (ed.), *Maori sovereignty: the Pakeha perspective*, Auckland: Hodder Moa Beckett Publishers, 1995, p. 34.

28 C. Laidlaw, 'Race reality', *Metro*, 140, February 1993, 42.

29 A clear history of the haka is Timoti Karetu's *Haka: the dance of a noble people*, Auckland: Reed Publishing, 1996.

30 R. Walker, 'Being Maori is forever', *Listener*, 11 February 1978, from M. Crockett, P. Little and T. Snow (eds), *The Listener Bedside Book*, Auckland: Wilson and Horton, 1997, 180.

31 R. Mulgan, 'Multiculturalism: a New Zealand perspective', from C. Kukathas (ed.), *Multicultural citizens: the philosophy and politics of identity*, Canberra: The Centre for Independent Studies Limited, 1993, p. 87.

32 Thakur, 'In defense of multiculturalism', from S. Greif (ed.), *Immigration and national identity in New Zealand*, Palmerston North: Dunmore Press, 1995, p. 272.

33 C. Laidlaw, 'Race reality', *Metro*, 140, February 1993, 46.

34 P. Spoonley, 'Being here and being Pakeha', from M. King (ed.), *Pakeha: The quest for identity in New Zealand*, Auckland: Penguin, 1991, p. 146.

35 P. Booth, 'Winston Peters: the man you want as Prime Minister', *North and South*, July 1990, 42.

36 W. Peters, from D. McLoughlin, 'The rise and rise of Winston Peters', *North and South*, July 1996, 54.

37 N. Legat, 'Immigration: what have we got to fear?' *North and South*, June 1996, 63.

38 A provocative and important research project by Malcolm McKinnon explores the role of Asia in New Zealand's future. Refer to his *Immigrants and citizens: New Zealanders and Asian immigration in historical context*, Wellington: Institute of Policy Studies, 1996.

39 David McLoughlin used this phrase in 'To be male is to beware', *North and South*, August 1997, 38.
40 T. Dalrymple, 'An amusement arcade masquerading as a museum', *New Statesman* 128, 4423, 12 February 1999, 33.
41 J. Phillips, *A man's country*, Auckland: Penguin, 1987, p. 130.
42 Ibid., p. 266.
43 Lynne Segal was particularly critical of 'popular feminist attachment to idealized views of women as inherently less aggressive than men', *Slow Motion*, London: Virago, 1990, p. 267.
44 T. Morton, *Altered mates: the man question*, St Leonards: Allen and Unwin, 1997, p. 138.
45 N. Wedgwood, '"Court" in the act: the informal reproduction of male power in pennant squash', *Sporting Traditions* 13, 1, November 1996, 46.
46 Ibid., 54.
47 S. Thompson, '"Thank the ladies for the plates": the incorporation of women into sport', *Leisure Studies* 9, 1990, 135–43.
48 D. Adair, J. Nauright and M. Phillips, 'Playing fields through battle fields: the development of Australian sporting manhood in its imperial context, c. 1850–1918', from C. Moore and K. Saunders (eds), *Australian masculinities: men and their histories*, St Lucia: University of Queensland Press, 1998, p. 54.
49 R. Horricks, *Male myths and icons*, Basingstoke: Macmillan, 1995, p. 151.
50 Ibid., p. 154.
51 Nauright, 'Introduction', pp. 2–3.
52 S. Zavos, *The gold and the black*, St Leonards: Allen and Unwin, 1995, p. 15.

## Conclusion

1 It is important to note that this game was played in the context of the Conservative leader Michael Howard's proposed 'crackdown' on immigration in the lead-up to the 2005 election. For a discussion about his immigration 'panic', refer to Diane Abbott, 'This racist appetite will never be sated', *Guardian*, 18 February 2005, 25.
2 Jon Magee wrote about this change to the player register of British football in 'Shifting balances of power in the new football economy', from J. Sugden and A. Tomlinson (eds), *Power games: a critical sociology of sport*, London: Routledge, 2002, pp. 216–39.
3 This headline – 'Are soccer's millionaires putting enough back into the game's grassroots?' – was featured on p. 1 of *Society Guardian*, 23 February 2005, 1. David Conn reported in his article 'The people's game', *Society Guardian*, 23 February 2005, 2, that 'despite the extraordinary wealth of the top professional football clubs, their investment in local community programmes is pitiful'.
4 J. O'Farrell, 'A league of their own', *Guardian*, 18 February 2005, 25.
5 M. Latham, 'Libraries in the 21st century learning society', *APLIS* 13, 4, December 2000, 146.
6 T. Bentley, *Learning beyond the classroom*, London: Routledge, 1998.
7 A web-based version of this document can be found at *A sporting future for all*, Department for Culture, Media and Sport, <www.culture.gov.uk/sport/index. html> (2001)(accessed 10 November 2002).
8 Refer to Hal Colebatch, 'World narrowing: notes on Britain's culture-war', *National Observer*, Winter 2002, 31–45.
9 Henry Winter reported this takeover as 'the Theatre of Dreams becomes Sold Trafford', from 'Revolt stirs for Sold Trafford', *The West Australian*, 14 May 2005, p. 192.

# Select bibliography

Andrews, D. and Jackson, S. *Sport stars: the cultural politics of sporting celebrity* (London: Routledge, 2001)

Atkinson, K. *Behind the scenes at the museum* (New York: Picador, 1995)

Ball, P. *An Englishman abroad: Beckham's Spanish adventure* (London: Ebury, 2004)

Barker, T. *The WACA: an Australian cricket success story* (St Leonards: Allen and Unwin, 1998)

Belich, J. *Making peoples: a history of New Zealanders* (Auckland: Penguin, 1996)

Bose, M. *A history of Indian cricket* (London: André Deutsch Limited, 2002)

Breckenridge, C. (ed.) *Consuming modernity: public culture in a South Asian world* (Minneapolis: University of Minnesota Press, 1995)

Burchill, J. *Burchill on Beckham* (London: Yellow Jersey Press, 2001)

Collins, T. and Vamplew, W. *Mud, sweat and beers: a cultural history of sport and alcohol* (Oxford: Berg, 2002)

Colman, M. and Edwards, K. *Eddie Gilbert: the true story of an Aboriginal cricketing legend* (Sydney: Australian Broadcasting Corporation, 2002)

Farred, G. (ed.) *Rethinking C.L.R. James* (Cambridge, MA: Blackwell, 1996)

Garland, J., Malcolm, D. and Rowe, M. (eds) *The future of football* (London: Frank Cass, 2000)

Geddes, M. *Remembering Bradman* (London: Penguin, 2002)

Giulianotti, R. and Williams, J. (eds) *Game without frontiers: football, identity and modernity* (Aldershot: Ashgate Publishing Limited, 1994)

Haigh, G. *The summer game: Australian Test cricket 1949–71* (Melbourne: Text Publishing, 1999)

Hignell, A. *Rain stops play* (London: Frank Cass, 2002)

Kavanagh, G. *Dream spaces* (London: Leicester University Press, 2000)

Kavanagh, G. (ed.) *Making histories in museums* (London: Leicester University Press, 1999)

Kell, P. *Good sports: Australian sport and the myth of the fair go* (Sydney: Pluto Press, 2000)

Klein, N. *No logo* (London: Flamingo, 2001)

Longman, J. *The girls of summer: the US women's soccer team and how it changed the world* (New York: HarperCollins Publishers, 2001)

Macdonald, S. and Fyfe, G. (eds) *Theorizing museums* (Oxford: Blackwell Publishing, 1999)

Maleuvre, D. *Museum memories: history, technology*, art (Stanford: Stanford University Press, 1999)

Mangan, J.A. (ed.) *Tribal identities: nationalism, Europe, sport* (London: Frank Cass, 1996)

Markovits, A. and Hellerman, S. *Offside: soccer and American exceptionalism* Princeton: Princeton University Press, 2001)

Marqusee, M. *Anyone but England: cricket and the national malaise* (London: Verso, 1994)

Moore, C. and Saunders, K. (eds) *Australian masculinities: men and their histories* (St Lucia: University of Queensland Press, 1998)

Moore, K. *Museums and popular culture* (London: Cassell, 1997)

Piesse, K. *The Taylor years* (London: Penguin, 2000)

Powell, W. *The Australians in England* (Stroud: Tempus Publishing Limited, 2001)

Redhead, S. *Football with attitude* (Manchester: Wordsmith, 1991)

Redhead, S. (ed.) *The passion and the fashion: football fandom in the New Europe* (Aldershot: Avebury, 1993)

Reynolds, H. *An indelible stain?* (Ringwood: Viking, 2001)

Rice, J. *One hundred Lord's Tests: a celebration of the home of cricket* (London: Methuen, 2001)

Samuel, R. *Theatres of memory* (London: Verso, 1994)

Sandiford, K. *Cricket nurseries of colonial Barbados* (Barbados: University of West Indies, The Press, 1998)

Searle, C. *Pitch of life: writings on cricket* (Manchester: Parrs Wood Press, 2001)

Solly, R. *Shoot out: the passion and the politics of soccer's fight for survival in Australia* (Milton: John Wiley & Sons, 2004)

Sugden, J. *Scum airways* (Edinburgh/London: Mainstream Press, 2003)

Sugden, J. and Bairner, A. *Sport, sectarianism and society in a divided Ireland* (Leicester: Leicester University Press, 1993)

Urry, J. *Global complexity* (Cambridge: Polity, 2003)

Urry, J. *Sociology beyond societies* (London: Routledge, 2000)

Urry, J. *The tourist gaze: leisure and travel in contemporary societies* (London: Sage, 1990)

Vasili, P. *The first black footballer: Arthur Wharton 1865–1930 – an absence of memory* (London: Frank Cass, 1998)

Walmsley, D. with Done, S. *The treasures of Liverpool FC* (London: Carlton Books, 2004)

Whimpress, B. *Passport to nowhere* (Sydney: Walla Walla Press, 2000)

Williams, J. *Cricket and England: a cultural and social history of the inter-war years* (London: Frank Cass, 1999)

Zavos, S. *The golden Wallabies: the story of Australia's rugby world champions* (Ringwood: Penguin, 2000)

# Index

Aberfan disaster 3, 75, 77, 79, 93, 97–100, 194; collective memory 99; media attention 87–89; relief fund 80; TV coverage 82, 87, 89–91, 100–01

Aboriginal cricket players 125, 129, 131, 137, 144; English tour 132; female player 144; racial taunts 132

Aboriginal people 126, 133, 137–39, 146–47, 153; sports persons 136; White Australia Policy 143

Aboriginal Protection Act 133, 139, 144; Protector of Aborigines, the 142

Afrikaners 182

Akhtar, Shoaib 134

Akram, Wasim 138

Alderman, Terry 102, 110

All Blacks 4, 102, 130, 179–84, 187–90, 192; Springbok rivalry 182–83

Ambleside 10–11, 16, 18, 59

Angel, Jo 102, 110

Antipodes 3–4, 21, 193

Aotearoa/New Zealand 176–77, 181, 187, 193

apartheid 148, 180, 182, 190

Arsenal Football Club 13, 41, 191; global brand 40; museum 43; nationality of playing squad 192

Association football 35, 61, 187; attendances at matches 29–30

Australian and Torres Strait Islander Commission (ATSIC) 133

Australian association football (Soccer) 92, 104, 110, 144

Australian cricket 105, 130, 187; captains 95; ethnicity of players 128

Australian Cricket Board 148; cancellation South African tour 148

Australian National Museum 200n6

Australian Rugby Union 181, 183

Australian Rules Football 36, 48, 104, 109, 121, 181

Australian Services Cricket Team 147

Australian women's soccer team 162

baggy green cap 128–29

Barlow, A.N. 141; see also illegal bowling action

Barmy Army 60

Barnes, John 95

Barnes, Simon 25

Barnsley Football Club 39

Beckham, David 4, 12, 155, 173–75, 191, 194

Beckham, Victoria 155

Bedser, Eric 135

Belich, Jamie 177

Benaud, Richie 95, 106, 147

Bend it like Beckham 4, 154–55, 158, 161, 164, 166, 193

Bentley, Tom; Learning beyond the classroom 193

Berger, John 20

Best, George 50–51, 53, 94, 96, 100, 173–74

Beveridge Report, the 101

Bhamra, Jess 154, 158, 165–66, 169, 173, 175

biculturalism 178, 183–84, 187, 190; Asian migrants in NZ 185, 223n37

Bill, Oscar Wendell 125

Birmingham 13, 96

Blackburn Rovers Football Club 23, 32

Blair government 31, 58, 94; new labour 98; *A sporting future for all* 194; equitable redistribution of sports revenue, 31
Blair, Tony 8, 94, 97, 193
Bledisloe Cup 60, 184
Bose, Mihir 166; *A History of Indian Cricket* 166
Boucher, Mark 121
Bradford disaster 33
Bradman, Sir Donald 3, 102, 117, 143, 146, 148, 193; bodyline series 128, 135; Burgmann letters 147–49; death 150; Freemasonry 127, 214n28; Gilbert dismissal 125, 140; his world standing 126, 132; oral history 147–49; statistics 134–35, 141; 'the little bastard' 135
Brayshaw, Ian 110
Brearley, Mike 164
Brooking, Sir Trevor 31
Bullocky 136; *see also* Aboriginal cricket players
Burchill, Julie 174
Burgmann, Meredith 147–49
Bury Football Club 15, 28
Bushell, Mark 33

Carlisle United 12
Carpenter, Alan 111–12
Cavalier tour (1986) 180
Chadha, Gurinder 154–55;
Charlton, Sir Bobby 91, 94
Chastain, Brandi 2, 156–58, 160–64, 170, 173
Chelsea Football Club 1, 13; Asian fans 168; global brand 40
Chisholm, Melanie (Sporty Spice) 169
Christchurch Commonwealth Games 180
City of Manchester Stadium 33
Clarke, Stuart 3, 7–40, 60; *England the Light* 17
Clinton, Bill 157
Coghlan, John 94
Cohen, Erik 18
Cole, King 132; *see also* Aboriginal cricket players
Collins, Tony 26
colonization 22, 104, 109, 125–31, 137, 165, 186; in NZ 173, 184,

Commonwealth Immigration Act 23, 97
Coward, Mike 104
Cowley, Jason 94, 96
Creed, Barbara 19
cricket 3, 21; racism 130; origins 193
Crow, Jim 132; *see also* Aboriginal cricket players
Crystal Palace, 191
cultural diversity 56, 77
cultural tourism 40, 60
Culture, Media and Sport, the department 58

Darwin, Australia 108
Davis, Sir Herbert; *see* Government Tribunal of Inquiry
Dick-a-Dick 132, 152; *see also* Aboriginal cricket players
Di Venuto, Michael 128
Duke, Vic 32
Dundee Football Club 13
Dundee United Football Club 13

Eden Park, Auckland 183; Cessna attack 183
England at WACA 104, 121
English Premier League 1, 11, 13, 15, 51, 191, 192; global marketing 19, 22, 44; regional past 36; safer facilities 30, 35; spectator target 32, 61, 175;
Englishness 18, 21, 23, 48, 77–78, 86, 129, 176; decline and isolation 92, 105; cricket supremacy 135
Euro 2004 17
European Women's Championship (UEFA) 33
Everton Football Club 13

Farmer, Graham (Polly) 136; *see also* Aboriginal people
Fédération Internationale de Football (FIFA) 48; FIFA Women's Player of the Year 158–59
female spectatorship 16, 19, 34, 60, 169
feminism 158, 181, 187–90
Ferguson, Sir Alex 1, 191
Football Association 11, 95
Football Foundation 11, 31
Football Trust, the 27, 29
Foucault, Michel 42

Freeman, Cathy 136; *see also* Aboriginal people
Frith, Simon 44
Frow, John 49
Fussell, Paul 75

Gaelic football 48
Gamman, Lorraine 19
Gascoigne, Paul 96, 173
Gatting, Mike 105
Gilbert, Eddie 4, 125, 127, 133, 136, 151–52, 192–93; Aboriginal Protection Act 139; Bradman comment 141; forgotten sportsman 146; illegal bowling action 140–41; illness and death 142; marriage 140; suspension and blazer retrieval 142; unmarked grave 150
Gilchrist, Adam 102, 106, 110, 121, 129
Gillespie, Jason 144, 151–52; *see also* Aboriginal cricket players
Gingrich, Newt 3
Glamorgan Cricket Club 105
Glasgow Rangers 29
Gleneagles agreement 183
Goss, Zoe 153
Greig, Tony 106
Gresford *see* mining disasters
Griffith Joyner, Florence 170

Hadlee, Richard 132
Haigh, Gideon 147; *The summer game* 147
haka; *see* Maori
Hall of Fame; *see* National Football Museum
Haller, Helmet 84
Haller, Jurgen 84
Hamm, Mia 158–59, 161
Hansen, Miriam 19
Hanson, Pauline 146, 186
Hayden, Matthew 102, 121
Healy, Ian 121
Henry, Albert 134, 136, 152; *see also* Aboriginal cricket players
*Herald of Free Enterprise* 80
heritage 49–52, 97; National Heritage Acts (1980 and 1983) 49
*Hertslet's commercial treaties* 178
Hewison, Robert 49
Heysel disaster 25, 33
Hignell, Andrew 108

Hillary, Edmund 189
Hillsborough tragedy 7–9, 15, 24–27, 80; hooligans 39; seating changes 32–33
historiographical debates 76
Hobart, Tasmania 108
Hobsbawm, Eric 105
Holyoake, Keith 182
Homes of Football 3, 7–40, 59–60, 192–93; patronage 12; website 10
homophobia in sport 2, 34, 43, 130, 168–71, 174
Hooper-Greenhill, Eilean 48
Hopkins, Eric 35
Hornby, Nick 40, 53–54, 57
Horricks, Roger 189
Howard, John 127, 143; affinity with test captains 143; Prime Minister's XI 152
Howard, Michael 192, 196n2
Howells, Kim; *see* (UK) Tourism, Minister for
Hughes, Kim 214n34
Hughes, Merv 102
Hurst, Sir Geoff 78, 84, 94
Hussain, Nasser 130, 165

illegal bowling action 134, 140–41
Indian cricket 105–06, 137, 152, 164, 166–67
Indigenous people 129, 131; rights 184; see Aboriginal cricket players
International Football Institute, (University of Central Lancashire) 46
Inverarity, John 110
Invincibles, the 130, 146–47

Jardine, Douglas 135
Jenkins, Keith 76
Johnes, Martin 79–80, 82, 87, 98–99
Jules Rimet Trophy; *see* World Cup
Juventus Football Club 25

Kureishi, Hanif 155
Kasprowicz, Michael 128
Kavanagh, Gaynor 47; *Dream spaces* 47
Kelso, Paul 25
Khan, Imran 132
Kop, the 1, 24–25, 29–31, 168; Spion Kop 30; 'You'll never walk alone' 84
Kournikova, Anna 170

Laidlaw, Chris 184
Laird, Bruce 102, 110
Lake District 14, 16, 60, 192
Lancashire C.C.C. 110, 172; facilities
    111, 115,
Langer, Justin 102, 110, 128
Lara, Brian 152–53
Latham, Mark 193
Lee, Brett 102, 104, 121, 129
Lehmann, Darren 127
Leicester City Football Club 30
Leicester University 27
Leitch, Archibald 29
Lennon, John 100
Lillee, D.K. 102, 110, 117; Fast Bowling
    Academy 114; Lillee Marsh
    grandstand 113; appointed President
    WACA 114
Liverpool Football Club 1, 13, 24–25;
    Asian fans 168; chant 24; global
    brand 40
Lloyd, Clive 138
Lomu, Jonah 180
Lords 102, 106, 108
Loughrigg Fell 15

McGrath, Glenn 102, 114, 129
McKenzie, Graham 102
McLean, Iain 80, 87, 98–99
Maleuvre, D 45
Mallett, Ashley 134, 151; coach
    Indigenous team 2001
Manchester 13; Commonwealth Games
    197n7; Creative Industries 51;
    declining industrialization 92; New
    Order 94
Manchester City 7, 31; chant 7, 35
Manchester Institute for Popular
    Culture 23
Manchester United 1, 13, 33, 52, 111,
    118–19, 155, 191; Asian fans 168,
    173; global brand 40; museum 43, 52,
    59, 61; superstore 119
Manchester United Enterprises 52
Maori 177–78, 185–87; colonial wars
    178; culture 183; haka 133, 185; in
    women's netball 190; kawanatanga
    (governance) 177–78; mana (pride)
    177; rugby involvement 183–85;
    Treaty of Waitangi, the 177–78, 182,
    184–85
Maradona, Diego 96
Marchioness 80, 98

Marsh, Rodney 102, 110, 121
Marsh, Geoff 110
Marsh, Jack 133–34, 136, 152; see also
    Aboriginal players
Marylebone Cricket Club, the 172
Massie, Bob 102, 110
Menzies, Sir Robert 143
Miller, Toby 125–26
mining disasters 93, 98
Moody, Tom 110
Moore, Bobby 77–78, 95–97, 101
Moore, Kevin 43, 46, 48, 61–62, 69, 83,
    116; world cup ball 85
Moorhouse, H.F. 47
Moran, Richie 22
Mourinho, José 156, 194, 196n1
Muldoon, Robert 183
Mullagh, Johnny 132–33; see also
    Aboriginal cricket players
multiculturalism 22, 145, 155, 167, 181,
    185–86, 190
Muralitharan, Muttiah 134
museum attendances 48; see also
    sporting museums
Museum of City of Manchester, the
    54–55
Museum of Photography, Film and
    Television, the 54
Museum of the Moving Image
    (MOMI), the 54
Museums and popular culture 201 n18;
    see Moore, Kevin
Muslim Cricket Club, Bombay 167

National Coal Board 80–81, 99
National Football Museum 3, 10, 33,
    41–51, 57–71, 193; Hall of Fame
    50–51; leadership in field 116;
    suggested relocation to London 57,
    96; world cup ball 84; world cup
    crossbar 78;
Native Land Act 177
New South Wales cricket 109, 125,
    133
New Zealand; cricket 105
New Zealand history 177; immigration
    187
New Zealand national women's rugby
    team 179
New Zealand rugby; see All Blacks
New Zealand Rugby Football Union
    181
Newcastle United Football Club 13

North End Football Club (Preston) 57, 61
Nottingham; Bradman century 135
Nottingham Forest Football Club 24

Old Etonians 23
Old Trafford 22, 52, 61, 111, 191
Olympic Games, Montreal 180
O'Reilly, W.J. (Bill) 127
Oval, the 108; *Rain stops play* 108
Owen, Michael 96, 167

Pacific Islanders 183, 187
Pakeha 176–77, 183, 186–88, 190; colonial wars 178
Pakistan; cricket 105–06, 130, 137, 164
Pantglas junior school *see* Aberfan disaster
Patterson, Patrick 138
Pelé 53, 62, 84, 95–96
Perth, Western Australia 102, 106, 117, 194
Peters, Winston 186
Phillips, Jock; *A man's country* 188
popular culture 2, 41, 61, 116, 120, 146, 171; film 61, 98, 155; in museums 43–48, 63, 69, 71; in New Zealand 176; in oral history 66, 76
popular memory 46, 98, 102, 116, 146, 153, 163; in museums 47; in sports 76, 92
post-colonialism 22, 193
post traumatic stress 88
Powell, Enoch 23
Preston, UK 3, 41, 58–59, 63; parliamentary member 58
Professional Footballers' Association 11

Queensland Cricket Association 109–10, 125, 140; coaching programme named in honour of Gilbert 151; Gilbert ban and blazer retrieval 142; Gilbert funeral costs 142;

Racial Discrimination act (of 1975) 137
racism in sport 2, 22–23, 132, 134–37, 182, 184, 186
Ramsay, Sir Alf; *see* World Cup (1966 England)
Real Madrid 155
Redhead, Steve 32–33, 197n3
Reid, Bruce 102

Reynolds, Henry 137; *An indelible stain* 137
Richards, Sir Vivian 110, 132, 138
Robens, Lord; Health and Safety at Work Act 81; *see also* National Coal board
Rogoff, Irit 8
Ronaldo 53, 95
Rooney, Wayne 2, 53, 95, 156, 175, 194
Rose, Lionel 136; *see also* Aboriginal people
rugby 3, 21, 36, 104, 110, 121, 176, 178, 189, 193; league 181, 188
Rugby World Cup 180–81
Rushdie, Salman 167
Rutherford, Ernest 189

Samoan rugby players 182, 184
Santa Clara University 160, 163
Savage, Jon 44
sexism in sport 2
Scottish 'Super League' 32
Scurry, Briana 163; African American 163
Senghennydd *see* mining disasters
Shankly, Bill 1–2; 'Shankly school' 191
Sheffield 13
Sheffield Shield competition 109, 113, 117
Sheffield United Blades 34
Sheffield Wednesday Owls 34
Silver Ferns, the 190
Simpson, Bob 112
Sinclair, Keith 178
Sir Norman Chester Centre for Football Research 22, 60
Slaton, Danielle 163
Sobers, Gary 132, 136
Solly, Ross 201n24
Sorenstam, Annika 160
South African Cricket tour to Australian cancelled 148
South African Springboks 180, 182; All Blacks rivalry 183
*Sport and British Politics since 1960* 94
sport, as Creative Industry 7, 39, 51
Sport England 30; redevelopment of Wembley 95; economic recommendations 30
Sporting Events (Control of Alcohol etc) Act 25
sporting memory 4, 49: nostalgia 50

sporting museums 41–71, 97, 187; at
  WACA 116–17; Twickenham Rugby
  Museum 120;
sporting tourism 8, 14, 16, 18, 29, 40,
  42, 52, 58–61, 97; at WACA
  115–20; Barmy Army 60; in
  Melbourne Vic 115
sports culture 39, 61
sports history and theory 3, 36, 38, 50,
  76, 82–83, 177
sports media 2, 108
Sports Tourism International Council
  198n10
Springboks rugby tour Australia 148
Springboks; see South African
  Springboks
Sri Lankan cricket 104, 106, 127, 137,
  164; admiration of Bradman 149
Staffordshire University 194
Story of Football 96
Subiaco Oval (Perth) 111–12
Sugden, John 92, 224n2
Sunderland supporters 21
'Sundown' 132; see also Aboriginal
  cricket players

Taff Valley, Wales see Aberfan
Taylor, D. J. 30, 87
Taylor, Lord Justice report 24, 30, 52
Taylor, Mark 106, 143
Tendulkar, Sachin 152
Te Papa 187–88
'terra nullius' 138
Thatcher, Margaret 25, 49, 77
Theatre of Dreams, the 1, 22
Thomas, Faith 144; see also Aboriginal
  cricket players
Thomson, Jeff 102, 140
Tomlinson, Alan 92, 224n2
Tongan rugby players 184
Tourism, Minister for 58
Tranmere Rovers 20, 41, 46, 61
Treaty of Waitangi, the; see Maori
Trueman, Fred 138
Trumper, Victor 132–33
Twopenny, John 136; see also
  Aboriginal cricket players

Umaga, Tana 180
Underwood, Derek 108
University of Otago, the 179
Urbis 54–55
Urry, John 19

U.S.A. Women's Soccer team 157
U.S. Soccer; Female Athlete of the
  Year 159
U.S. Soccer; male participation 154,
  161, 194; World Cup 17, 48

Vamplew, Wray 26
Veletta, Mike 110
Verwoerd, Hendrick 182
Vorster, John 182

WACA (cricket ground) 2, 102–4,
  106–8, 110, 114, 120; museum
  117–20; wicket soil composition
  112–14
Walker, Ranginui 185
Wallabies 179, 181
Walsall Museum 62
Walters, Doug; Doug Walters' Stand
  130
Walvin, James 23
Warne, Shane 127–28
Watford Football Club 37
Waugh, Mark 127
Waugh, Stephen 106, 128–29, 132,
  143; Waugh/Ponting era 179
Webber, Saskia 163
Wembley Stadium 29, 58, 79, 92,
  95–96, 101
West Indies cricket 137, 152
Western Australian Cricket Association
  107; President appointment
  114–15
Western Australian Government Sports
  Minister 111
Western Australian isolation 107,
  109
Western Warriors 108, 113
Whannel, Garry 173
White Australia Policy 143
Williams, John 27, 92, 168, 173
Wilson, Harold 100
Winstanley, Ian see mining disasters
Wisden Cricket Monthly 105
Wolstenholme, Kenneth 79, 91
women's cricket 129–30, 144, 153, 172,
  216n72
women's football 2, 33–34, 48, 54; 154,
  156, 158–59, 201n23
women's golf 160
Women's National Basketball
  Association 159
women's rugby 179, 184, 187–88

women's squash 189
Women's United Soccer Association
  158–61, 163, 170
Wood, Graeme 102, 110
Worcestershire county; 135
World Cup (1966 England) 23, 41, 75,
  77, 79, 94, 101; attendance 78; red
  ball 82, 86; Wolstenholme
  commentary; 79, 91;
World Cup (1970 Mexico) 96
World Cup (1994 USA) 17, 48

World Cup (2002 Japan/Korea) 12, 16
World Cup (2006 Germany) 11
World Cup Women, (1999 USA)
  156–57
World Series Cricket 114

Yardley, Bruce 102
Yorkshire County Cricket Club 110;
  'birthright' 138

Zoehrer, Tim 102, 110

T - #0123 - 270225 - C0 - 234/156/13 - PB - 9780415484923 - Gloss Lamination